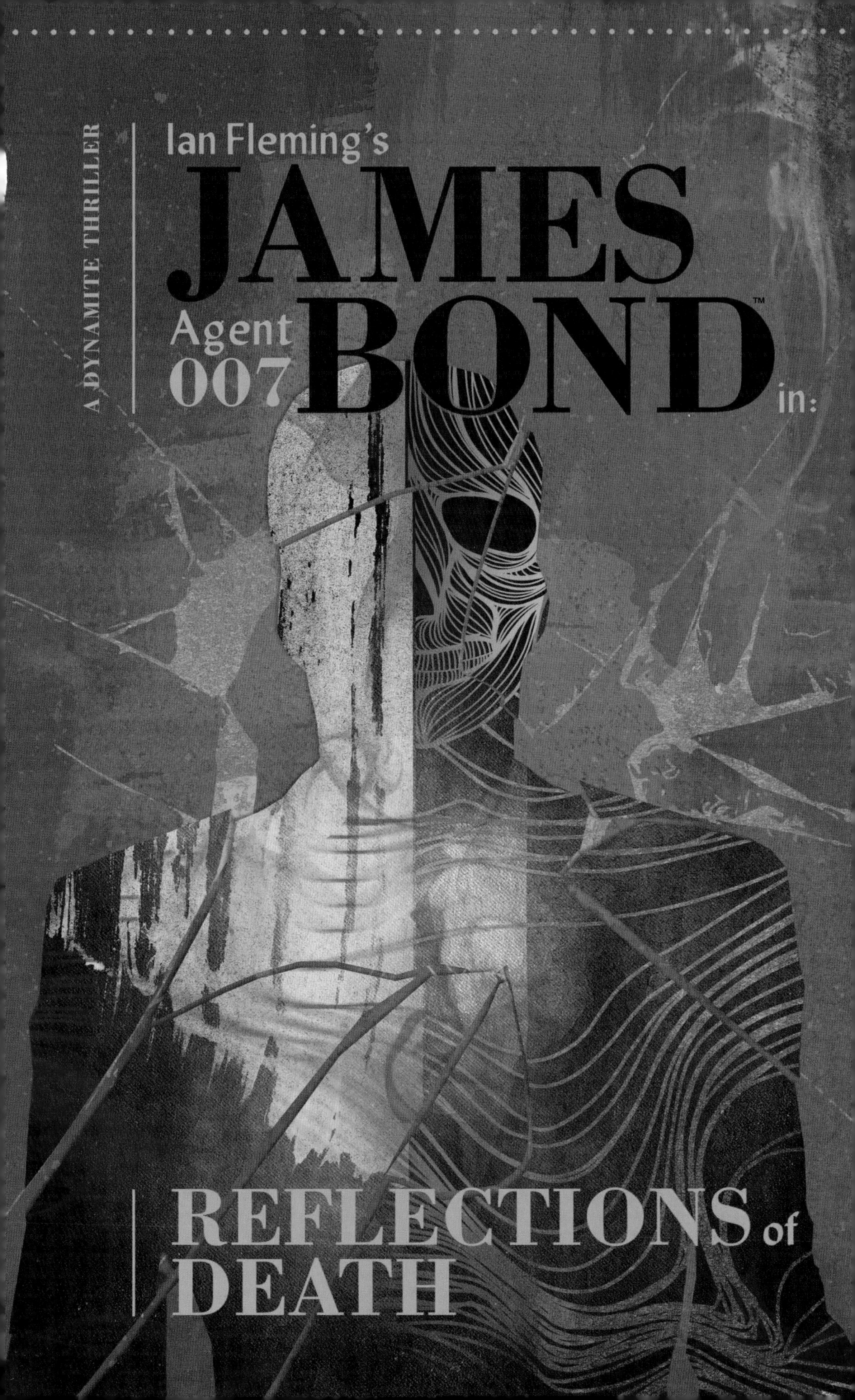
A DYNAMITE THRILLER
Ian Fleming's
JAMES
Agent
007
BOND™
in:
REFLECTIONS of
DEATH

CHAPTER ONE

The Broker

Script: Vita Ayala & Danny Lore
Art: Jordi Perez
Color: Kike J. Diaz

CHAPTER TWO

The Rare Dinner

Script: Benjamin Percy
Art: Kewber Baal
Color: Celeste Woods

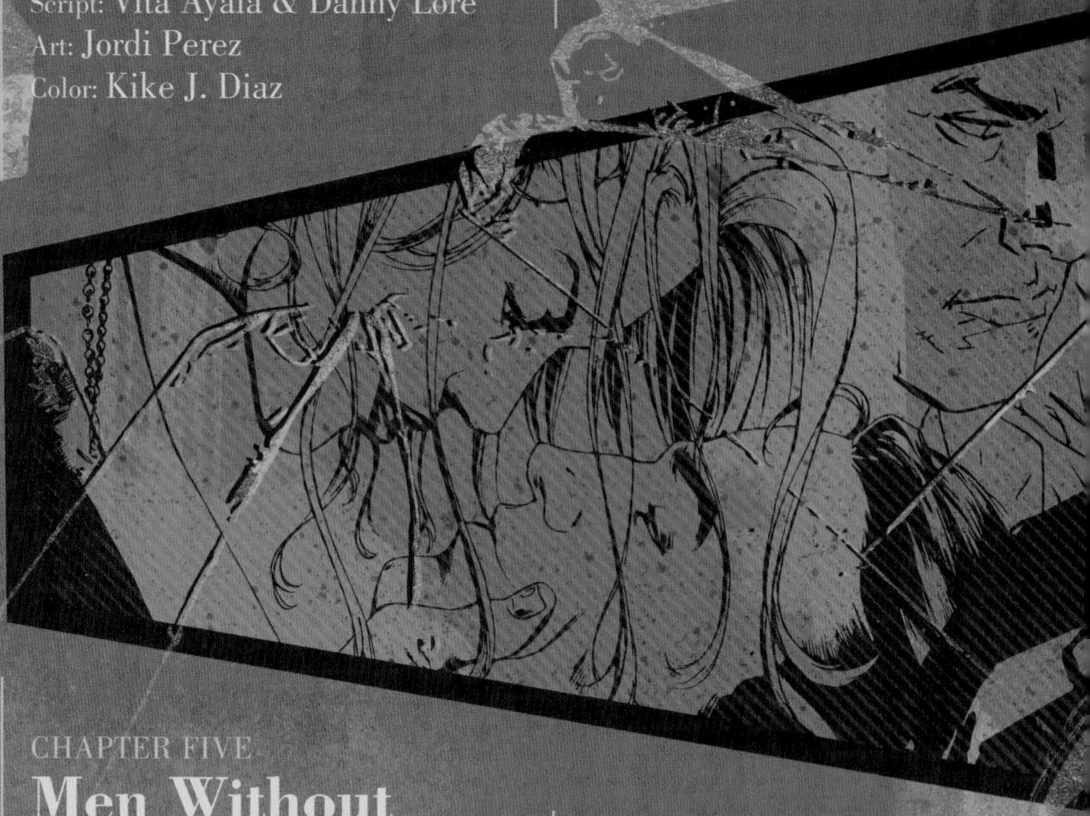

CHAPTER FIVE

Men Without A Country

Script: Mark Russell
Art: Robert Carey
Color: Roshan Kurichiyanil

CHAPTER SIX

The Hook

Script: Andy Diggle
Art: Luca Casalanguida
Color: Celeste Woods

CHAPTER THREE

The Oddest Job

Script: Greg Pak
Art: Dean Kotz
Color: Kike J. Diaz

CHAPTER FOUR

One Pistol, Three Silencers

Script: Gail Simone
Art: Eoin Marron
Color: Dearbhla Kelly

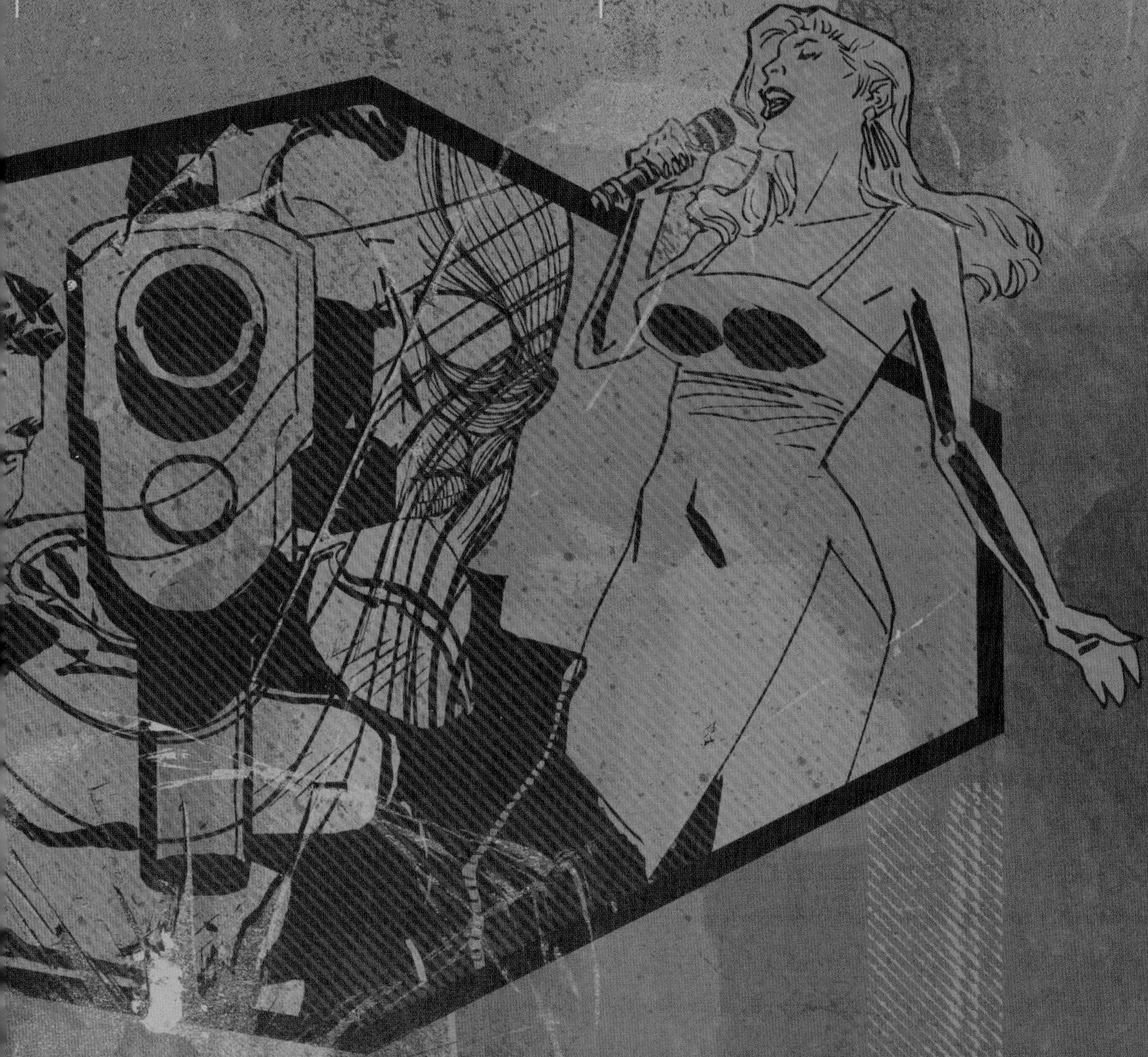

Letters: Ariana Maher
Collection Cover: Fay Dalton
Collection Design: Cathleen Heard
Editors: Nate Cosby, Matt Idelson, Kevin Ketner

Editorial Consultant: Michael Lake

Special Thanks To: Josephine Lane, Corinne Turner, Diggory Laycock at Ian Fleming Publications Ltd.

Jonny Geller at Curtis Brown

IAN FLEMING PUBLICATIONS LIMITED
www.IanFleming.com

IAN FLEMING PUBLICATIONS LIMITED

www.IanFleming.com

DYNAMITE®

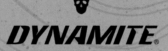

Nick Barrucci CEO/Publisher
Juan Collado President/COO
Brandon Primavera V.P. of IT and Operations

Joseph Rybandt Executive Editor
Matt Idelson Senior Editor
Kevin Ketner Editor

Cathleen Heard Art Director
Rachel Kilbury Digital Multimedia Associate
Alexis Persson Graphic Designer
Katie Hidalgo Graphic Designer

Alan Payne V.P. of Sales and Marketing
Pat O'Connell Sales Manager
Vincent Faust Marketing Coordinator

Jay Spence Director of Product Development
Mariano Nicieza Director of Research & Development

Amy Jackson Administrative Coordinator

Online **www.DYNAMITE.com**
Facebook **/Dynamitecomics**
Instagram **/Dynamitecomics**
Tumblr **dynamitecomics.tumblr.com**
Twitter **@dynamitecomics**

Standard Edition ISBN: 978-1-5241-1501-2
Signed Edition ISBN: 978-1-5241-1536-4

First Printing 10 9 8 7 6 5 4 3 2 1

For media rights, foreign rights, promotions, licensing, and advertising:
marketing@dynamite.com

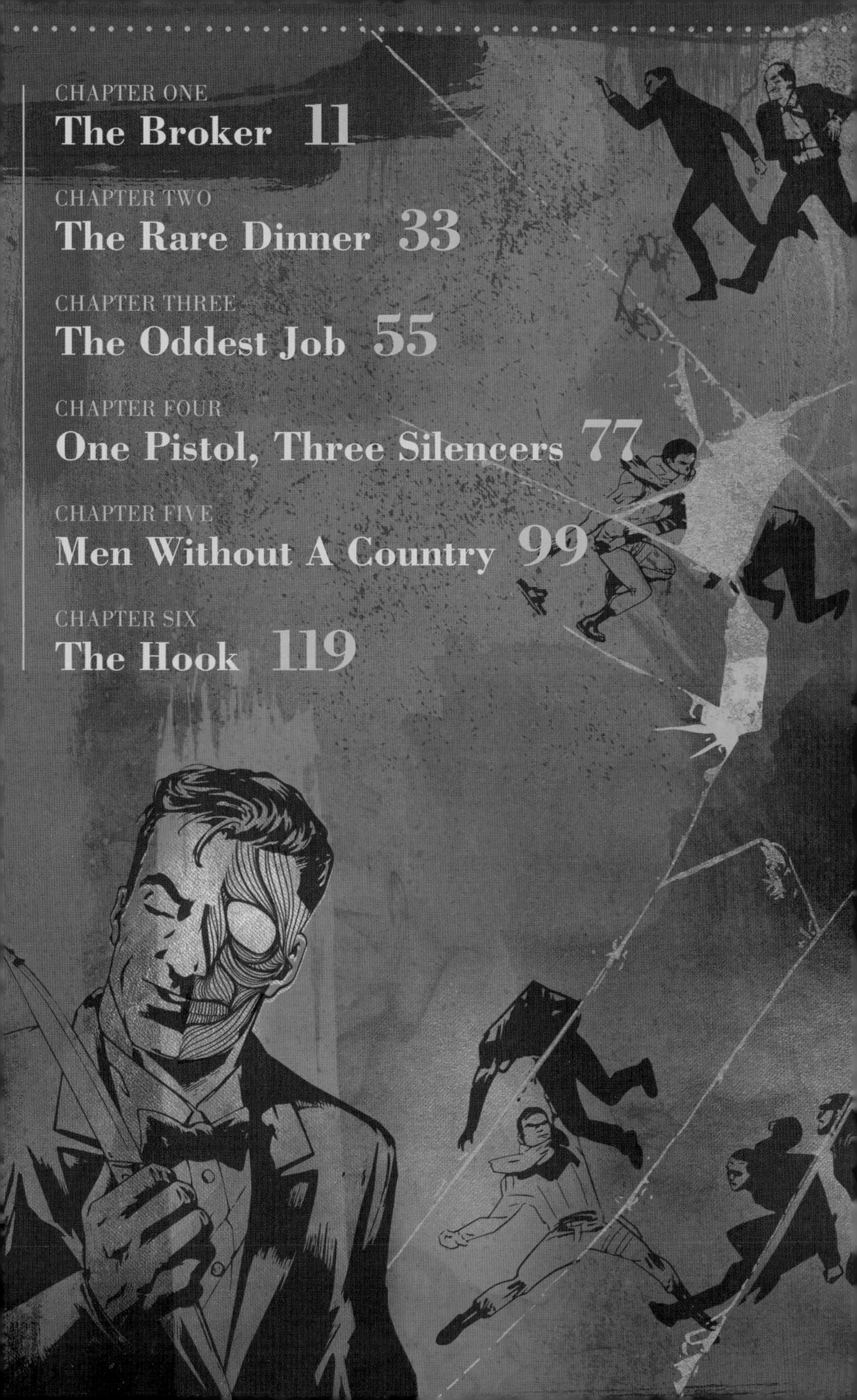

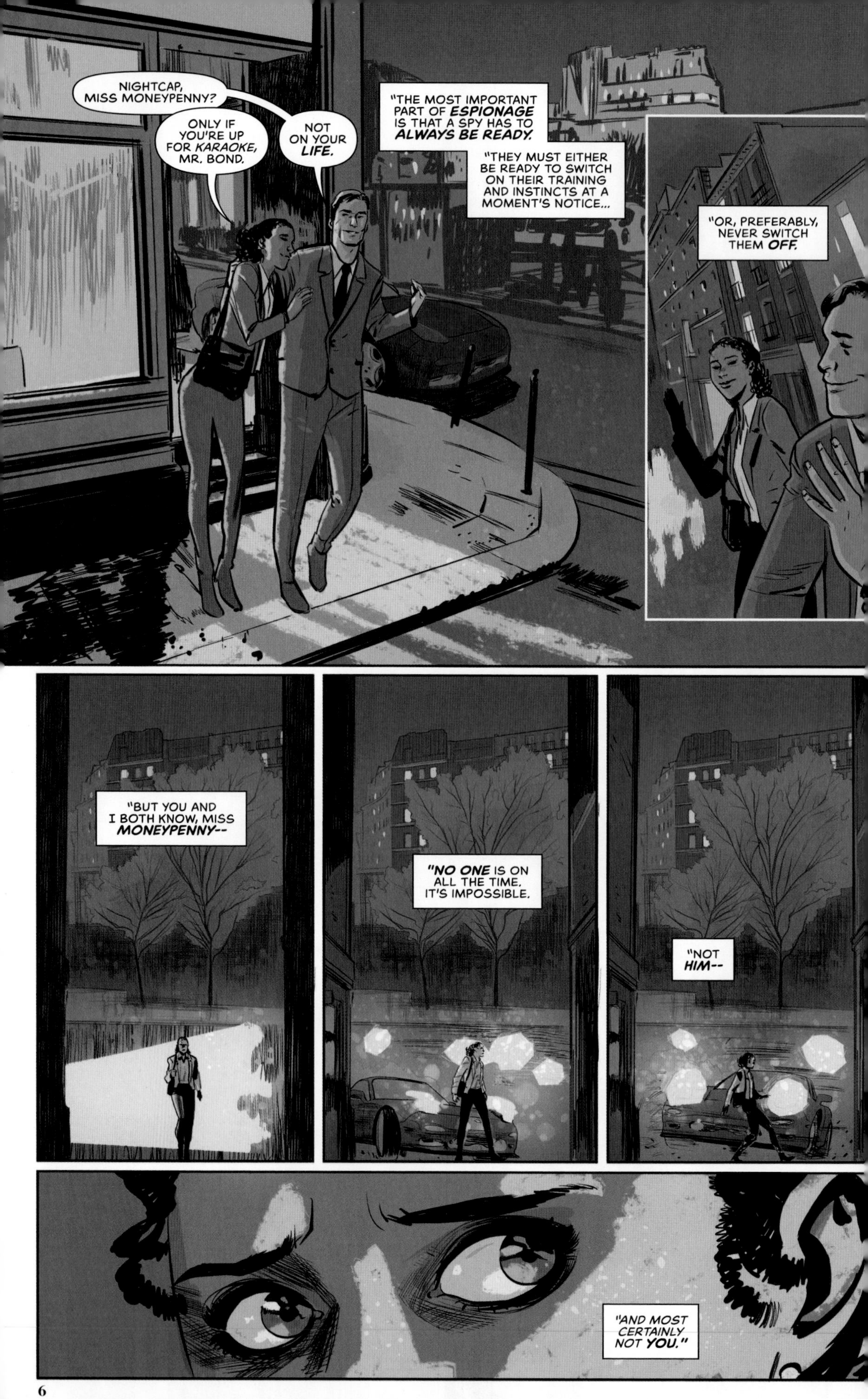
NIGHTCAP, MISS MONEYPENNY?
ONLY IF YOU'RE UP FOR KARAOKE, MR. BOND.
NOT ON YOUR LIFE.
"THE MOST IMPORTANT PART OF ESPIONAGE IS THAT A SPY HAS TO ALWAYS BE READY.
"THEY MUST EITHER BE READY TO SWITCH ON THEIR TRAINING AND INSTINCTS AT A MOMENT'S NOTICE...
"OR, PREFERABLY, NEVER SWITCH THEM OFF.
"BUT YOU AND I BOTH KNOW, MISS MONEYPENNY--
"NO ONE IS ON ALL THE TIME. IT'S IMPOSSIBLE.
"NOT HIM--
"AND MOST CERTAINLY NOT YOU."

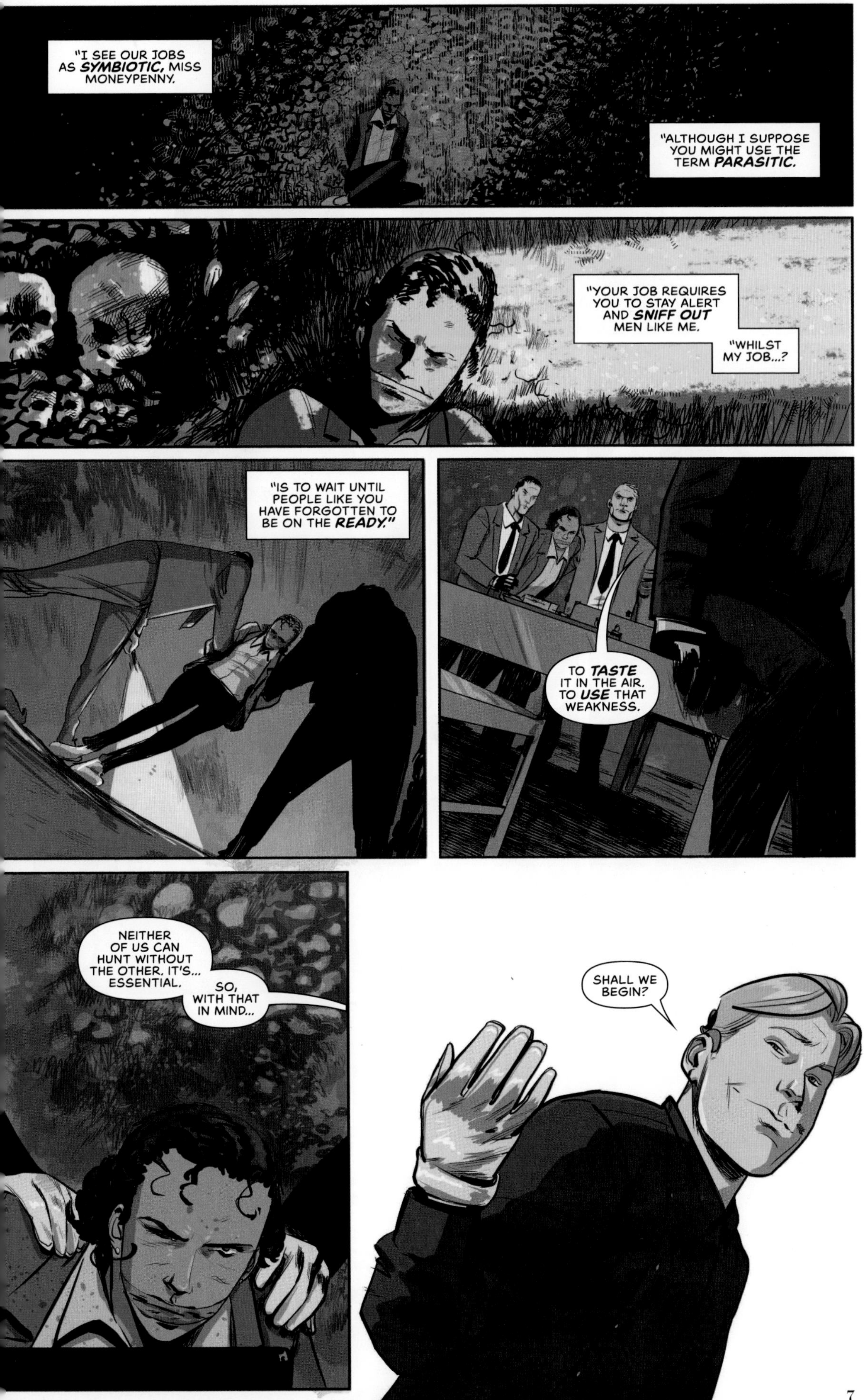
"I SEE OUR JOBS AS SYMBIOTIC, MISS MONEYPENNY.
"ALTHOUGH I SUPPOSE YOU MIGHT USE THE TERM PARASITIC.
"YOUR JOB REQUIRES YOU TO STAY ALERT AND SNIFF OUT MEN LIKE ME.
"WHILST MY JOB...?
"IS TO WAIT UNTIL PEOPLE LIKE YOU HAVE FORGOTTEN TO BE ON THE READY."
TO TASTE IT IN THE AIR. TO USE THAT WEAKNESS.
NEITHER OF US CAN HUNT WITHOUT THE OTHER. IT'S... ESSENTIAL.
SO, WITH THAT IN MIND...
SHALL WE BEGIN?

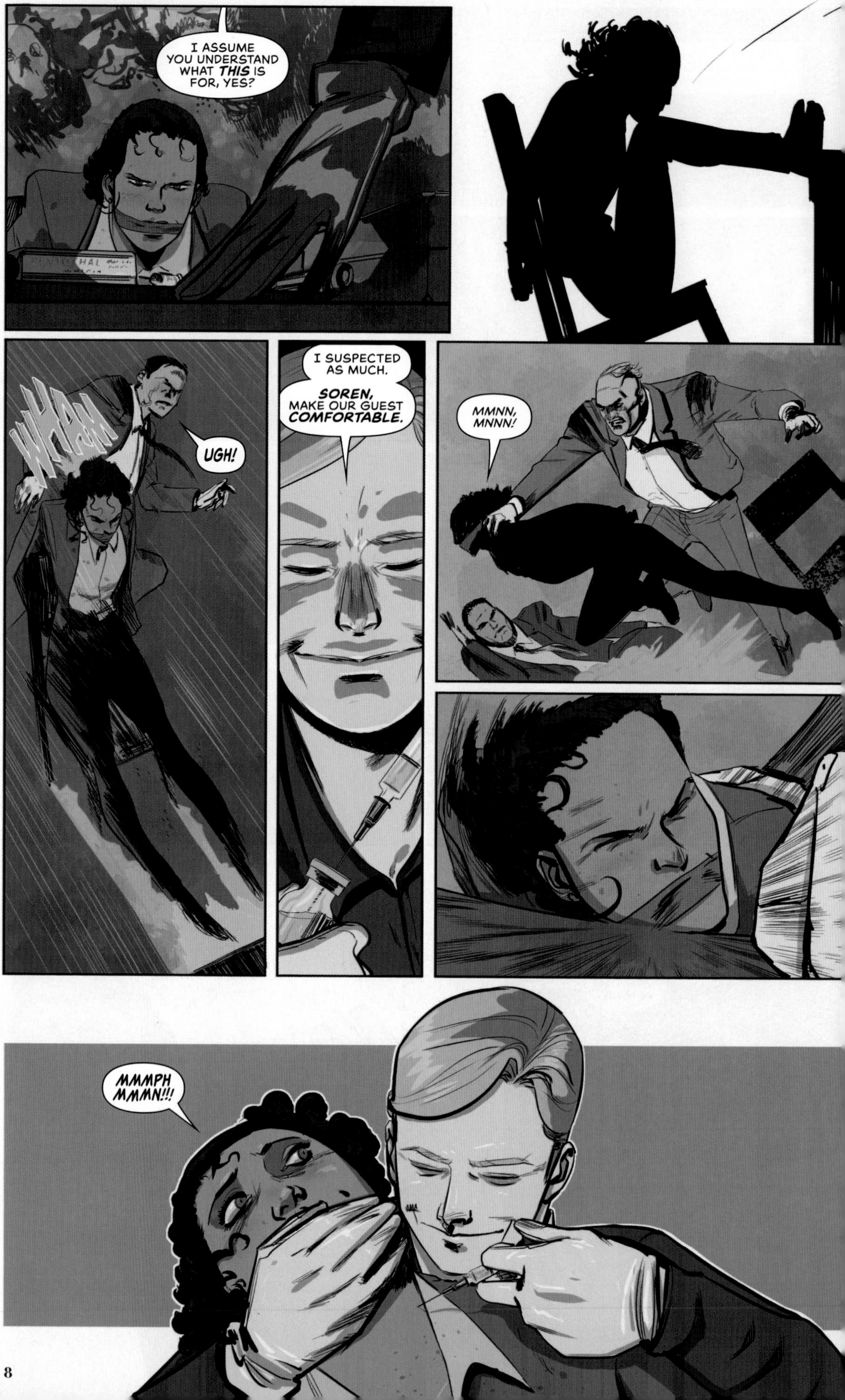
I ASSUME YOU UNDERSTAND WHAT THIS IS FOR, YES?
WHAM
UGH!
I SUSPECTED AS MUCH.
SOREN, MAKE OUR GUEST COMFORTABLE.
MMNN, MNNN!
MMMPH MMMN!!!

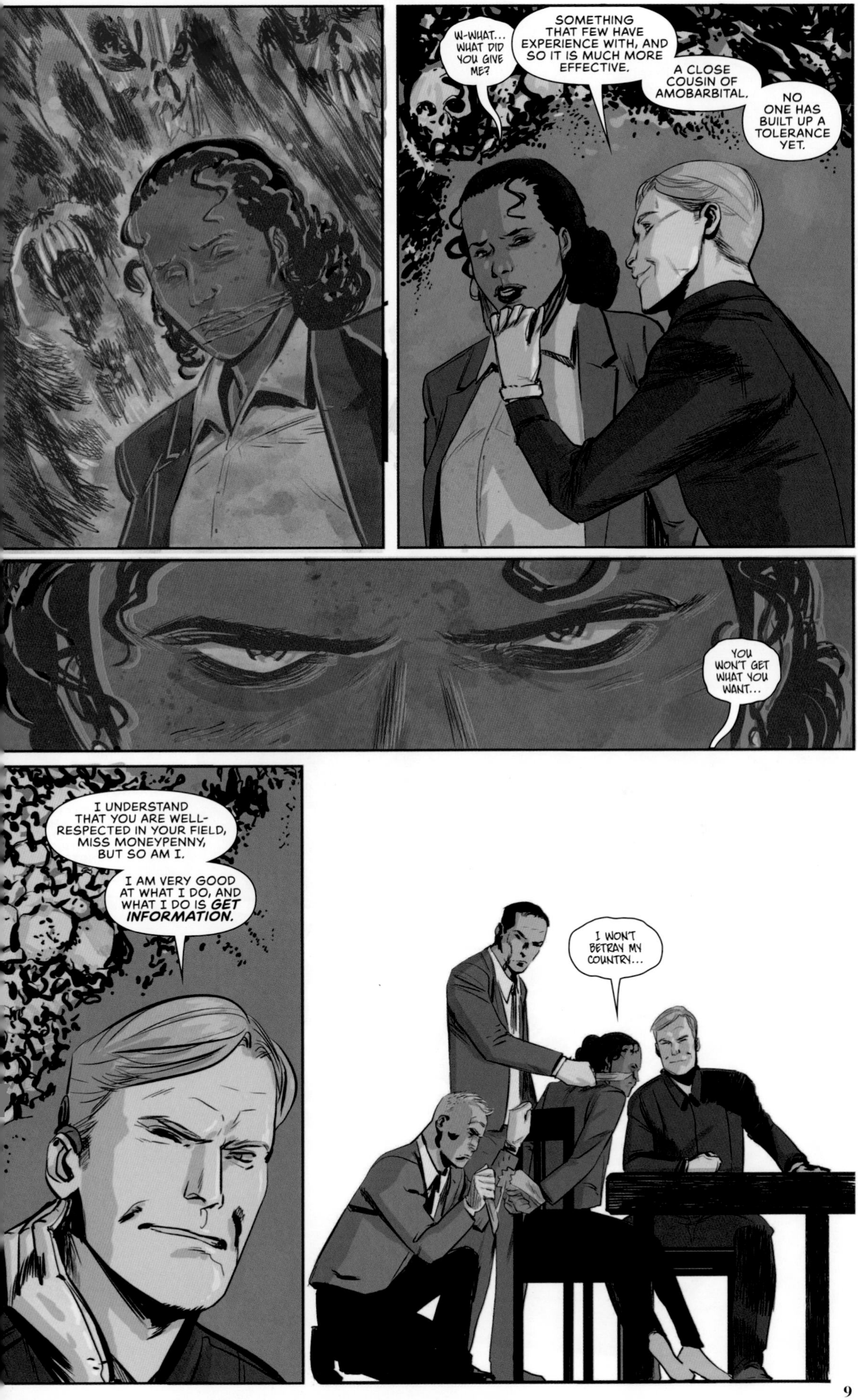
W-WHAT... WHAT DID YOU GIVE ME?
SOMETHING THAT FEW HAVE EXPERIENCE WITH, AND SO IT IS MUCH MORE EFFECTIVE.
A CLOSE COUSIN OF AMOBARBITAL.
NO ONE HAS BUILT UP A TOLERANCE YET.
YOU WON'T GET WHAT YOU WANT...
I UNDERSTAND THAT YOU ARE WELL-RESPECTED IN YOUR FIELD, MISS MONEYPENNY, BUT SO AM I.
I AM VERY GOOD AT WHAT I DO, AND WHAT I DO IS ***GET INFORMATION.***
I WON'T BETRAY MY COUNTRY...

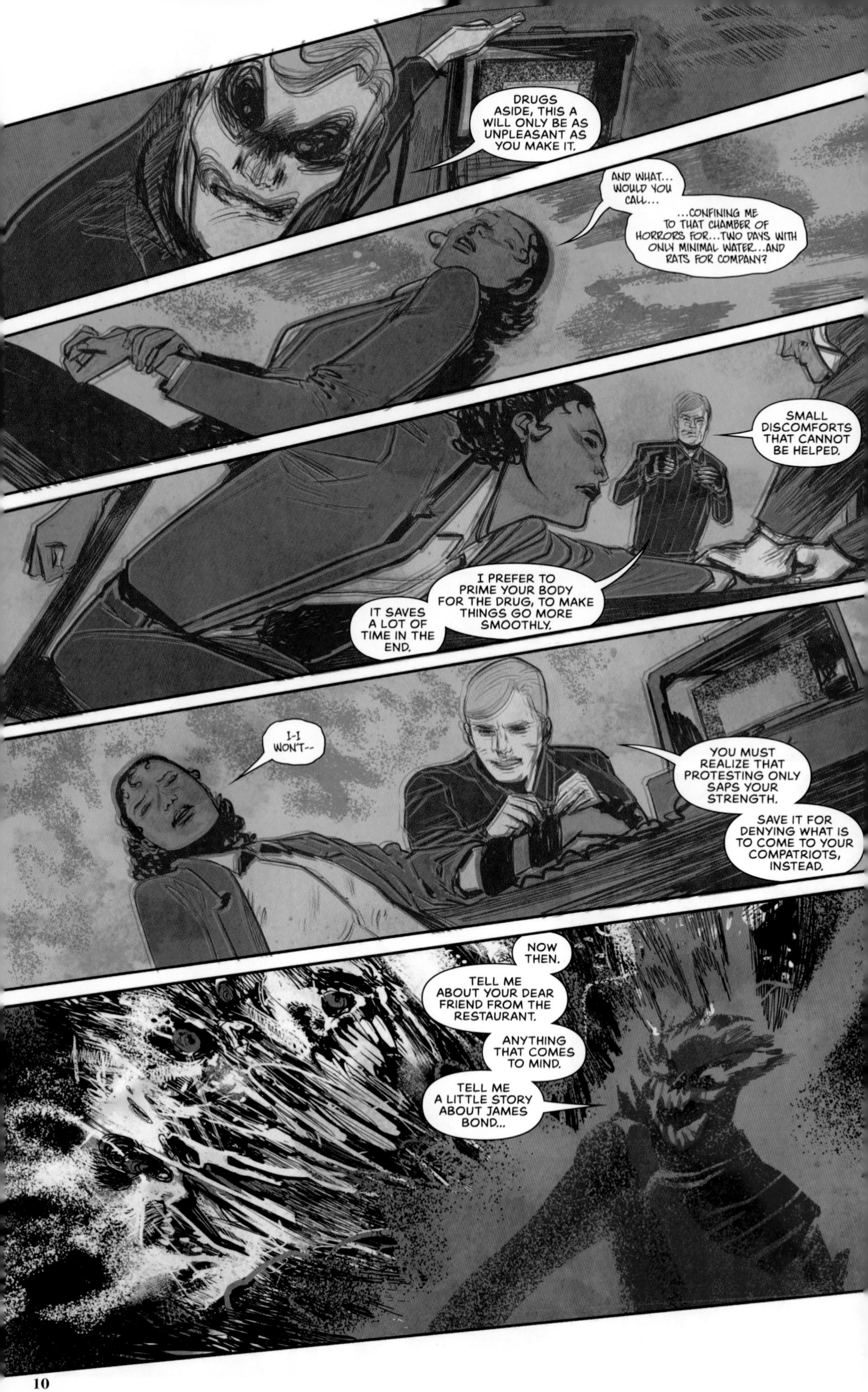
DRUGS ASIDE, THIS A WILL ONLY BE AS UNPLEASANT AS YOU MAKE IT.
AND WHAT... WOULD YOU CALL...
...CONFINING ME TO THAT CHAMBER OF HORRORS FOR...TWO DAYS WITH ONLY MINIMAL WATER...AND RATS FOR COMPANY?
SMALL DISCOMFORTS THAT CANNOT BE HELPED.
I PREFER TO PRIME YOUR BODY FOR THE DRUG, TO MAKE THINGS GO MORE SMOOTHLY.
IT SAVES A LOT OF TIME IN THE END.
I-I WON'T--
YOU MUST REALIZE THAT PROTESTING ONLY SAPS YOUR STRENGTH.
SAVE IT FOR DENYING WHAT IS TO COME TO YOUR COMPATRIOTS, INSTEAD.
NOW THEN.
TELL ME ABOUT YOUR DEAR FRIEND FROM THE RESTAURANT.
ANYTHING THAT COMES TO MIND.
TELL ME A LITTLE STORY ABOUT JAMES BOND...

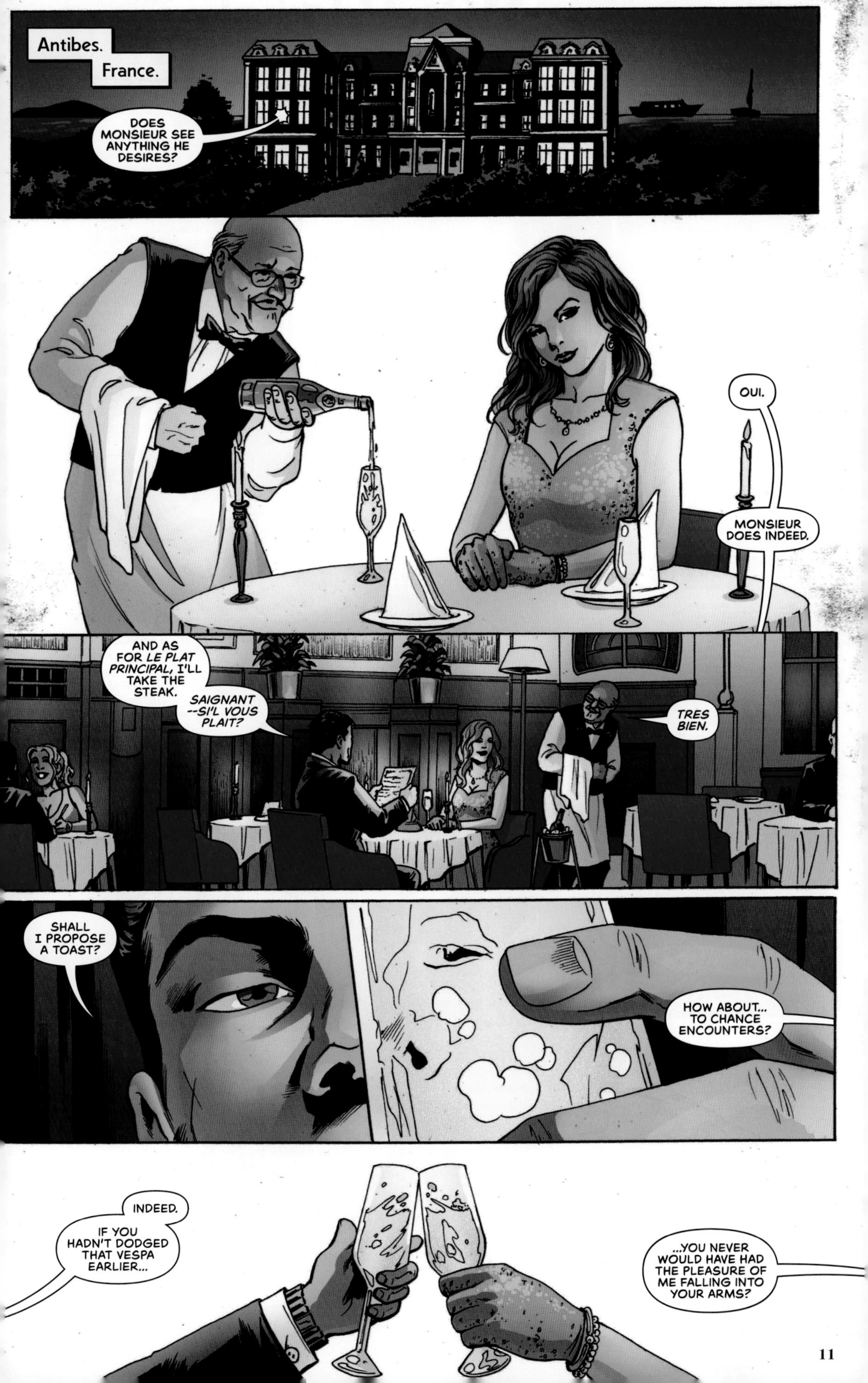
Antibes.
France.
DOES MONSIEUR SEE ANYTHING HE DESIRES?
OUI.
MONSIEUR DOES INDEED.
AND AS FOR LE PLAT PRINCIPAL, I'LL TAKE THE STEAK.
SAIGNANT --SI'L VOUS PLAIT?
TRES BIEN.
SHALL I PROPOSE A TOAST?
HOW ABOUT... TO CHANCE ENCOUNTERS?
INDEED.
IF YOU HADN'T DODGED THAT VESPA EARLIER...
...YOU NEVER WOULD HAVE HAD THE PLEASURE OF ME FALLING INTO YOUR ARMS?

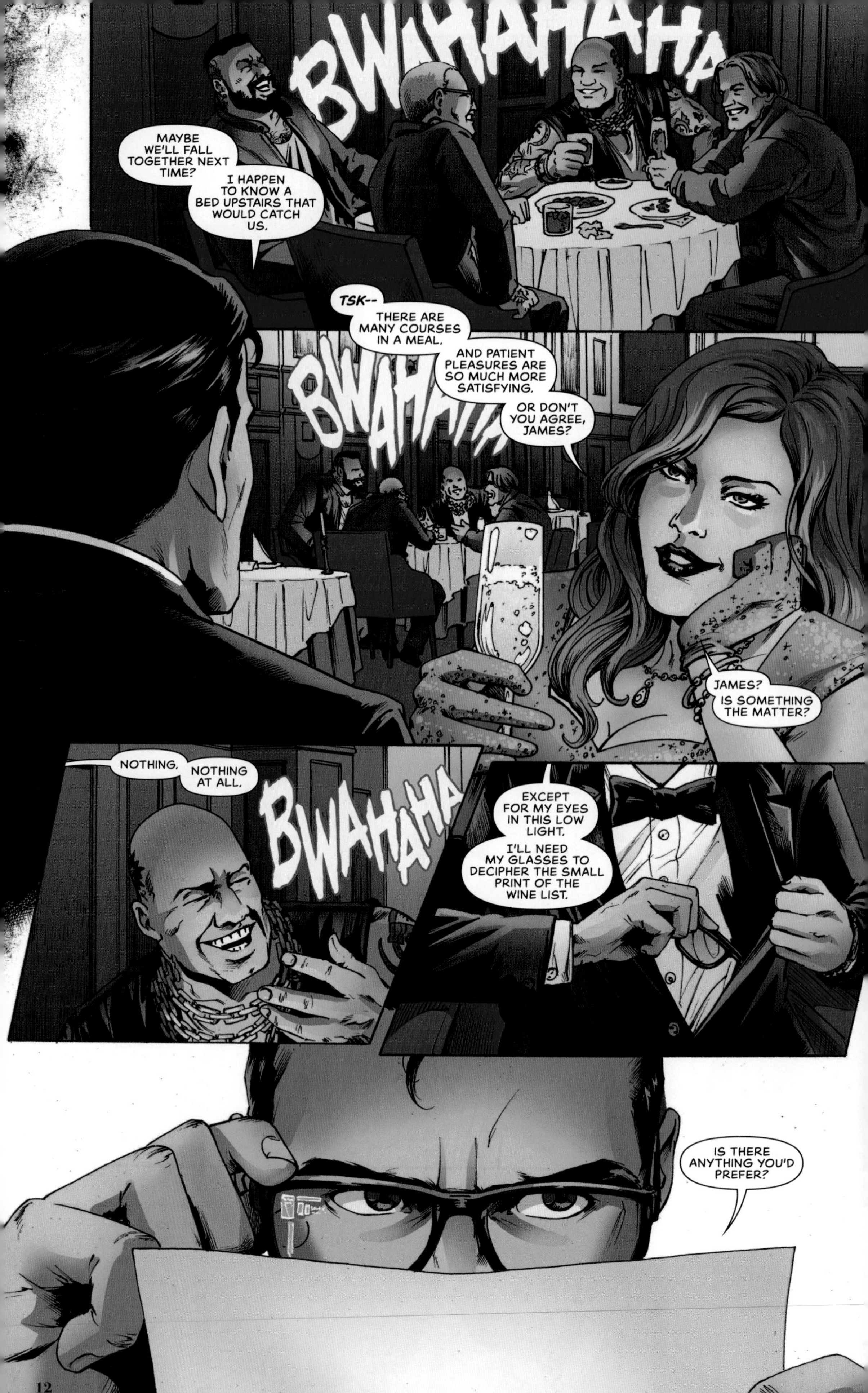
BWAHAHAHAHA
MAYBE WE'LL FALL TOGETHER NEXT TIME?
I HAPPEN TO KNOW A BED UPSTAIRS THAT WOULD CATCH US.
TSK--
THERE ARE MANY COURSES IN A MEAL.
AND PATIENT PLEASURES ARE SO MUCH MORE SATISFYING.
OR DON'T YOU AGREE, JAMES?
JAMES?
IS SOMETHING THE MATTER?
NOTHING.
NOTHING AT ALL.
BWAHAHA
EXCEPT FOR MY EYES IN THIS LOW LIGHT.
I'LL NEED MY GLASSES TO DECIPHER THE SMALL PRINT OF THE WINE LIST.
IS THERE ANYTHING YOU'D PREFER?

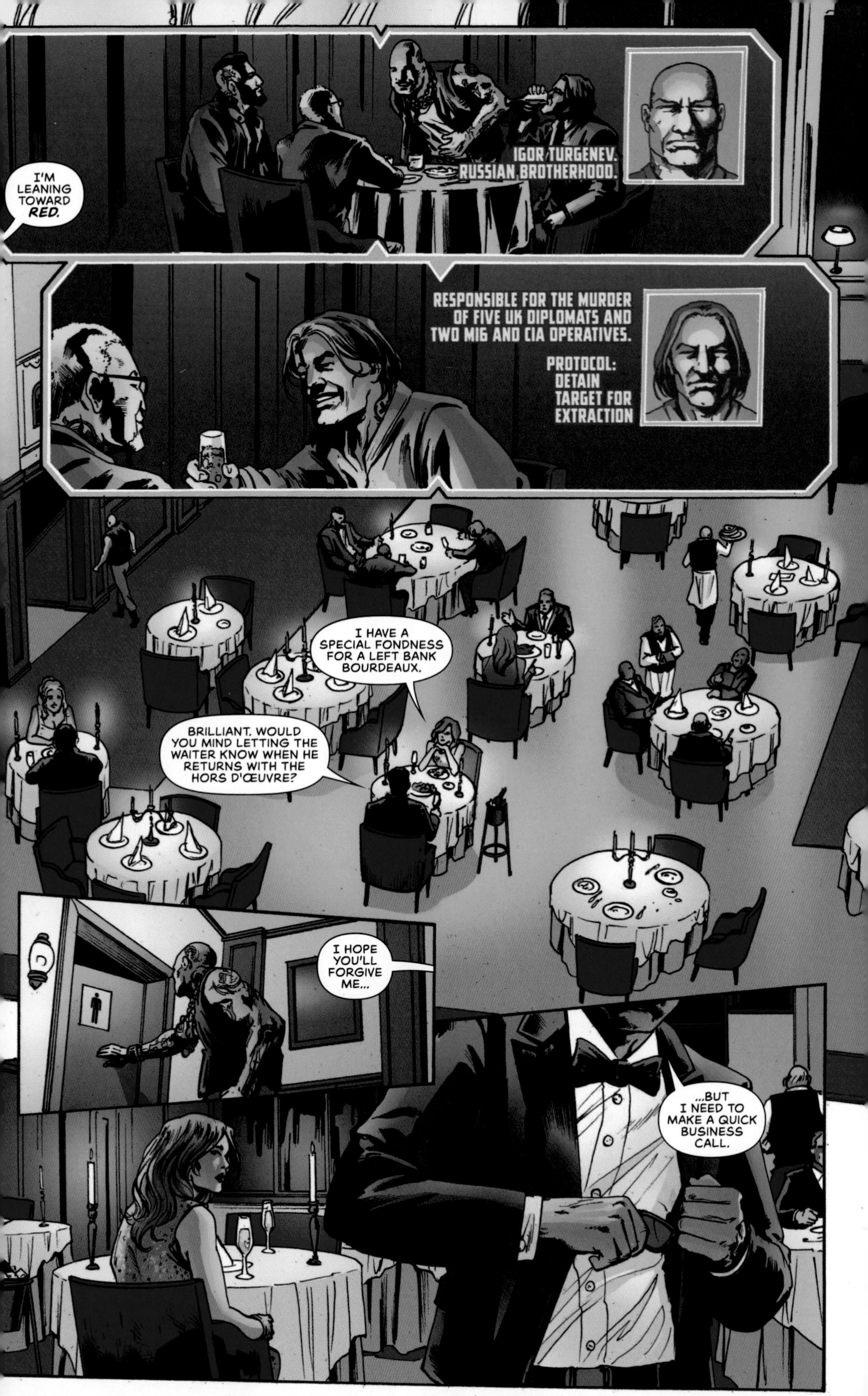
I'M LEANING TOWARD *RED.*
IGOR TURGENEV. RUSSIAN BROTHERHOOD.
RESPONSIBLE FOR THE MURDER OF FIVE UK DIPLOMATS AND TWO MI6 AND CIA OPERATIVES.
PROTOCOL: DETAIN TARGET FOR EXTRACTION
I HAVE A SPECIAL FONDNESS FOR A LEFT BANK BOURDEAUX.
BRILLIANT. WOULD YOU MIND LETTING THE WAITER KNOW WHEN HE RETURNS WITH THE HORS D'ŒUVRE?
I HOPE YOU'LL FORGIVE ME...
...BUT I NEED TO MAKE A QUICK BUSINESS CALL.

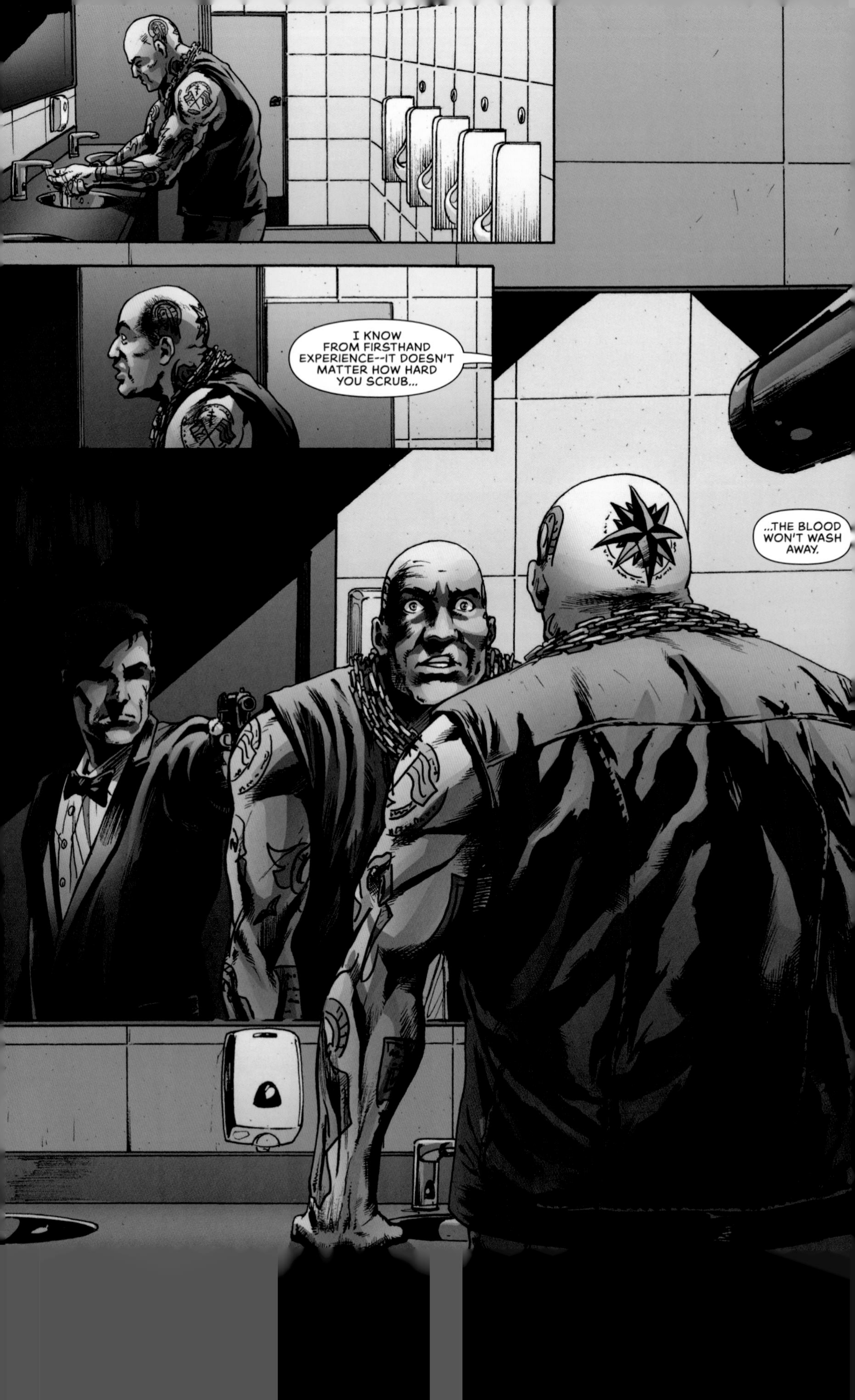
I KNOW FROM FIRSTHAND EXPERIENCE--IT DOESN'T MATTER HOW HARD YOU SCRUB...
...THE BLOOD WON'T WASH AWAY.

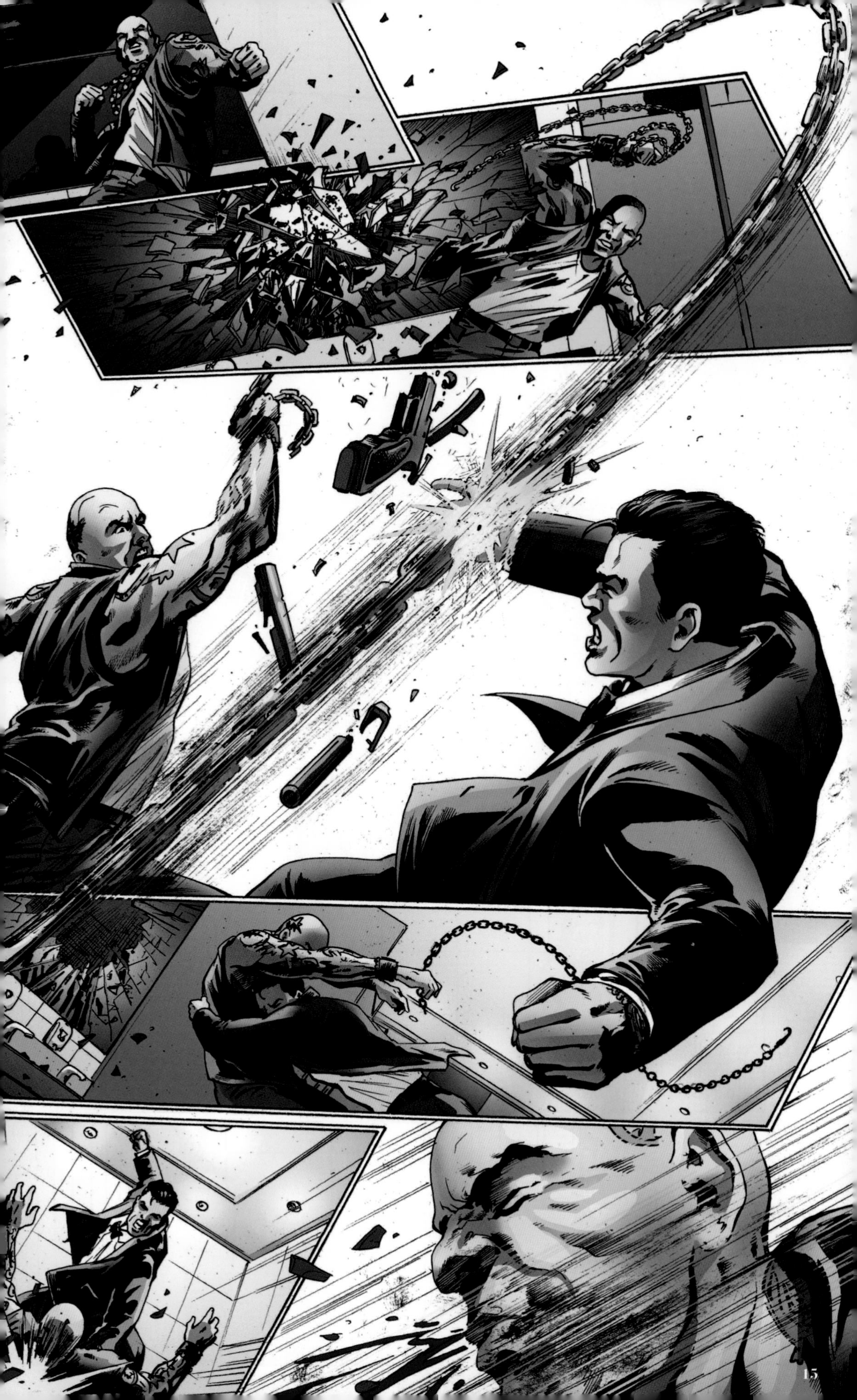

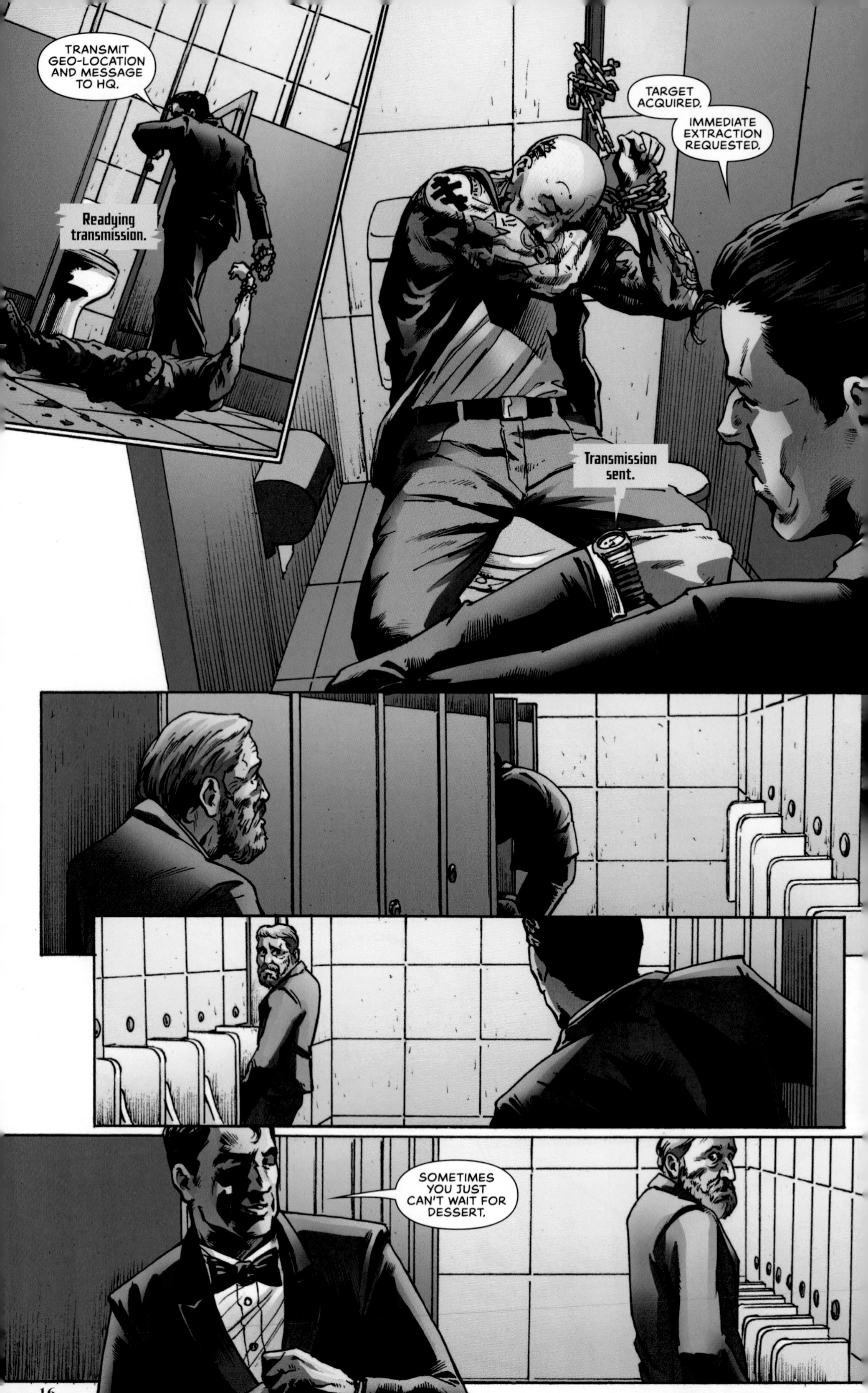
TRANSMIT GEO-LOCATION AND MESSAGE TO HQ.
Readying transmission.
TARGET ACQUIRED.
IMMEDIATE EXTRACTION REQUESTED.
Transmission sent.
SOMETIMES YOU JUST CAN'T WAIT FOR DESSERT.

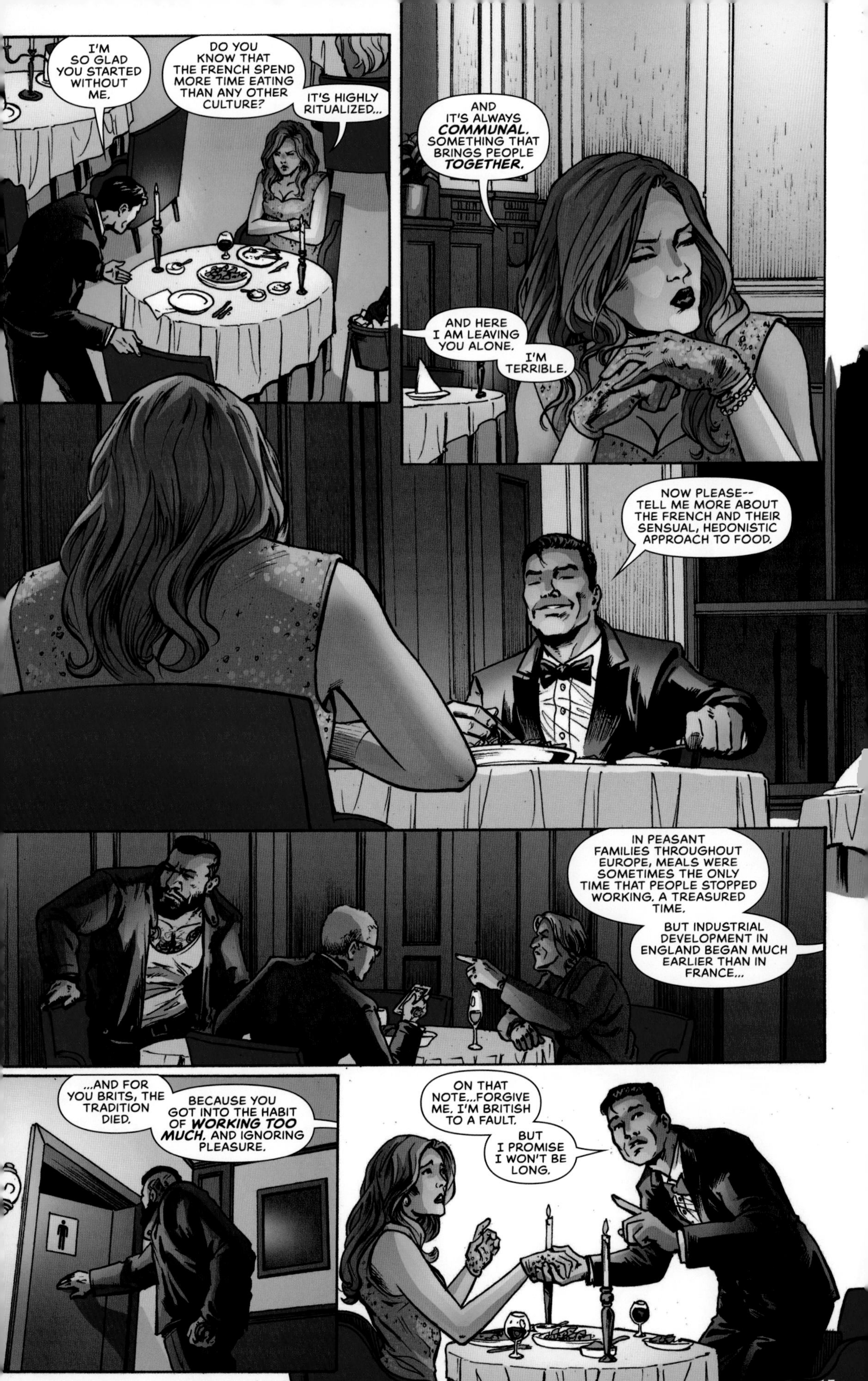

I'M SO GLAD YOU STARTED WITHOUT ME.
DO YOU KNOW THAT THE FRENCH SPEND MORE TIME EATING THAN ANY OTHER CULTURE?
IT'S HIGHLY RITUALIZED...
AND IT'S ALWAYS COMMUNAL, SOMETHING THAT BRINGS PEOPLE TOGETHER.
AND HERE I AM LEAVING YOU ALONE.
I'M TERRIBLE.
NOW PLEASE-- TELL ME MORE ABOUT THE FRENCH AND THEIR SENSUAL, HEDONISTIC APPROACH TO FOOD.
IN PEASANT FAMILIES THROUGHOUT EUROPE, MEALS WERE SOMETIMES THE ONLY TIME THAT PEOPLE STOPPED WORKING, A TREASURED TIME.
BUT INDUSTRIAL DEVELOPMENT IN ENGLAND BEGAN MUCH EARLIER THAN IN FRANCE...
...AND FOR YOU BRITS, THE TRADITION DIED,
BECAUSE YOU GOT INTO THE HABIT OF WORKING TOO MUCH, AND IGNORING PLEASURE.
ON THAT NOTE...FORGIVE ME. I'M BRITISH TO A FAULT.
BUT I PROMISE I WON'T BE LONG.

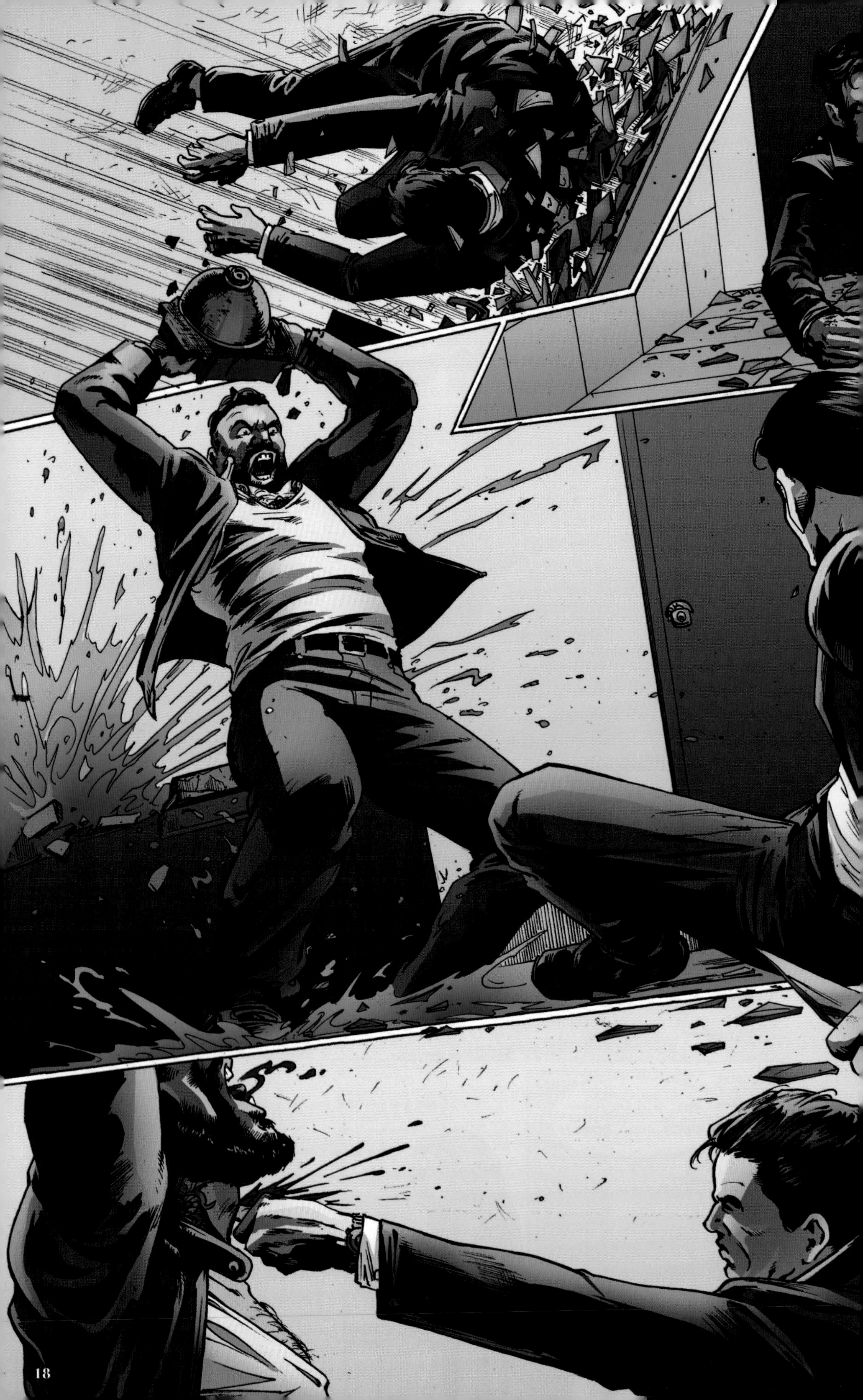

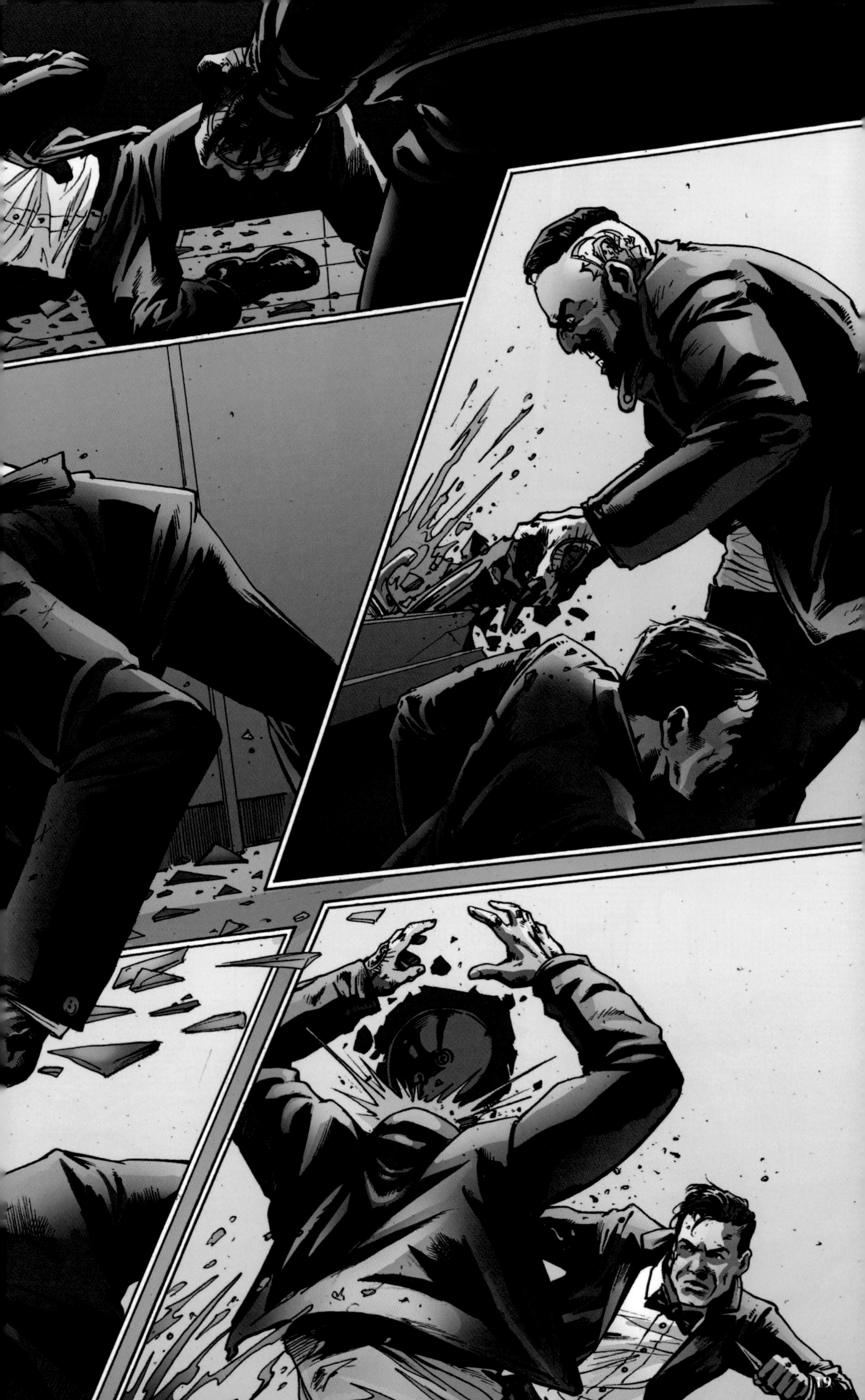

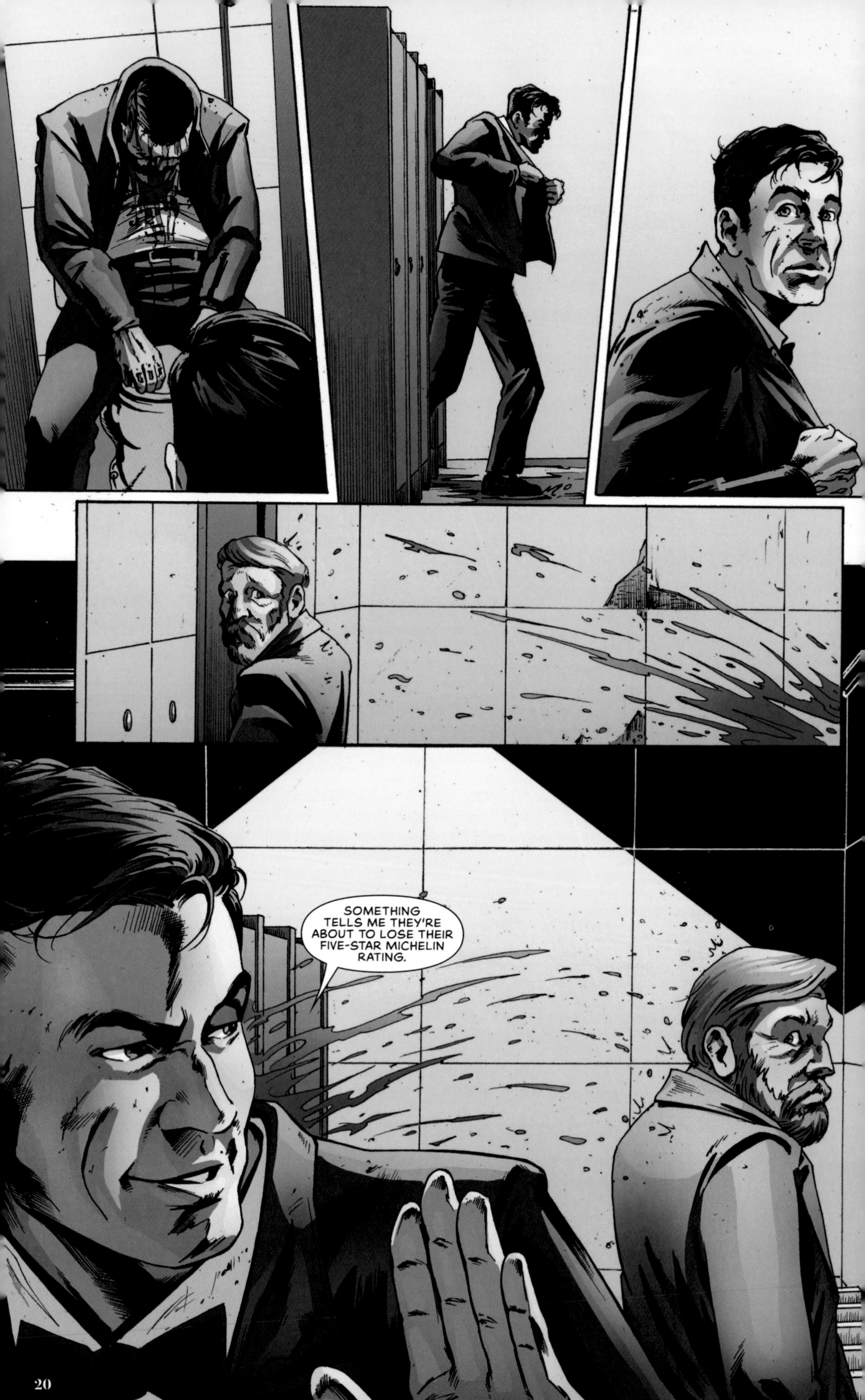
SOMETHING TELLS ME THEY'RE ABOUT TO LOSE THEIR FIVE-STAR MICHELIN RATING.

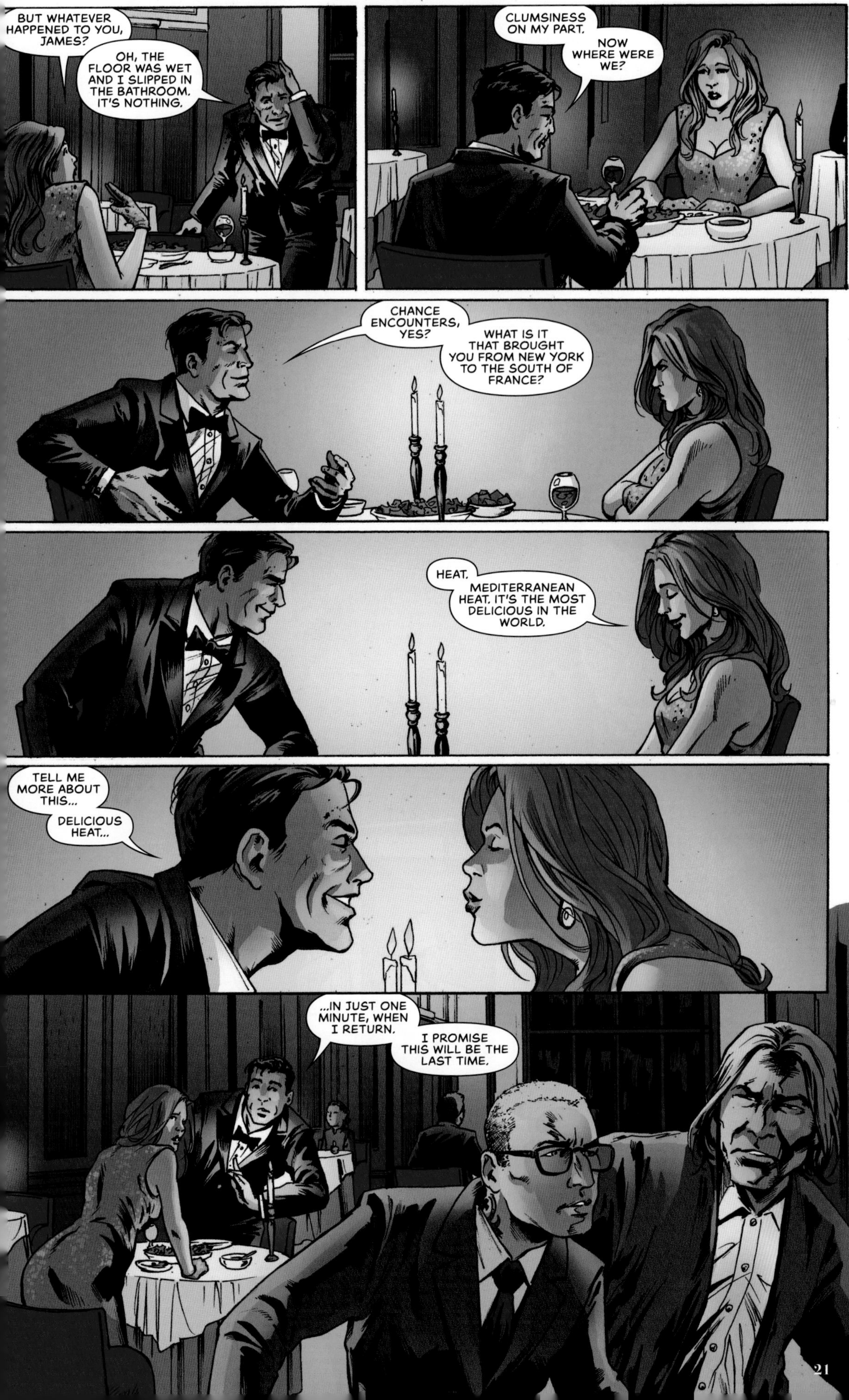

BUT WHATEVER HAPPENED TO YOU, JAMES?
OH, THE FLOOR WAS WET AND I SLIPPED IN THE BATHROOM. IT'S NOTHING.
CLUMSINESS ON MY PART.
NOW WHERE WERE WE?
CHANCE ENCOUNTERS, YES?
WHAT IS IT THAT BROUGHT YOU FROM NEW YORK TO THE SOUTH OF FRANCE?
HEAT.
MEDITERRANEAN HEAT. IT'S THE MOST DELICIOUS IN THE WORLD.
TELL ME MORE ABOUT THIS...
DELICIOUS HEAT...
...IN JUST ONE MINUTE, WHEN I RETURN.
I PROMISE THIS WILL BE THE LAST TIME.

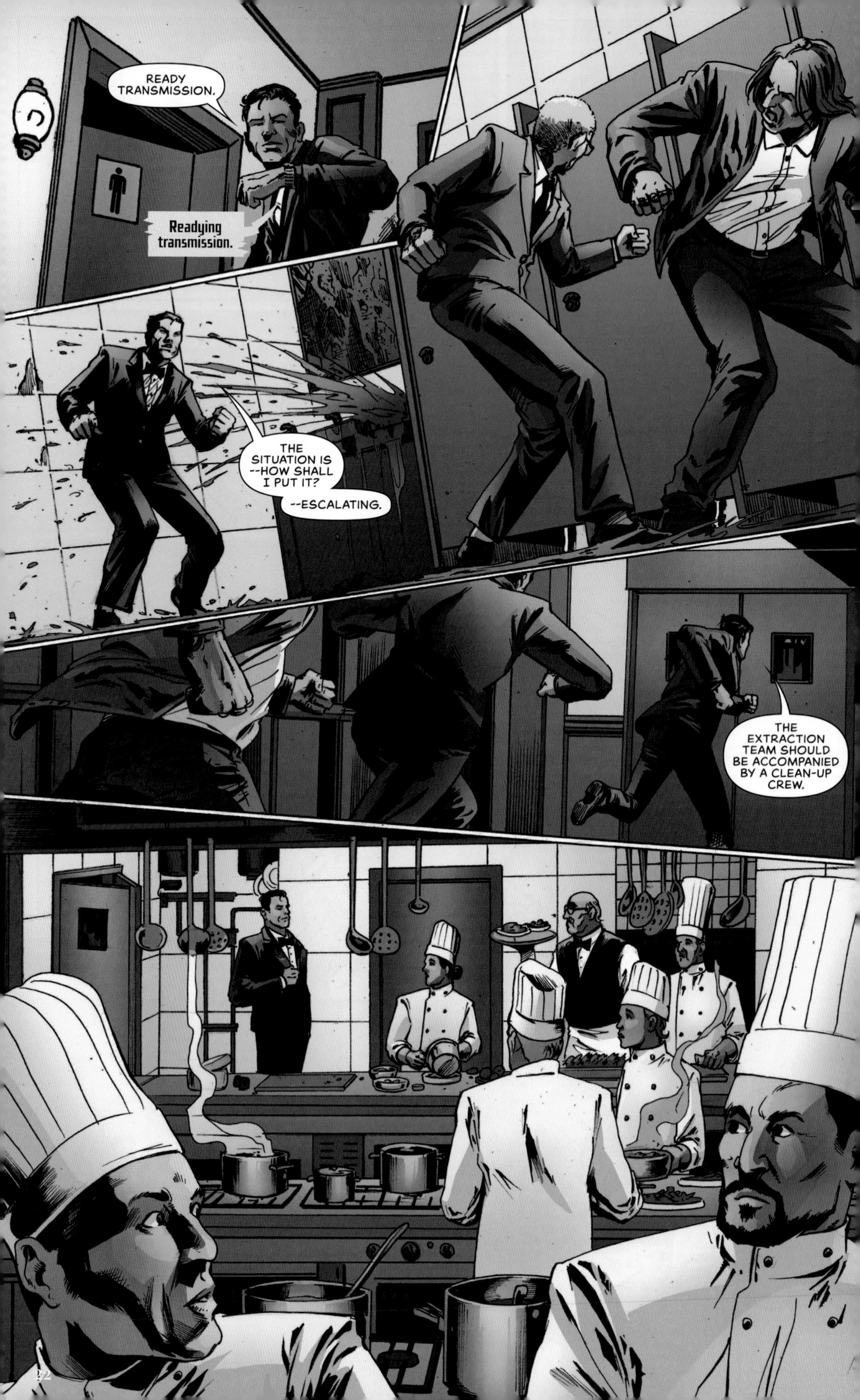
READY TRANSMISSION.
Readying transmission.
THE SITUATION IS --HOW SHALL I PUT IT?
--ESCALATING.
THE EXTRACTION TEAM SHOULD BE ACCOMPANIED BY A CLEAN-UP CREW.

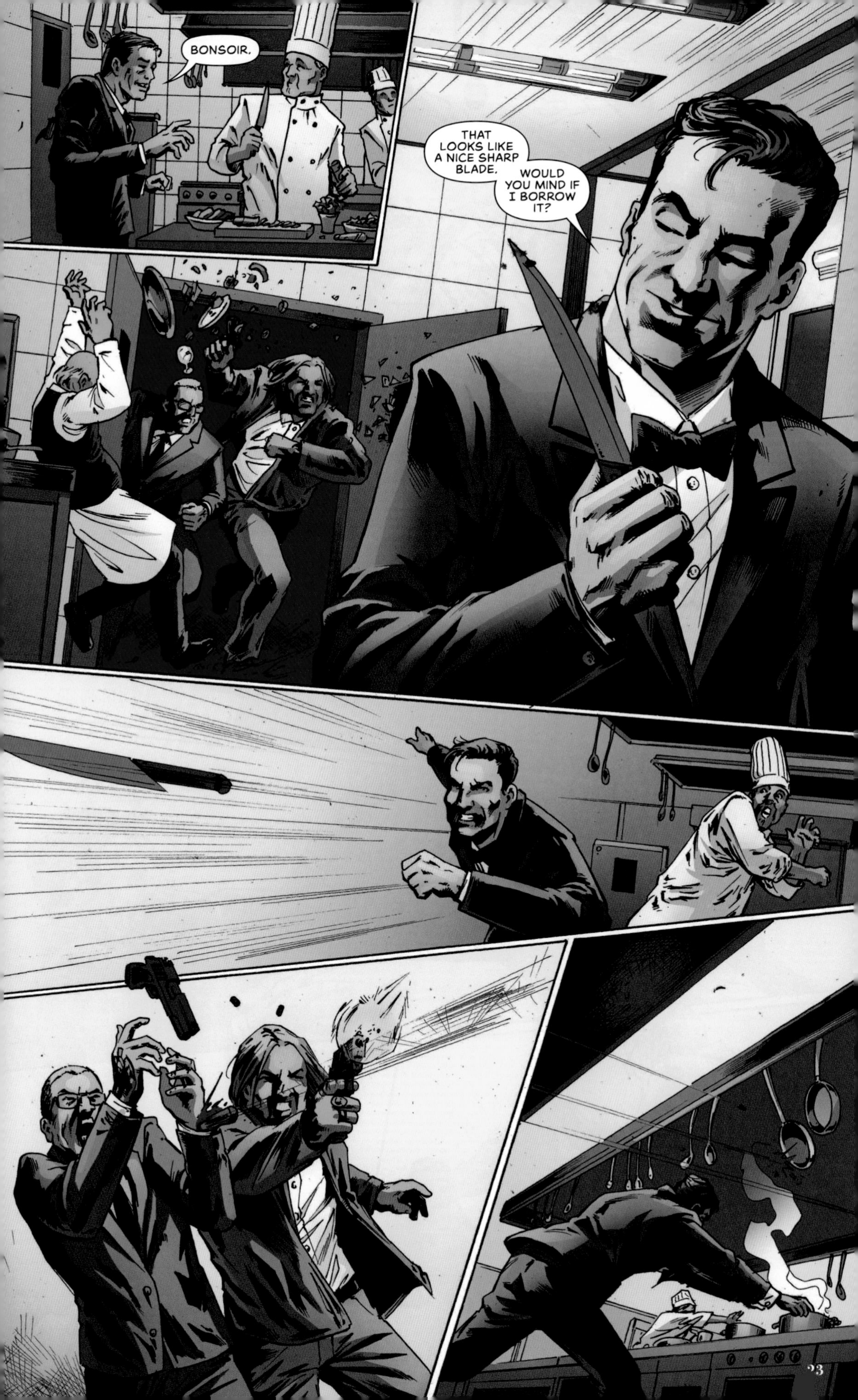
BONSOIR.
THAT LOOKS LIKE A NICE SHARP BLADE.
WOULD YOU MIND IF I BORROW IT?

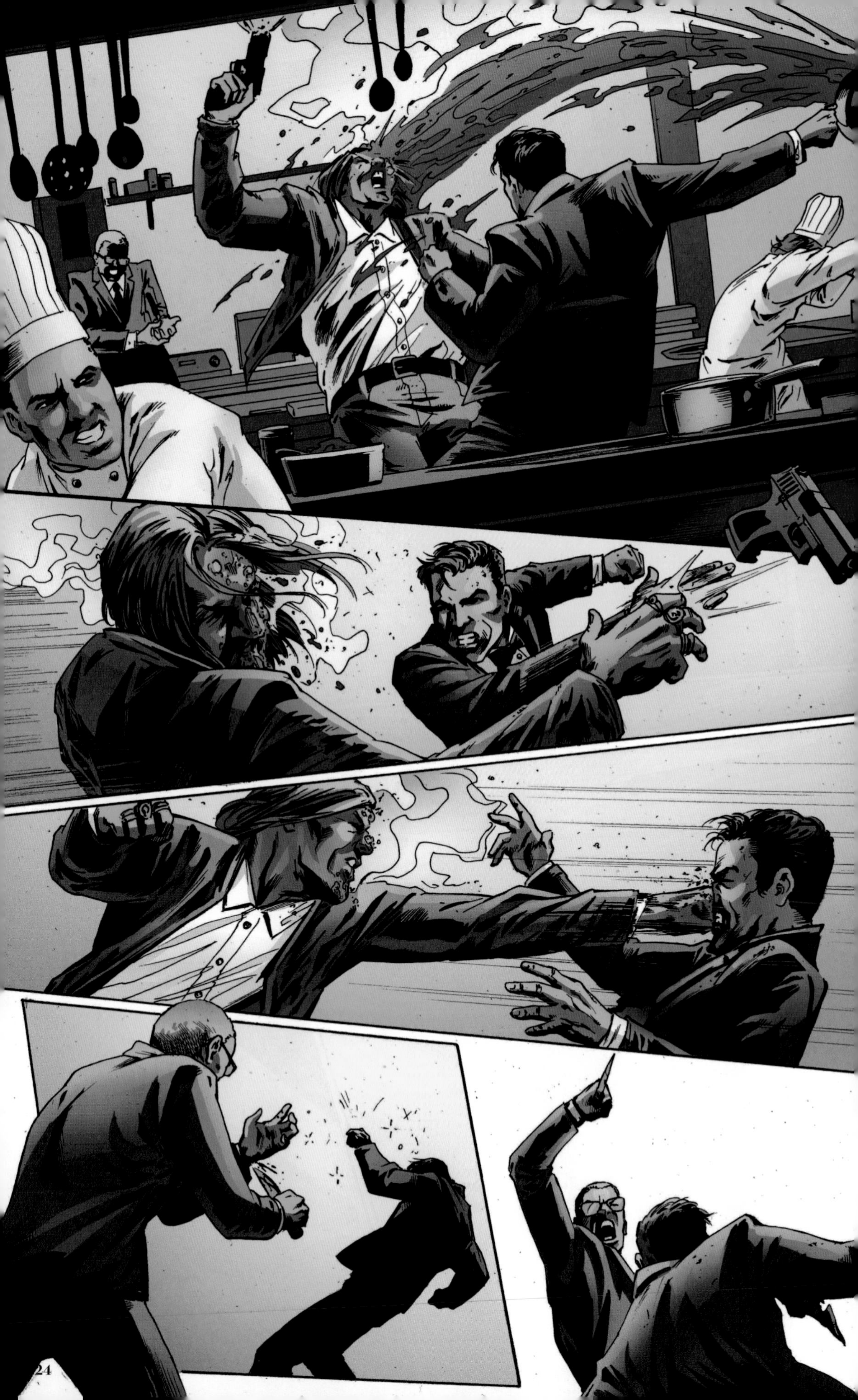

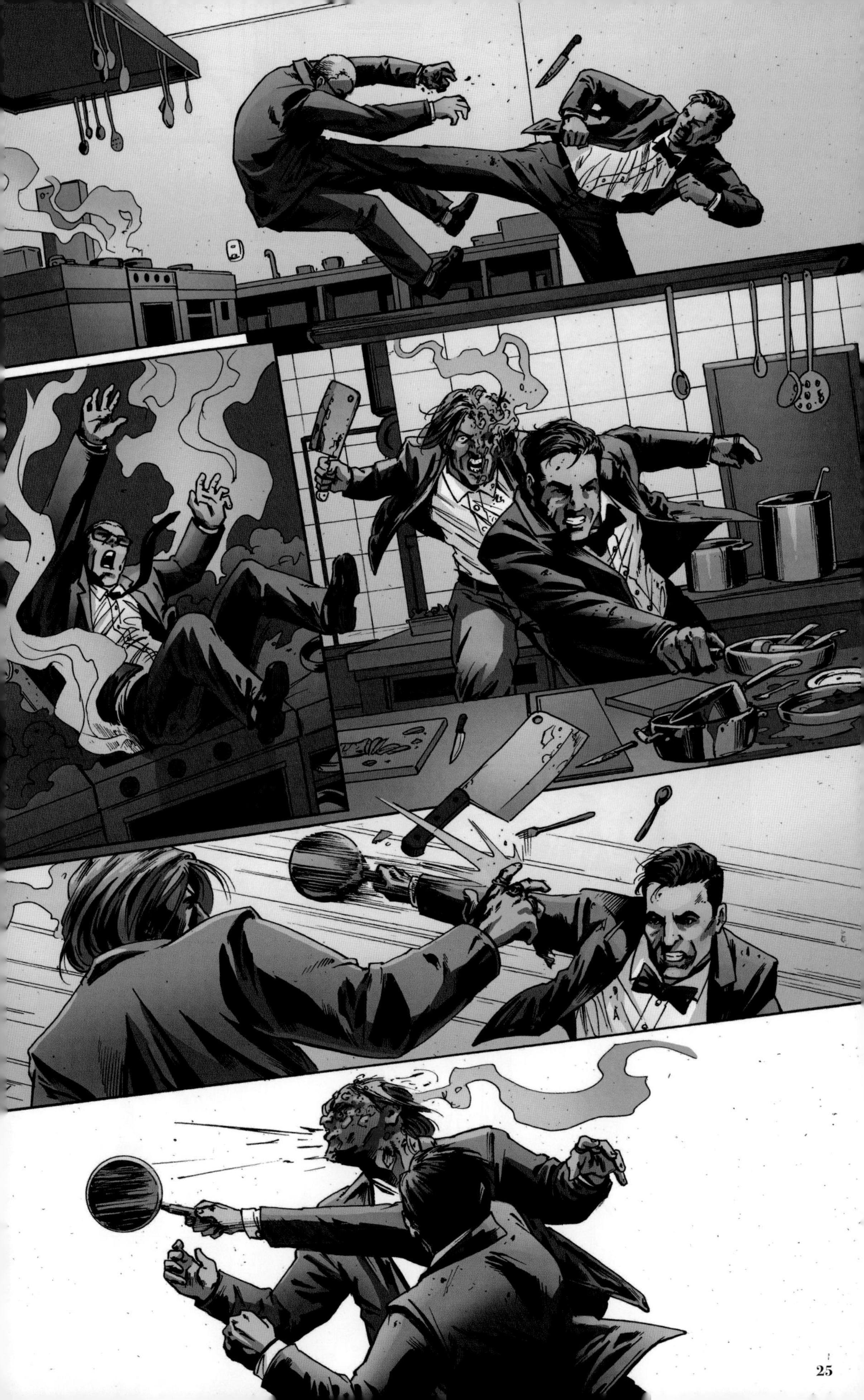

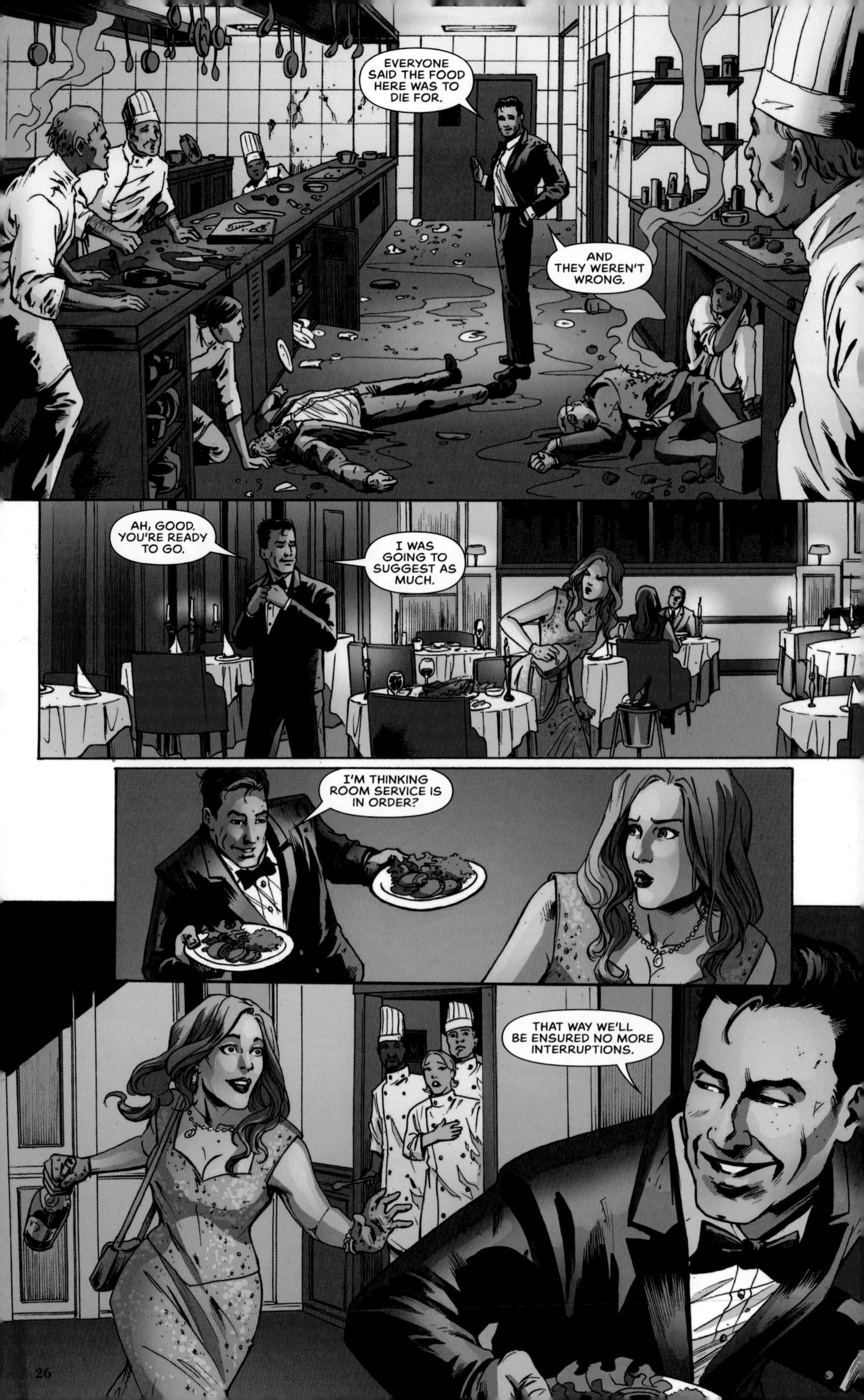
EVERYONE SAID THE FOOD HERE WAS TO DIE FOR.
AND THEY WEREN'T WRONG.
AH, GOOD. YOU'RE READY TO GO.
I WAS GOING TO SUGGEST AS MUCH.
I'M THINKING ROOM SERVICE IS IN ORDER?
THAT WAY WE'LL BE ENSURED NO MORE INTERRUPTIONS.

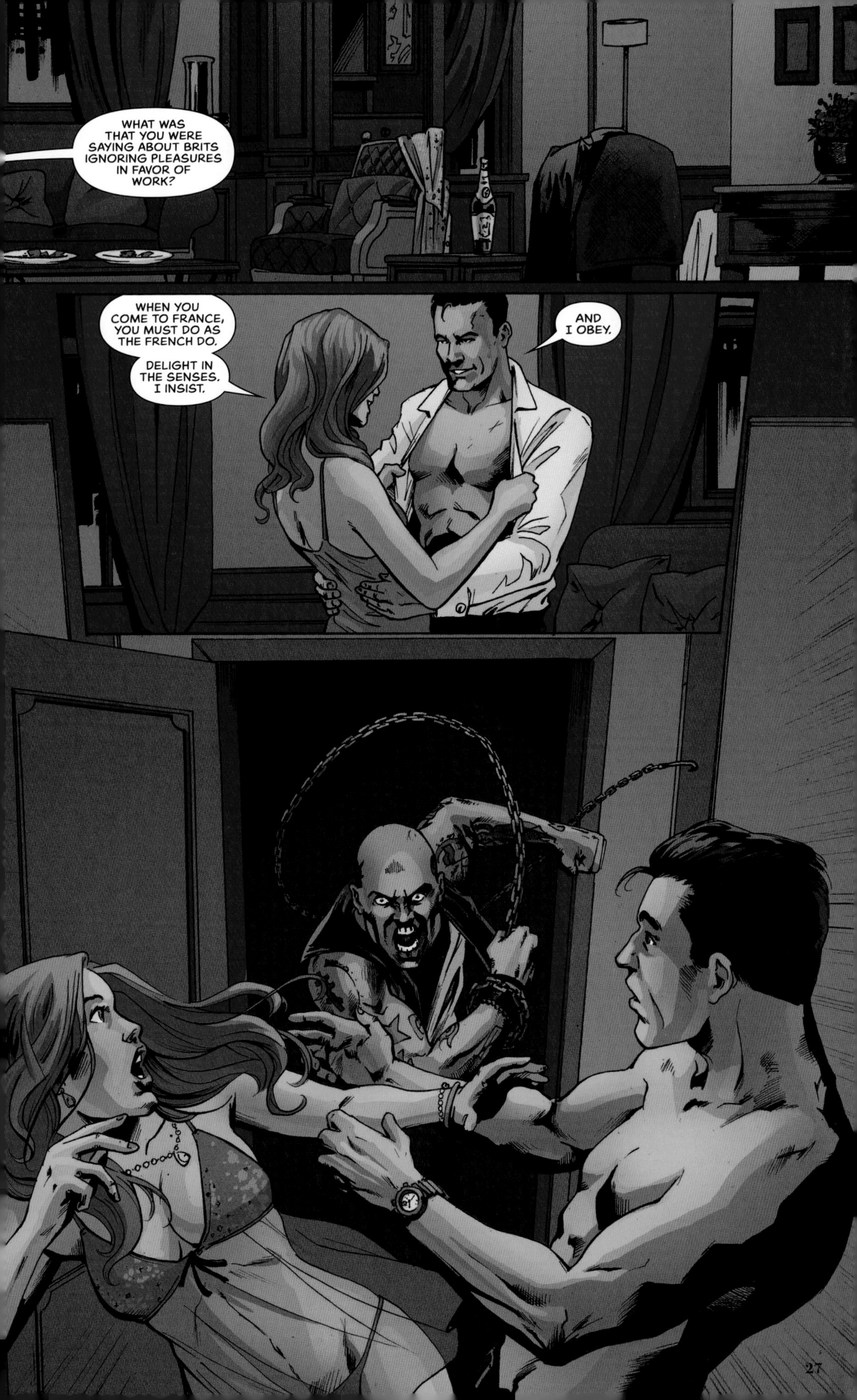
WHAT WAS THAT YOU WERE SAYING ABOUT BRITS IGNORING PLEASURES IN FAVOR OF WORK?
WHEN YOU COME TO FRANCE, YOU MUST DO AS THE FRENCH DO.
DELIGHT IN THE SENSES. I INSIST.
AND I OBEY.

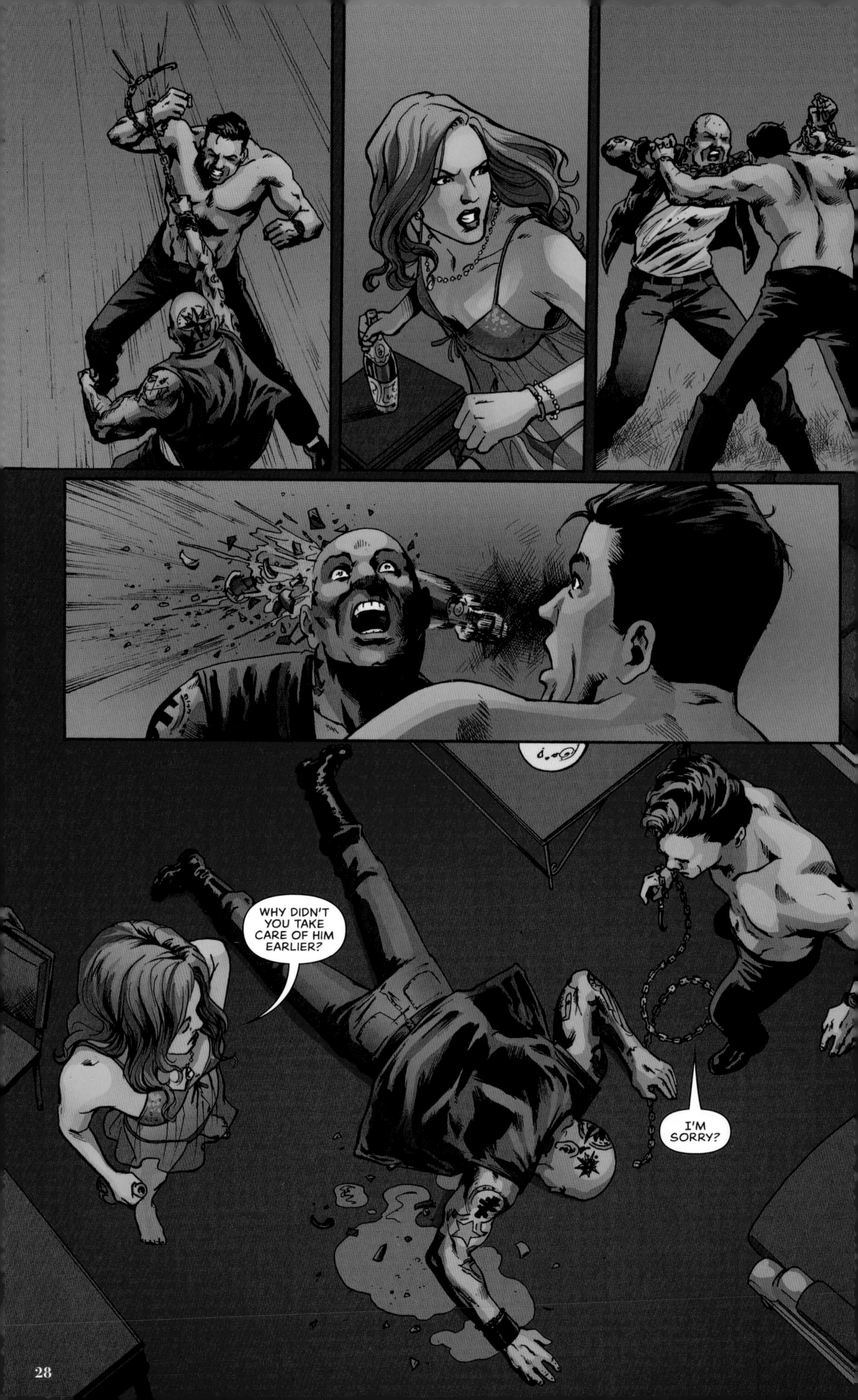
WHY DIDN'T YOU TAKE CARE OF HIM EARLIER?
I'M SORRY?

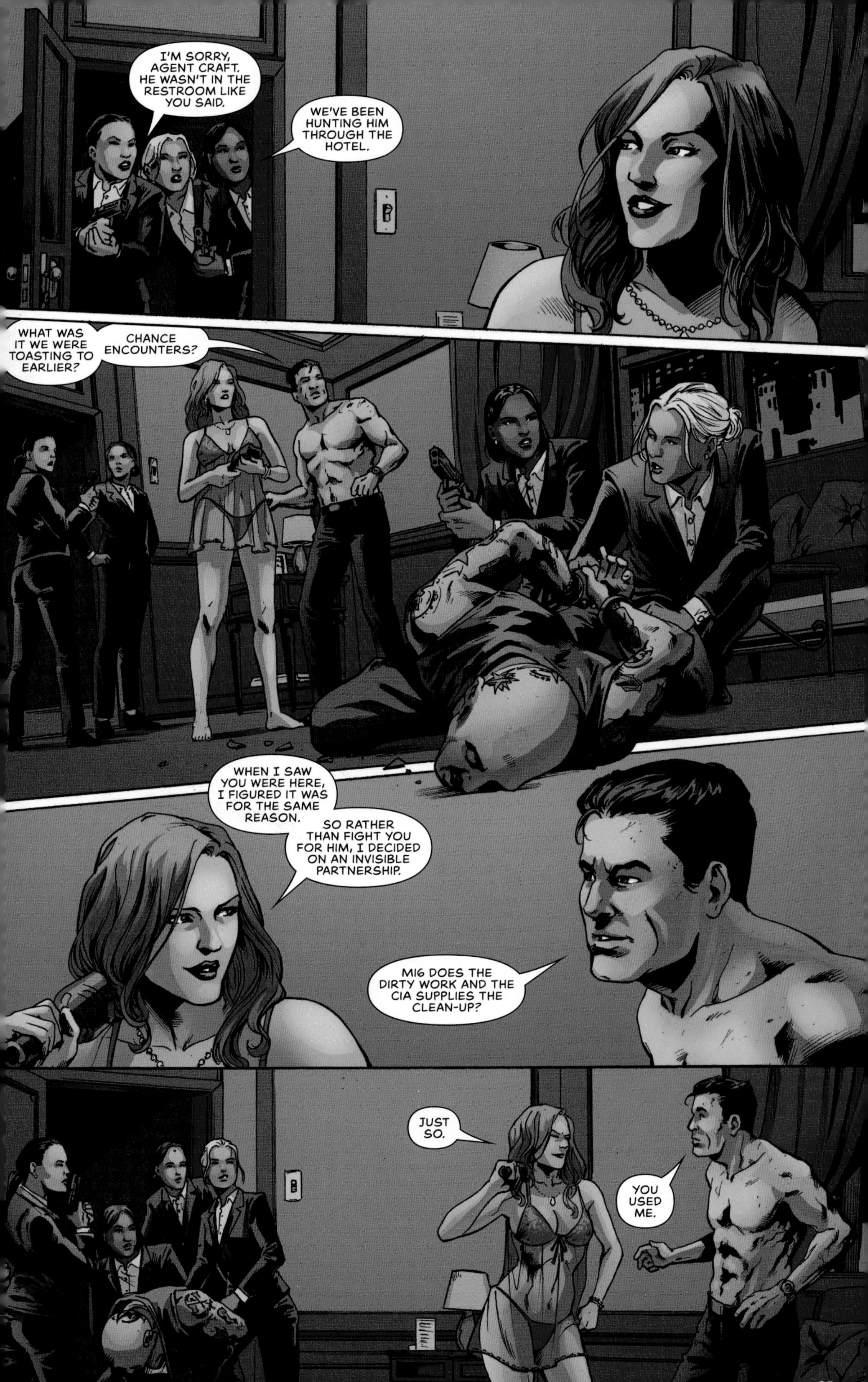
I'M SORRY, AGENT CRAFT. HE WASN'T IN THE RESTROOM LIKE YOU SAID.
WE'VE BEEN HUNTING HIM THROUGH THE HOTEL.
WHAT WAS IT WE WERE TOASTING TO EARLIER?
CHANCE ENCOUNTERS?
WHEN I SAW YOU WERE HERE, I FIGURED IT WAS FOR THE SAME REASON.
SO RATHER THAN FIGHT YOU FOR HIM, I DECIDED ON AN INVISIBLE PARTNERSHIP.
MI6 DOES THE DIRTY WORK AND THE CIA SUPPLIES THE CLEAN-UP?
JUST SO.
YOU USED ME.

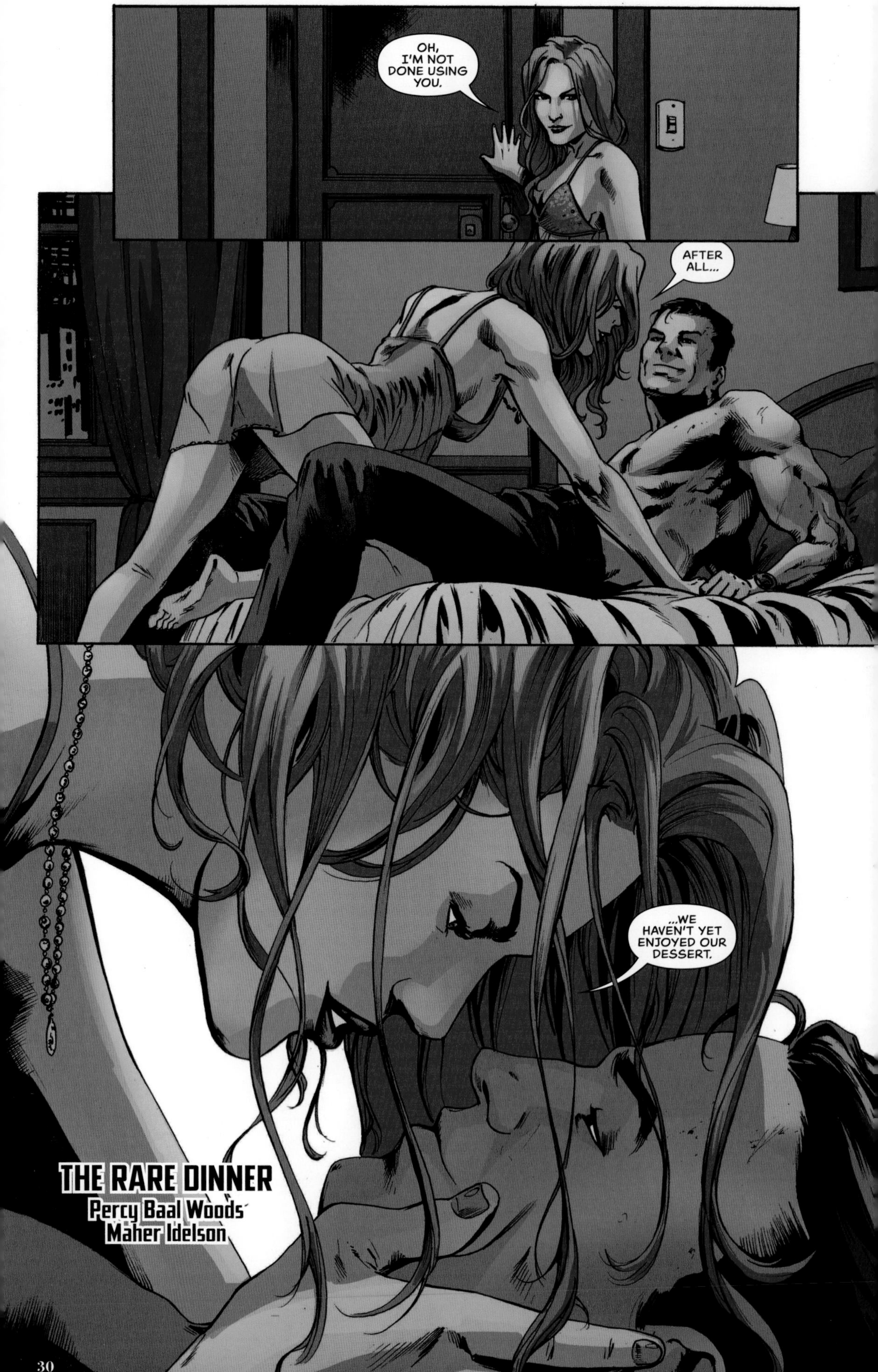
OH, I'M NOT DONE USING YOU.
AFTER ALL...
...WE HAVEN'T YET ENJOYED OUR DESSERT.
THE RARE DINNER
Percy Baal Woods
Maher Idelson

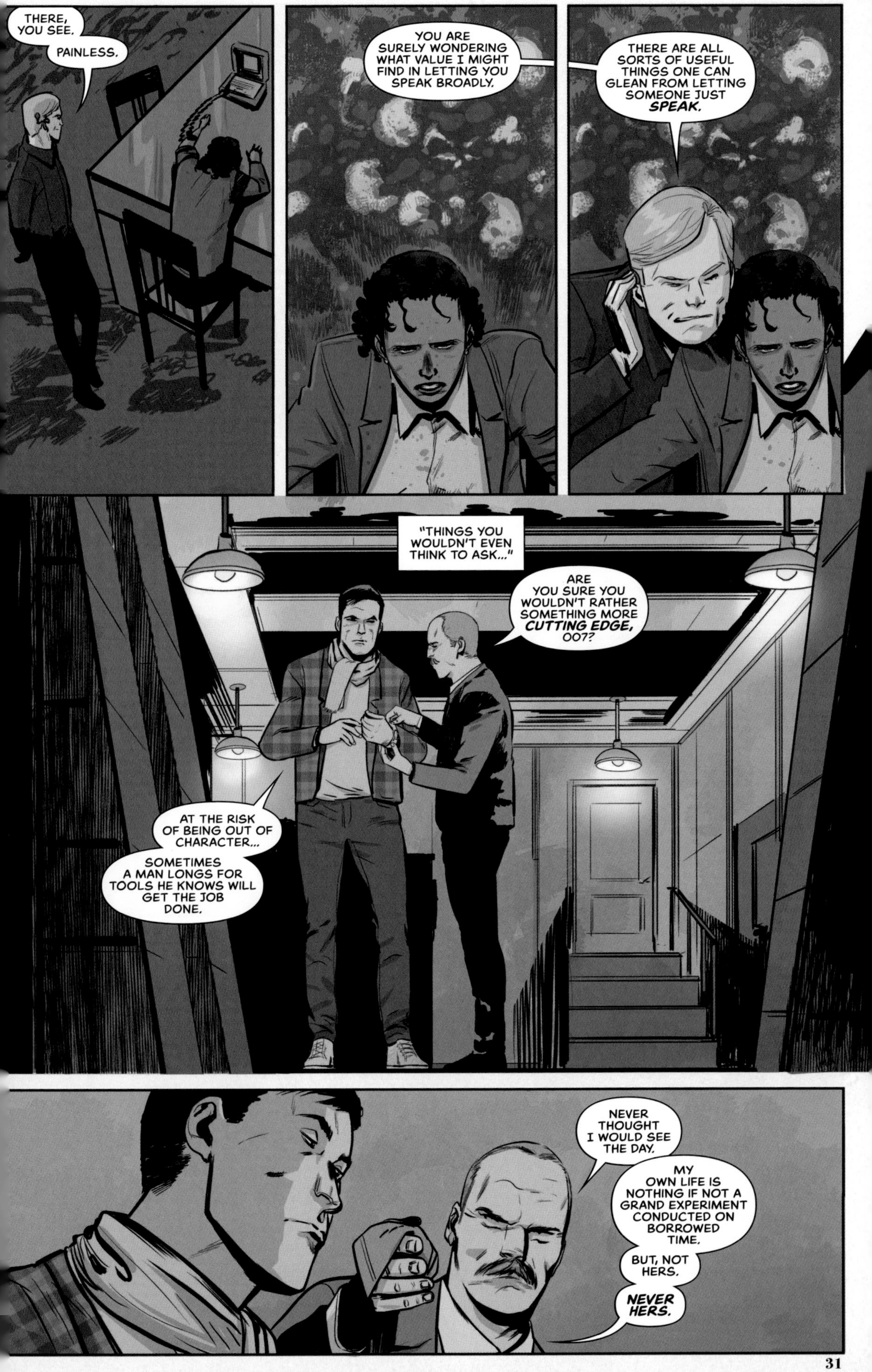
THERE, YOU SEE.
PAINLESS.
YOU ARE SURELY WONDERING WHAT VALUE I MIGHT FIND IN LETTING YOU SPEAK BROADLY.
THERE ARE ALL SORTS OF USEFUL THINGS ONE CAN GLEAN FROM LETTING SOMEONE JUST *SPEAK.*
"THINGS YOU WOULDN'T EVEN THINK TO ASK..."
ARE YOU SURE YOU WOULDN'T RATHER SOMETHING MORE *CUTTING EDGE,* 007?
AT THE RISK OF BEING OUT OF CHARACTER...
SOMETIMES A MAN LONGS FOR TOOLS HE KNOWS WILL GET THE JOB DONE.
NEVER THOUGHT I WOULD SEE THE DAY.
MY OWN LIFE IS NOTHING IF NOT A GRAND EXPERIMENT CONDUCTED ON BORROWED TIME.
BUT, NOT HERS.
NEVER HERS.

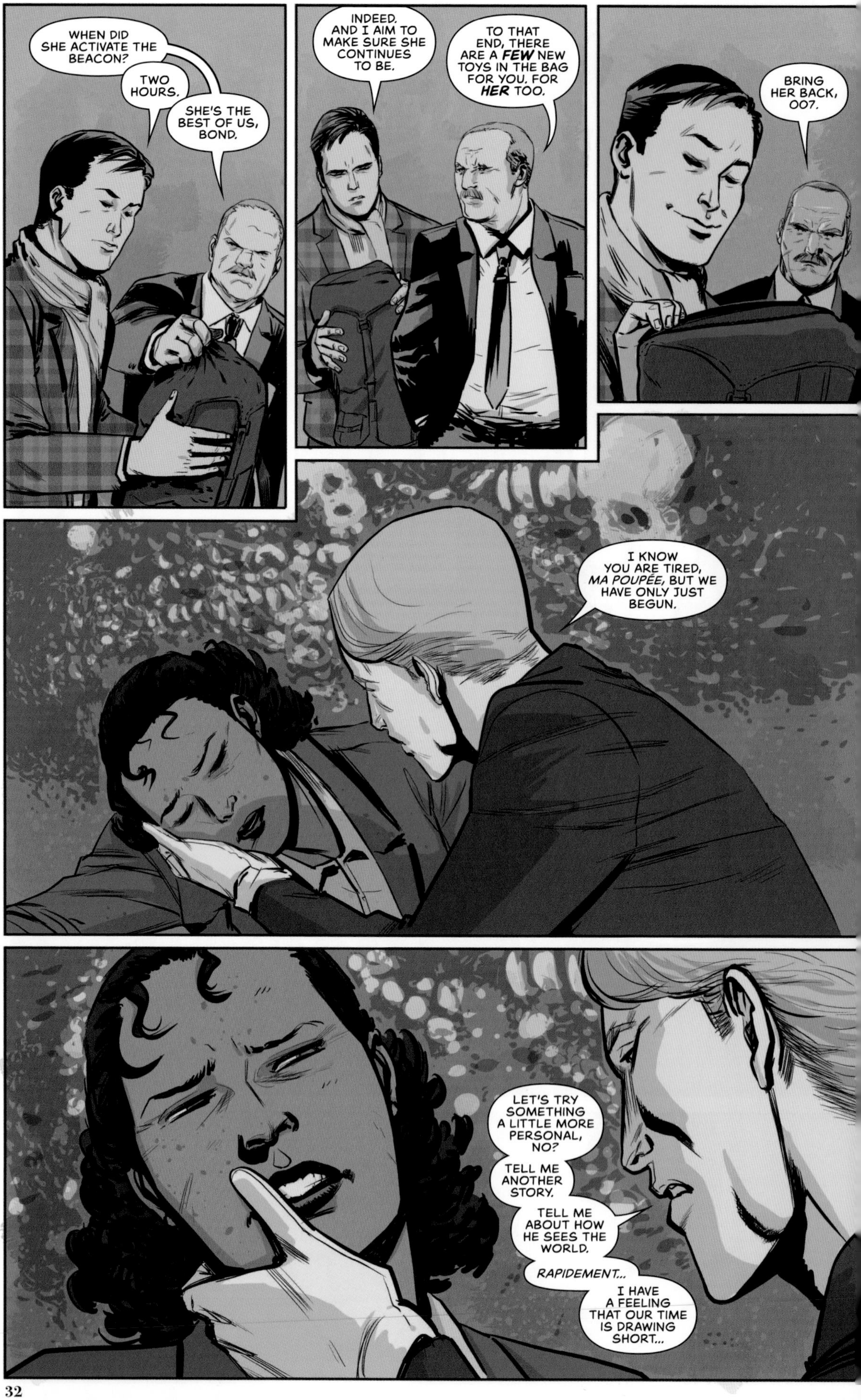
WHEN DID SHE ACTIVATE THE BEACON?
TWO HOURS.
SHE'S THE BEST OF US, BOND.
INDEED. AND I AIM TO MAKE SURE SHE CONTINUES TO BE.
TO THAT END, THERE ARE A FEW NEW TOYS IN THE BAG FOR YOU. FOR HER TOO.
BRING HER BACK, 007.
I KNOW YOU ARE TIRED, MA POUPÉE, BUT WE HAVE ONLY JUST BEGUN.
LET'S TRY SOMETHING A LITTLE MORE PERSONAL, NO?
TELL ME ANOTHER STORY.
TELL ME ABOUT HOW HE SEES THE WORLD.
RAPIDEMENT...
I HAVE A FEELING THAT OUR TIME IS DRAWING SHORT...

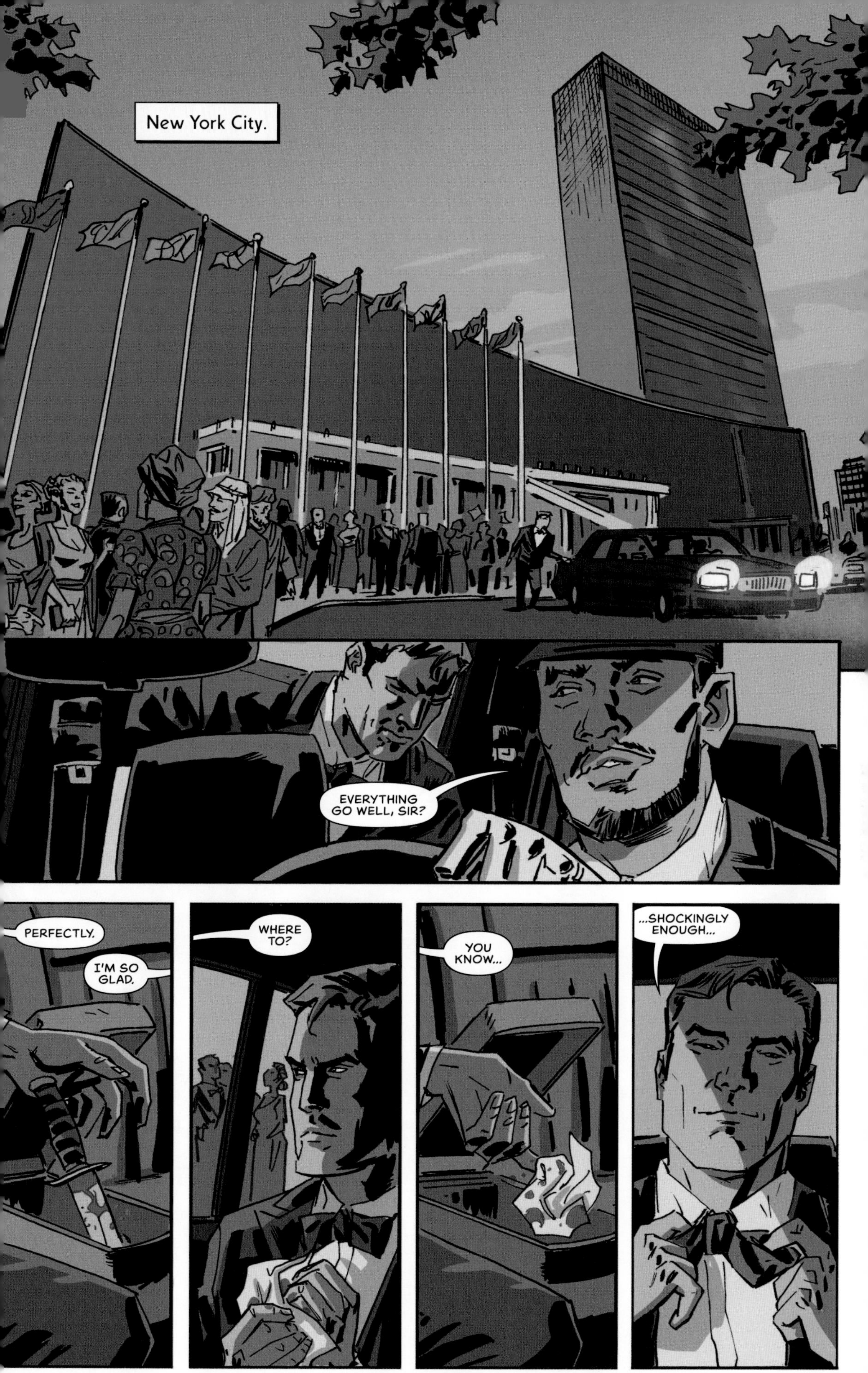
New York City.
EVERYTHING GO WELL, SIR?
PERFECTLY.
I'M SO GLAD.
WHERE TO?
YOU KNOW...
...SHOCKINGLY ENOUGH...

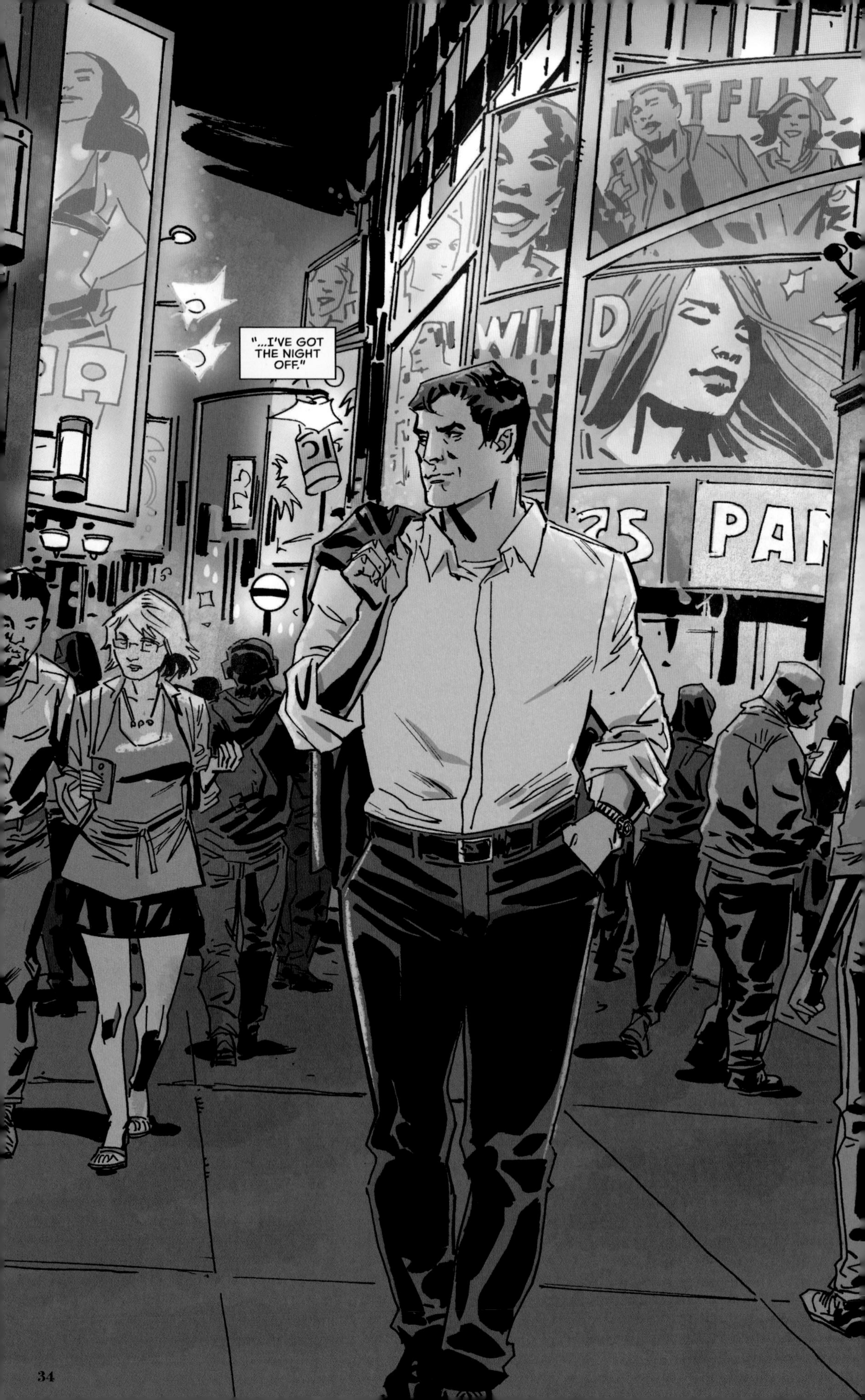
"...I'VE GOT THE NIGHT OFF."

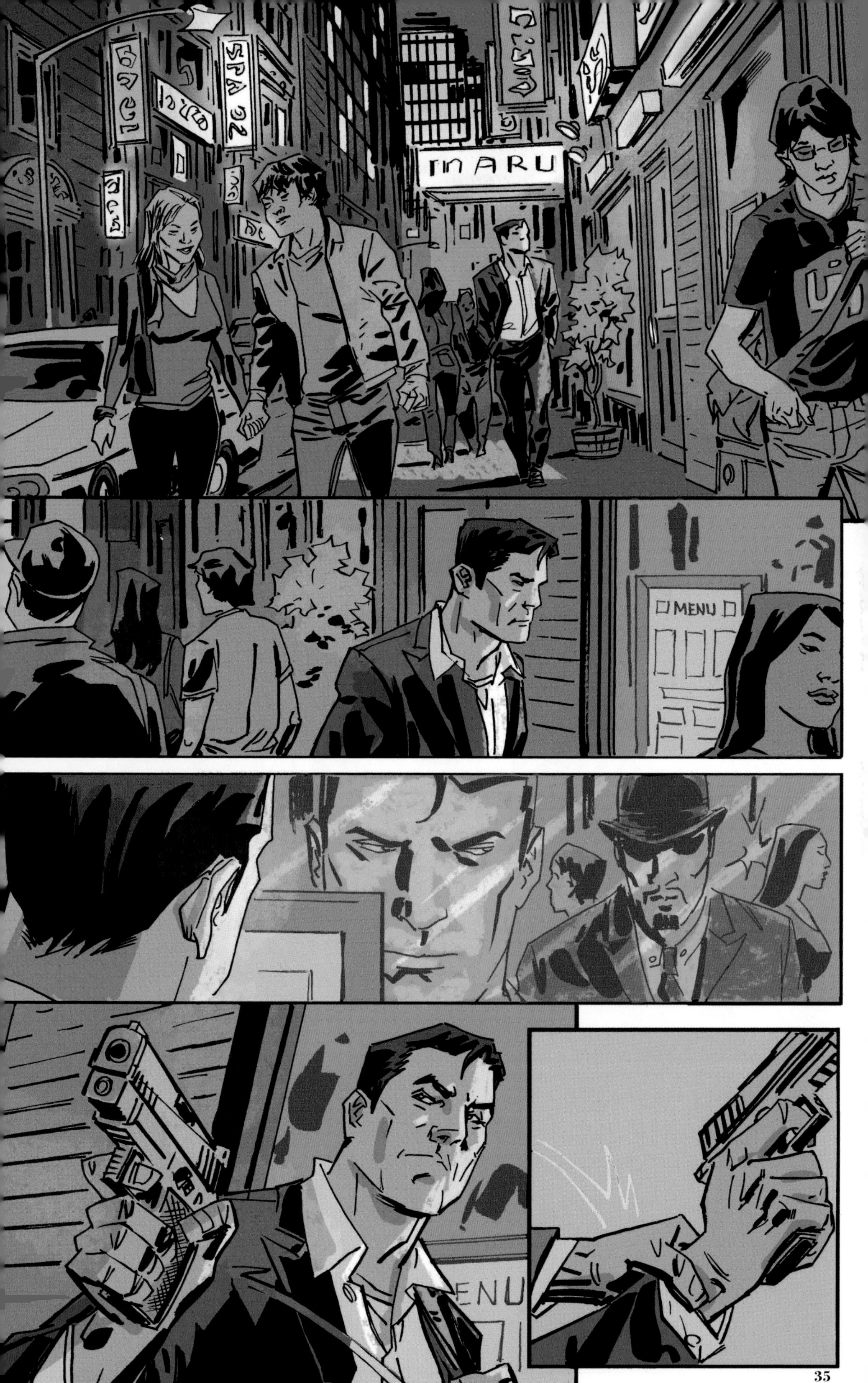
MARU
MENU
ENU

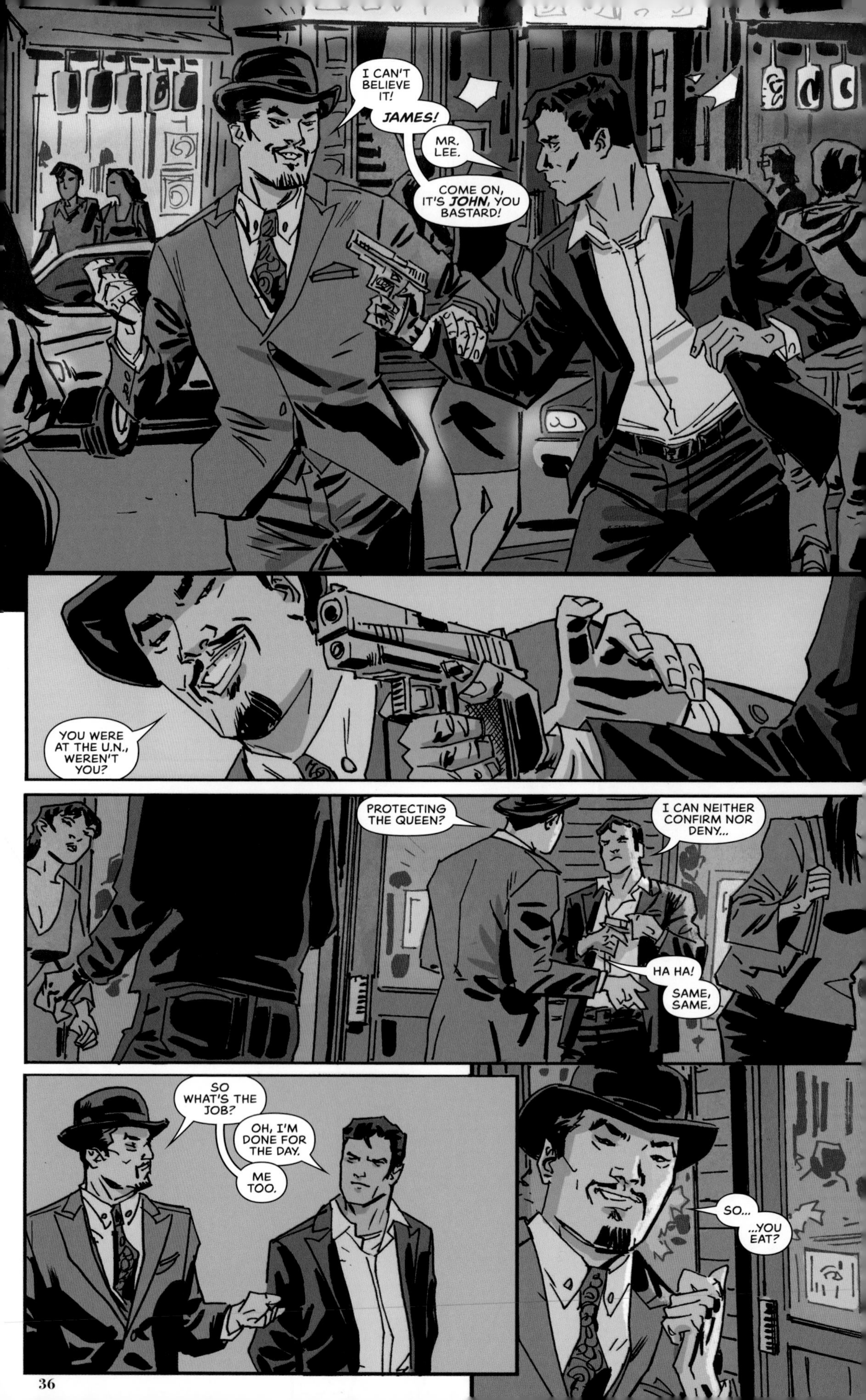
I CAN'T BELIEVE IT!
JAMES!
MR. LEE.
COME ON, IT'S JOHN, YOU BASTARD!
YOU WERE AT THE U.N., WEREN'T YOU?
PROTECTING THE QUEEN?
I CAN NEITHER CONFIRM NOR DENY...
HA HA!
SAME, SAME.
SO WHAT'S THE JOB?
OH, I'M DONE FOR THE DAY.
ME TOO.
SO...
...YOU EAT?

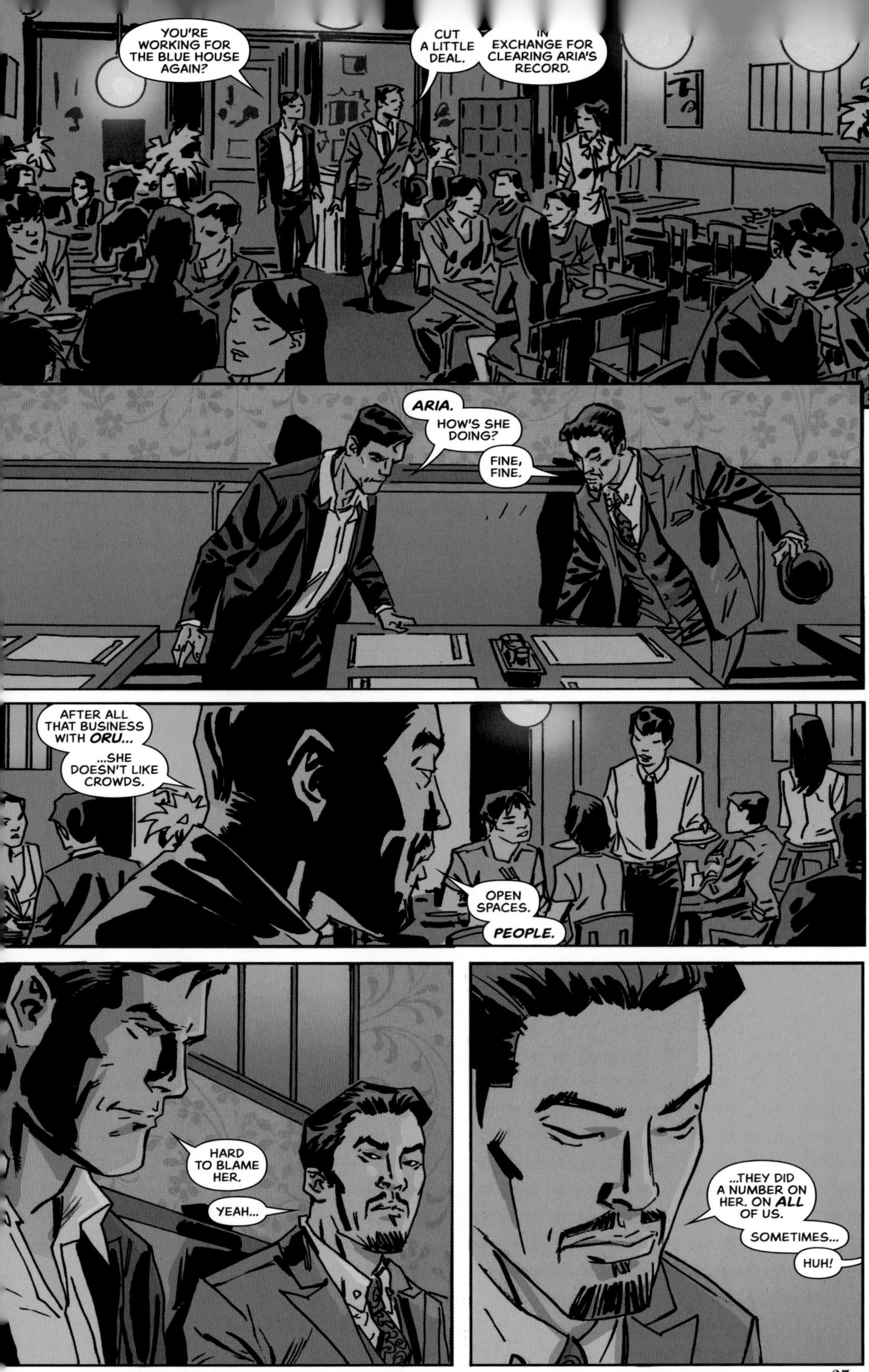
YOU'RE WORKING FOR THE BLUE HOUSE AGAIN?
CUT A LITTLE DEAL.
IN EXCHANGE FOR CLEARING ARIA'S RECORD.
ARIA.
HOW'S SHE DOING?
FINE, FINE.
AFTER ALL THAT BUSINESS WITH ORU...
...SHE DOESN'T LIKE CROWDS.
OPEN SPACES.
PEOPLE.
HARD TO BLAME HER.
YEAH...
...THEY DID A NUMBER ON HER. ON ALL OF US.
SOMETIMES...
HUH!

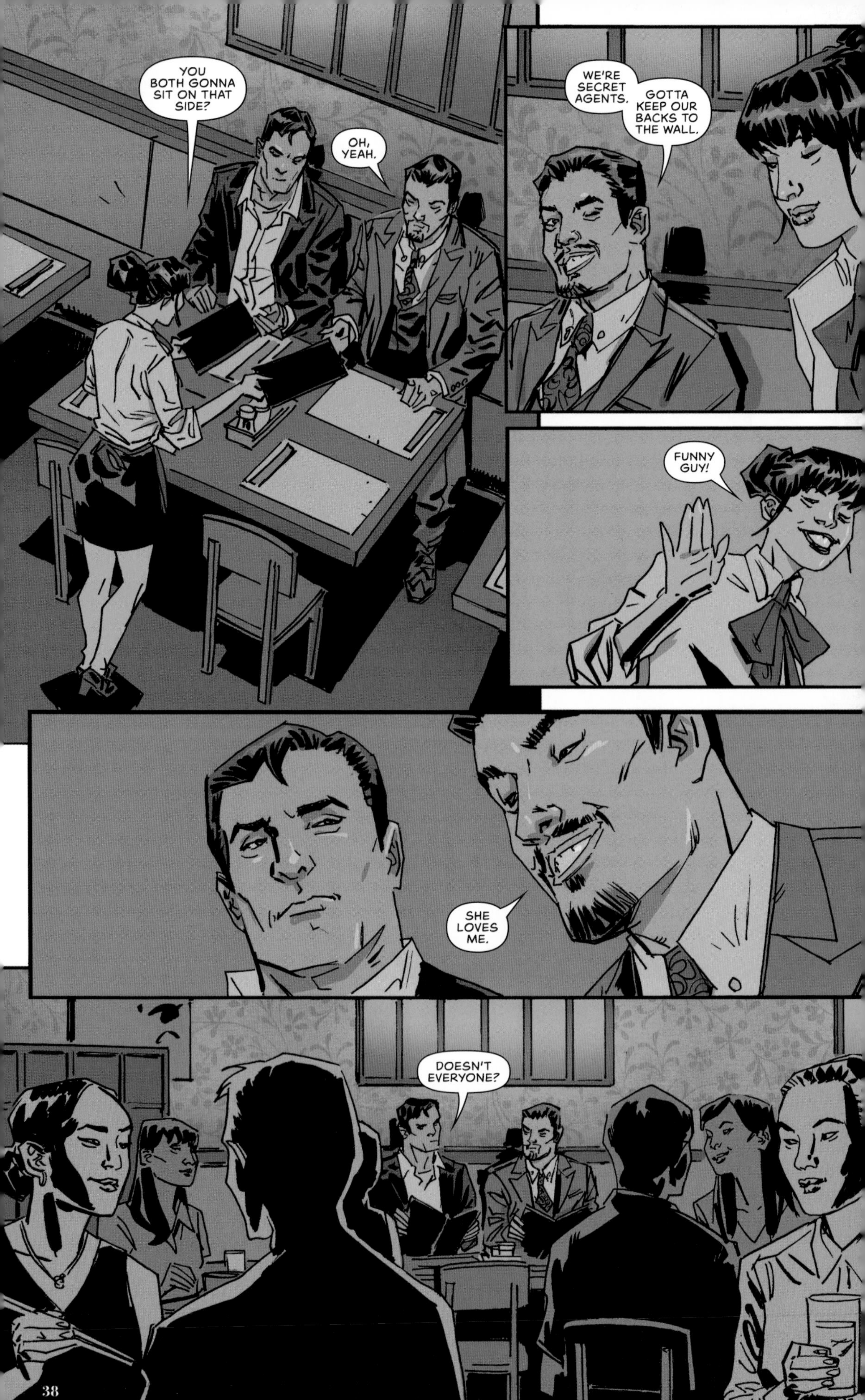
YOU BOTH GONNA SIT ON THAT SIDE?
OH, YEAH.
WE'RE SECRET AGENTS.
GOTTA KEEP OUR BACKS TO THE WALL.
FUNNY GUY!
SHE LOVES ME.
DOESN'T EVERYONE?

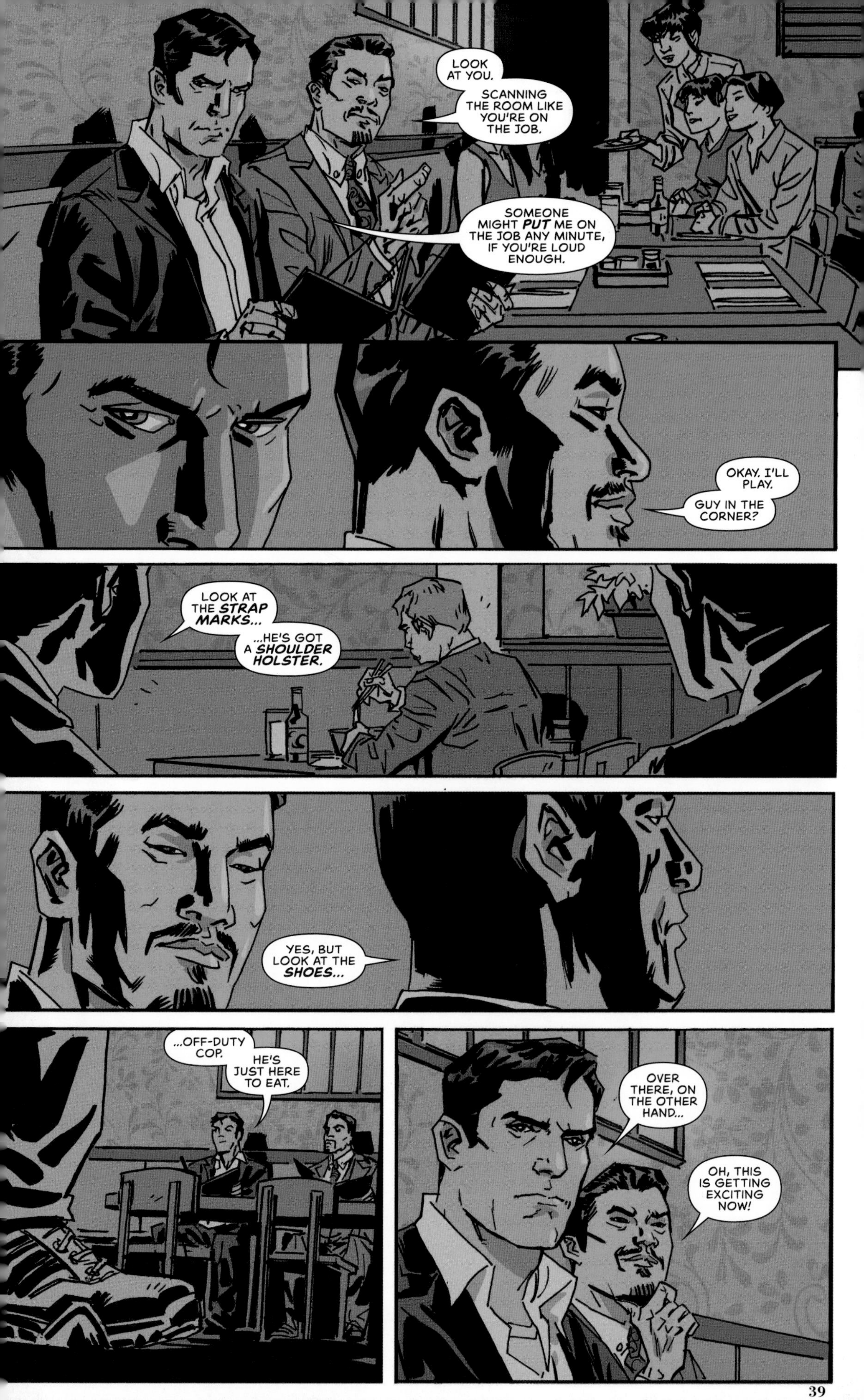
LOOK AT YOU.
SCANNING THE ROOM LIKE YOU'RE ON THE JOB.
SOMEONE MIGHT PUT ME ON THE JOB ANY MINUTE, IF YOU'RE LOUD ENOUGH.
OKAY. I'LL PLAY.
GUY IN THE CORNER?
LOOK AT THE STRAP MARKS...
...HE'S GOT A SHOULDER HOLSTER.
YES, BUT LOOK AT THE SHOES...
...OFF-DUTY COP.
HE'S JUST HERE TO EAT.
OVER THERE, ON THE OTHER HAND...
OH, THIS IS GETTING EXCITING NOW!

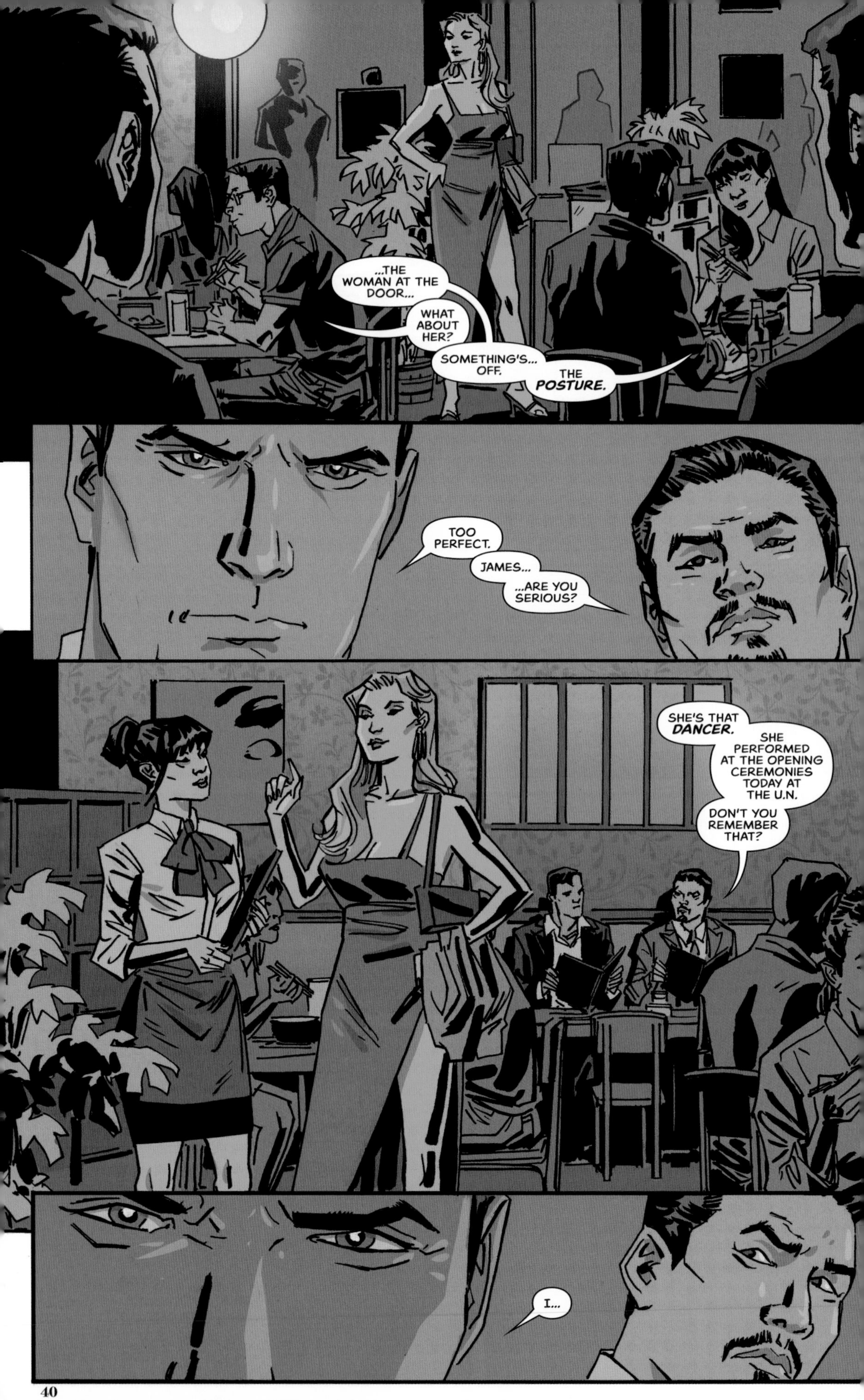
...THE WOMAN AT THE DOOR...
WHAT ABOUT HER?
SOMETHING'S... OFF.
THE *POSTURE.*
TOO PERFECT.
JAMES...
...ARE YOU SERIOUS?
SHE'S THAT *DANCER.*
SHE PERFORMED AT THE OPENING CEREMONIES TODAY AT THE U.N.
DON'T YOU REMEMBER THAT?
I...

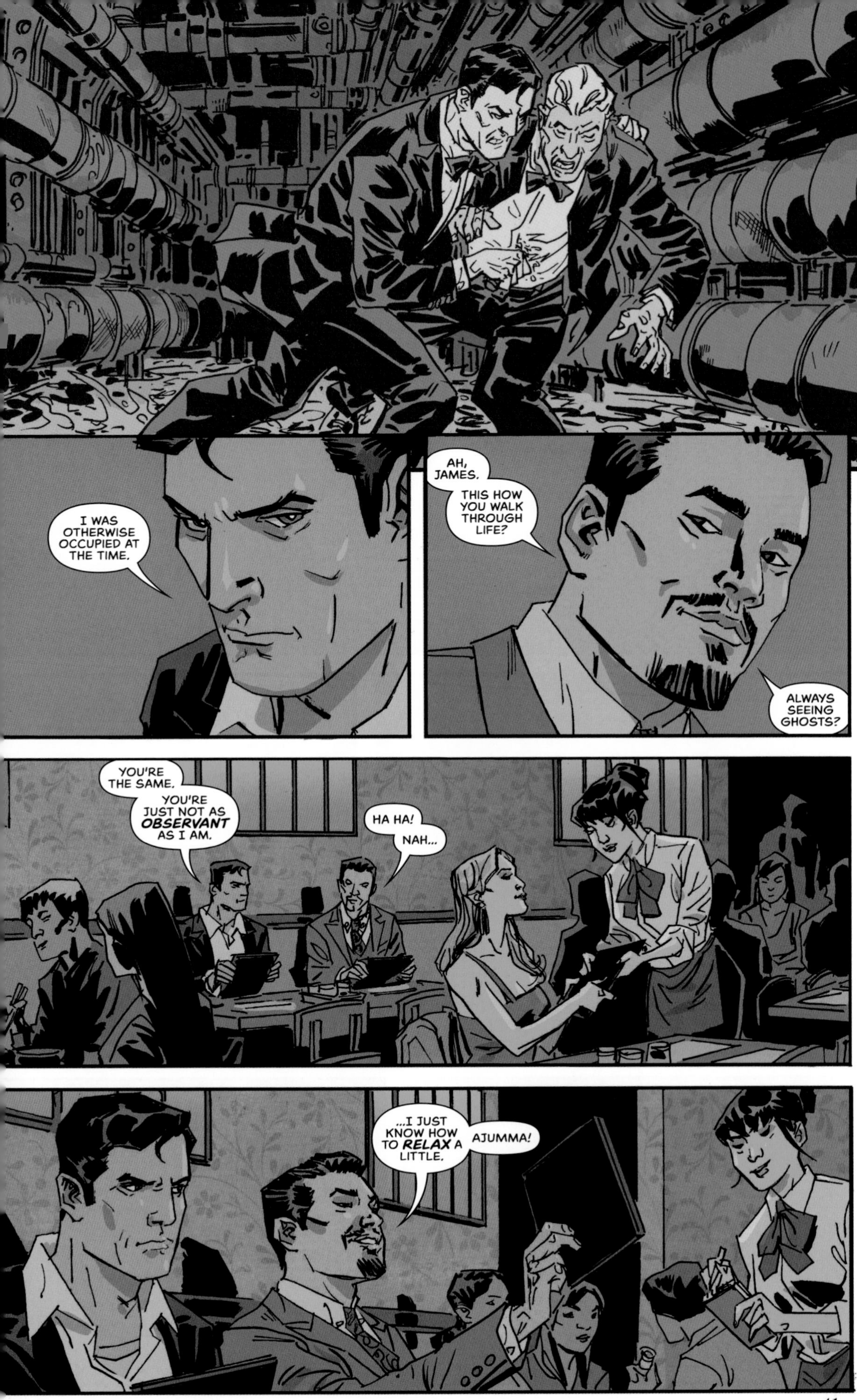
I WAS OTHERWISE OCCUPIED AT THE TIME.
AH, JAMES.
THIS HOW YOU WALK THROUGH LIFE?
ALWAYS SEEING GHOSTS?
YOU'RE THE SAME.
YOU'RE JUST NOT AS OBSERVANT AS I AM.
HA HA!
NAH...
...I JUST KNOW HOW TO RELAX A LITTLE.
AJUMMA!

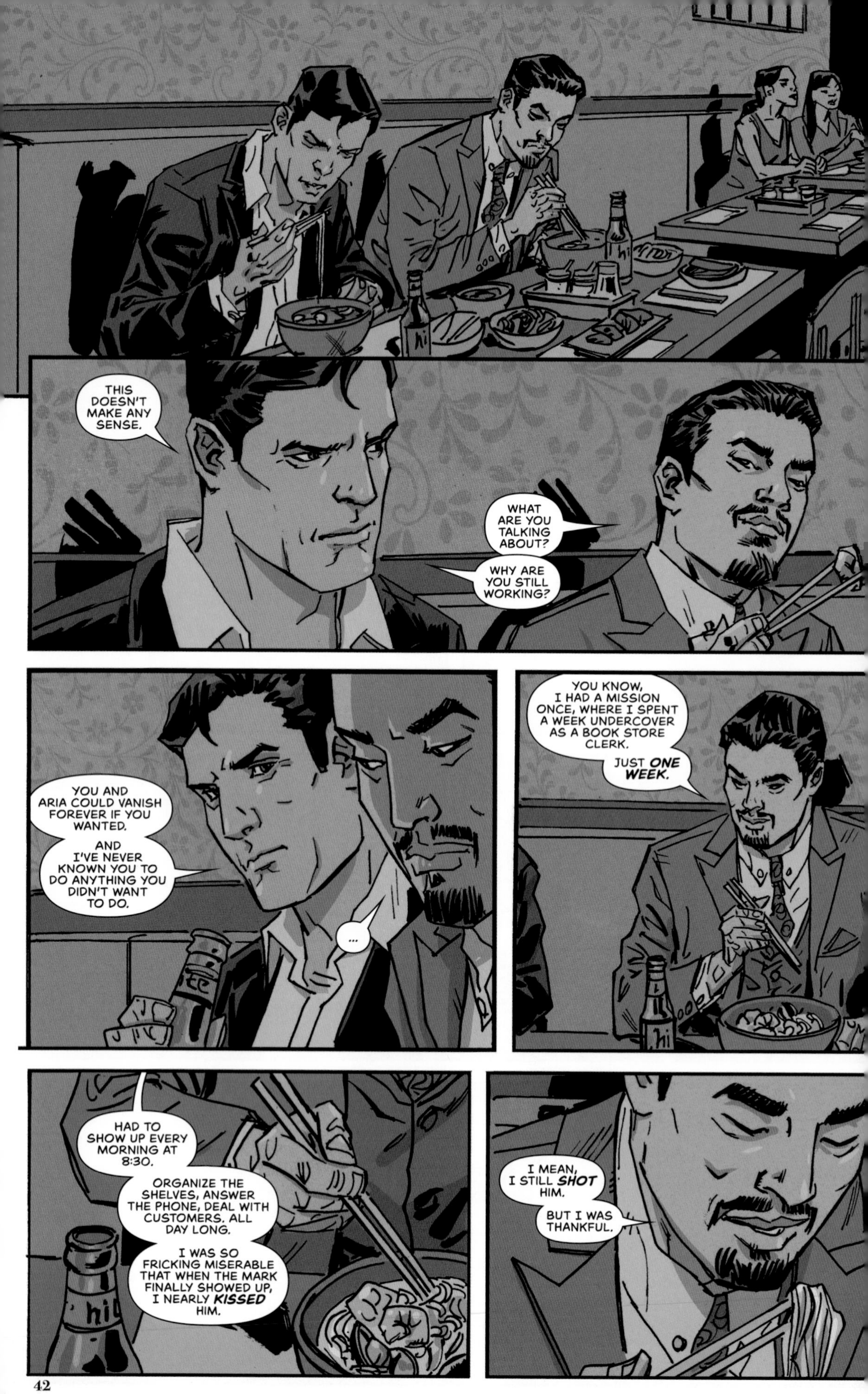
THIS DOESN'T MAKE ANY SENSE.
WHAT ARE YOU TALKING ABOUT?
WHY ARE YOU STILL WORKING?
YOU AND ARIA COULD VANISH FOREVER IF YOU WANTED.
AND I'VE NEVER KNOWN YOU TO DO ANYTHING YOU DIDN'T WANT TO DO.
...
YOU KNOW, I HAD A MISSION ONCE, WHERE I SPENT A WEEK UNDERCOVER AS A BOOK STORE CLERK.
JUST ***ONE WEEK.***
HAD TO SHOW UP EVERY MORNING AT 8:30.
ORGANIZE THE SHELVES, ANSWER THE PHONE, DEAL WITH CUSTOMERS. ALL DAY LONG.
I WAS SO FRICKING MISERABLE THAT WHEN THE MARK FINALLY SHOWED UP, I NEARLY ***KISSED*** HIM.
I MEAN, I STILL ***SHOT*** HIM.
BUT I WAS THANKFUL.

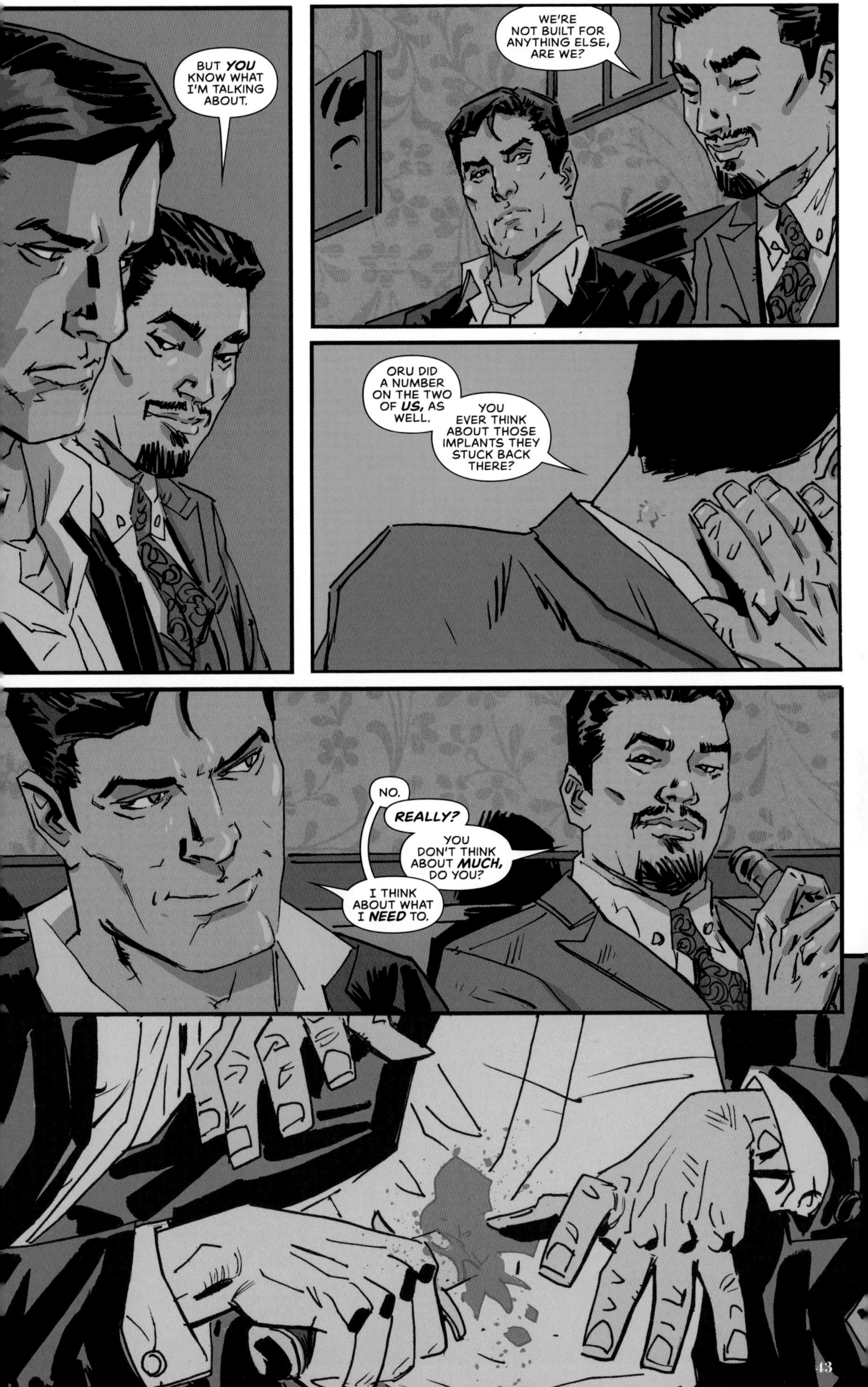
BUT *YOU* KNOW WHAT I'M TALKING ABOUT.
WE'RE NOT BUILT FOR ANYTHING ELSE, ARE WE?
ORU DID A NUMBER ON THE TWO OF *US,* AS WELL.
YOU EVER THINK ABOUT THOSE IMPLANTS THEY STUCK BACK THERE?
NO.
REALLY?
YOU DON'T THINK ABOUT *MUCH,* DO YOU?
I THINK ABOUT WHAT I *NEED* TO.

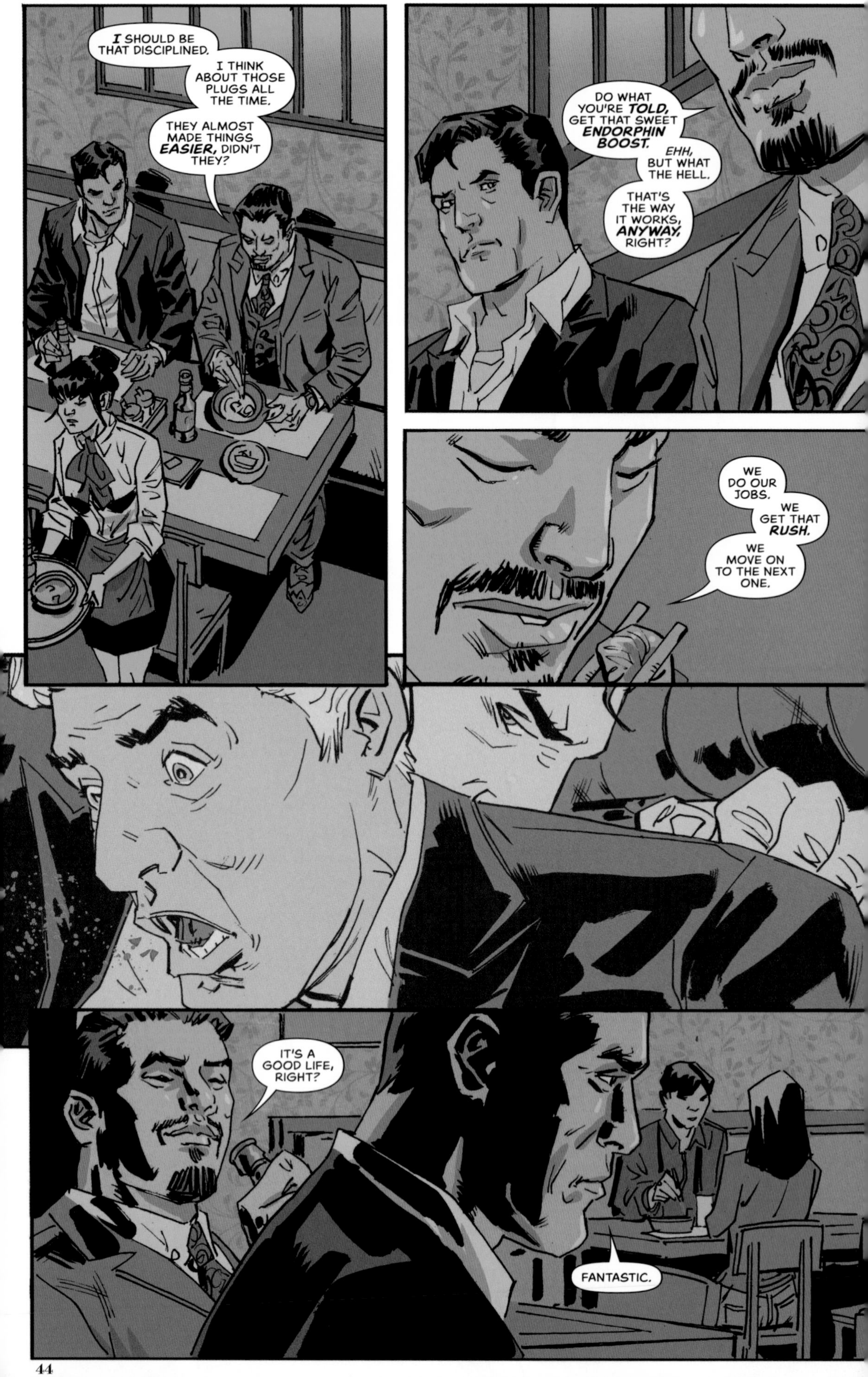
I SHOULD BE THAT DISCIPLINED.
I THINK ABOUT THOSE PLUGS ALL THE TIME.
THEY ALMOST MADE THINGS EASIER, DIDN'T THEY?
DO WHAT YOU'RE TOLD, GET THAT SWEET ENDORPHIN BOOST.
EHH, BUT WHAT THE HELL.
THAT'S THE WAY IT WORKS, ANYWAY, RIGHT?
WE DO OUR JOBS.
WE GET THAT RUSH.
WE MOVE ON TO THE NEXT ONE.
IT'S A GOOD LIFE, RIGHT?
FANTASTIC.

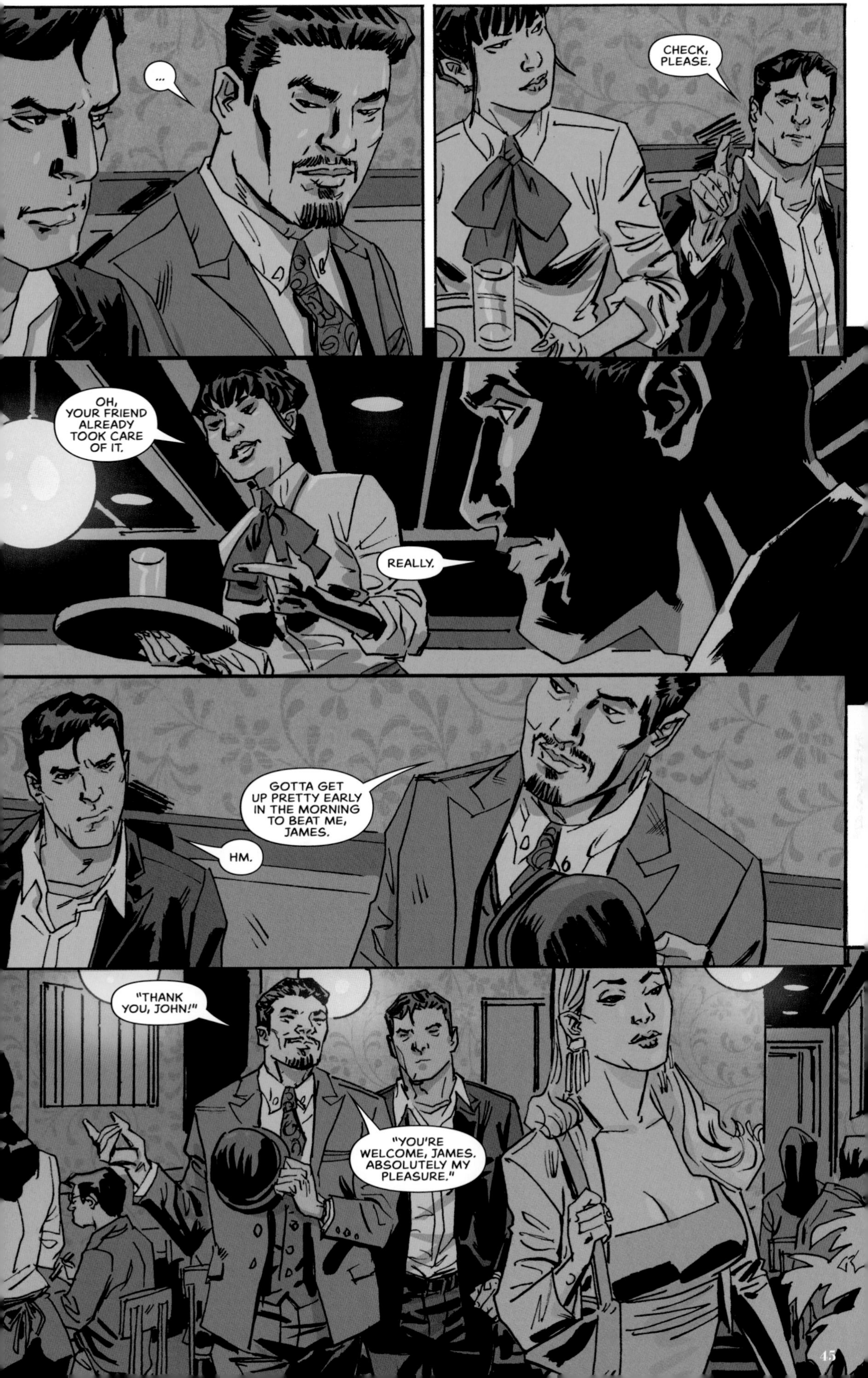

...
CHECK, PLEASE.
OH, YOUR FRIEND ALREADY TOOK CARE OF IT.
REALLY.
GOTTA GET UP PRETTY EARLY IN THE MORNING TO BEAT ME, JAMES.
HM.
"THANK YOU, JOHN!"
"YOU'RE WELCOME, JAMES. ABSOLUTELY MY PLEASURE."

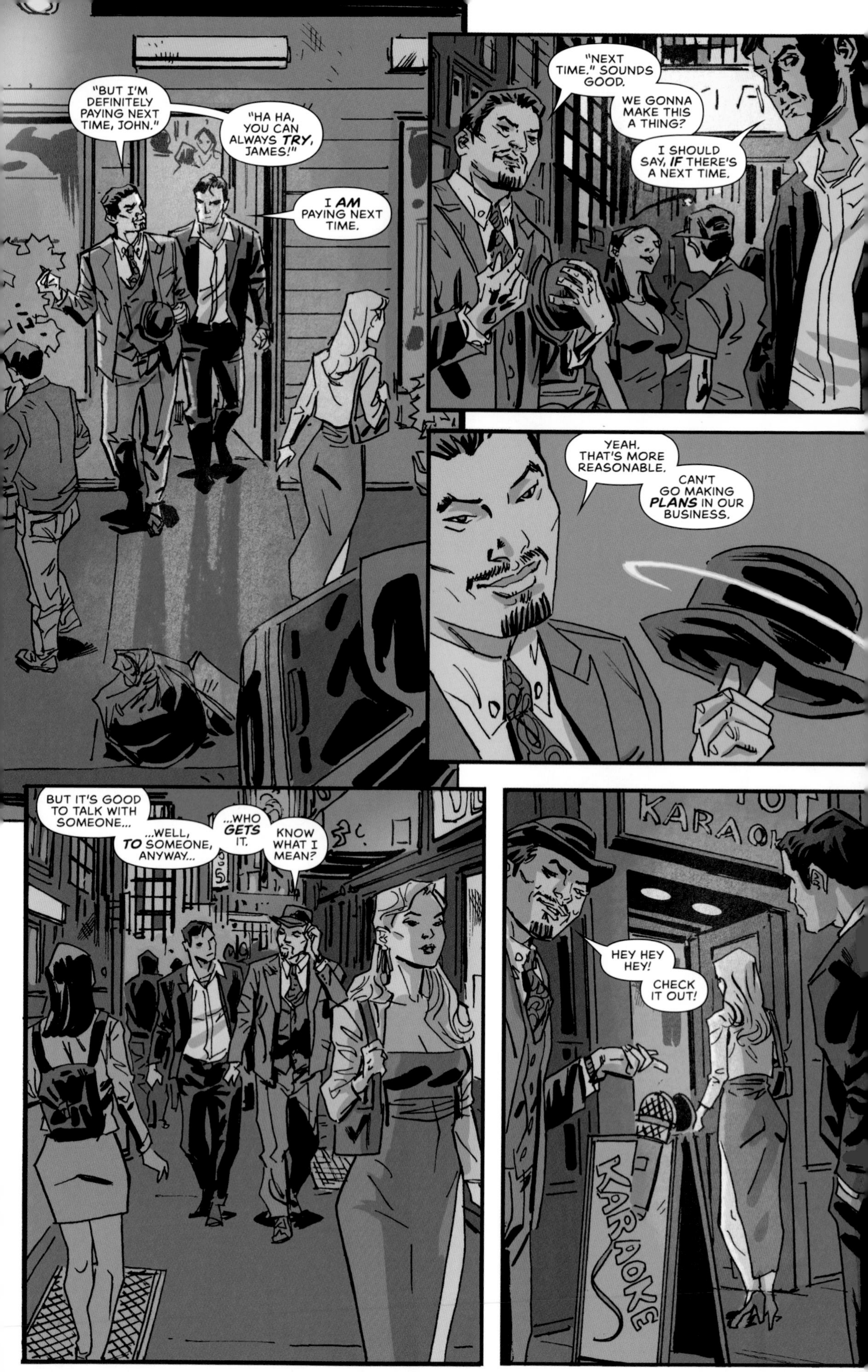
"BUT I'M DEFINITELY PAYING NEXT TIME, JOHN."
"HA HA, YOU CAN ALWAYS TRY, JAMES!"
I AM PAYING NEXT TIME.
"NEXT TIME," SOUNDS GOOD.
WE GONNA MAKE THIS A THING?
I SHOULD SAY, IF THERE'S A NEXT TIME.
YEAH. THAT'S MORE REASONABLE.
CAN'T GO MAKING PLANS IN OUR BUSINESS.
BUT IT'S GOOD TO TALK WITH SOMEONE...
...WELL, TO SOMEONE, ANYWAY...
...WHO GETS IT.
KNOW WHAT I MEAN?
KARAOKE
HEY HEY HEY!
CHECK IT OUT!
KARAOKE

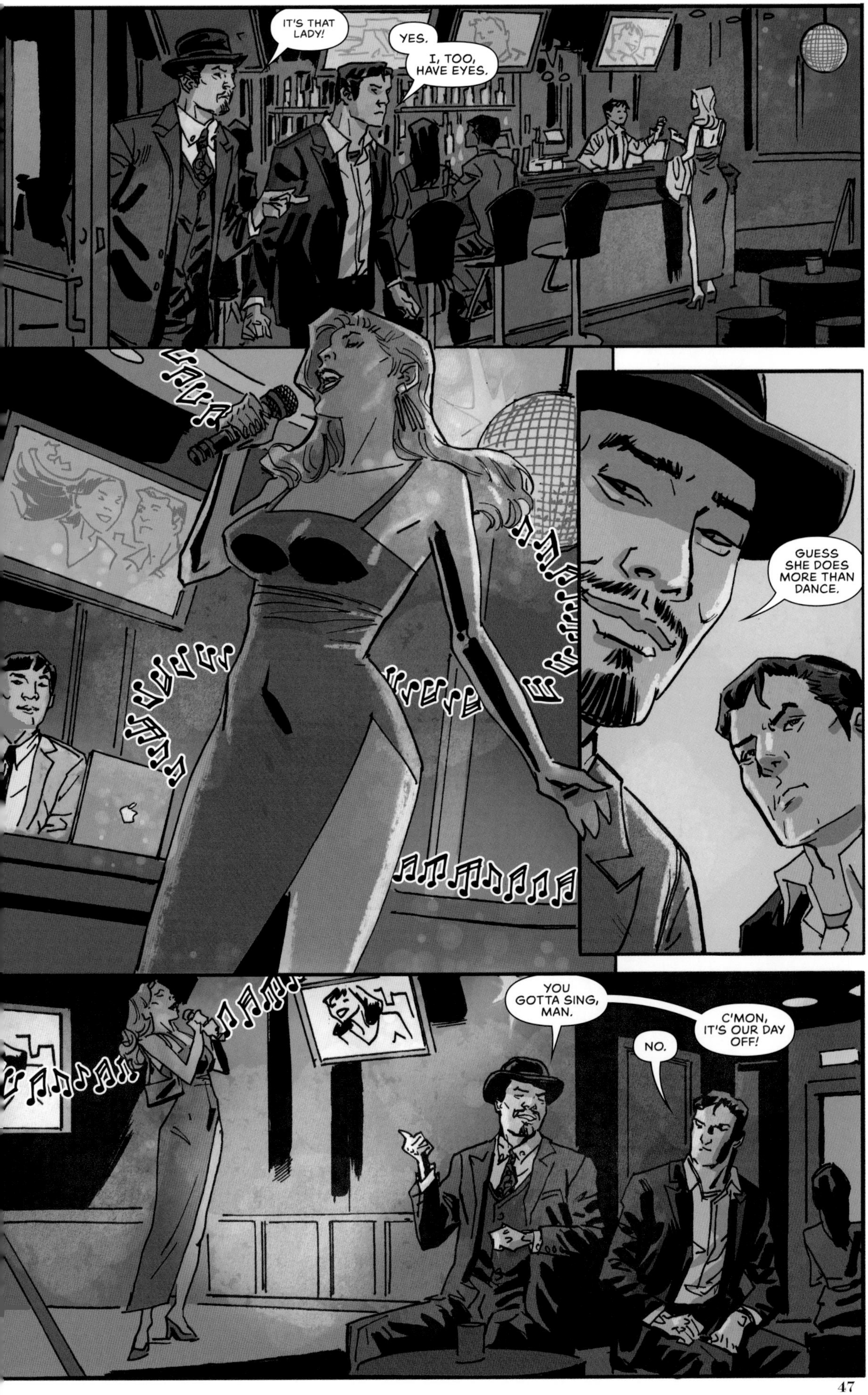
IT'S THAT LADY!
YES.
I, TOO, HAVE EYES.
GUESS SHE DOES MORE THAN DANCE.
YOU GOTTA SING, MAN.
NO.
C'MON, IT'S OUR DAY OFF!

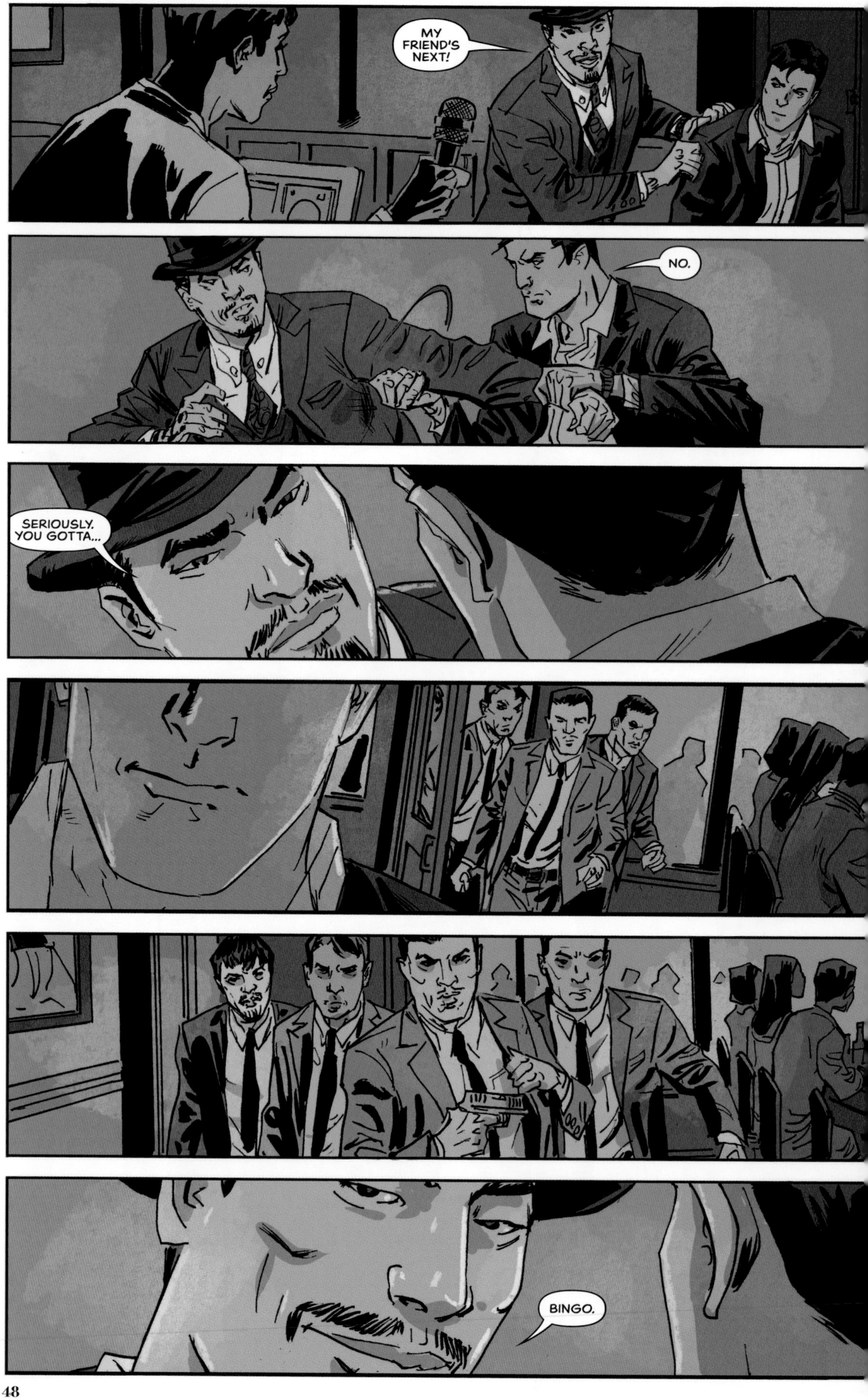
MY FRIEND'S NEXT!
NO.
SERIOUSLY. YOU GOTTA...
BINGO.

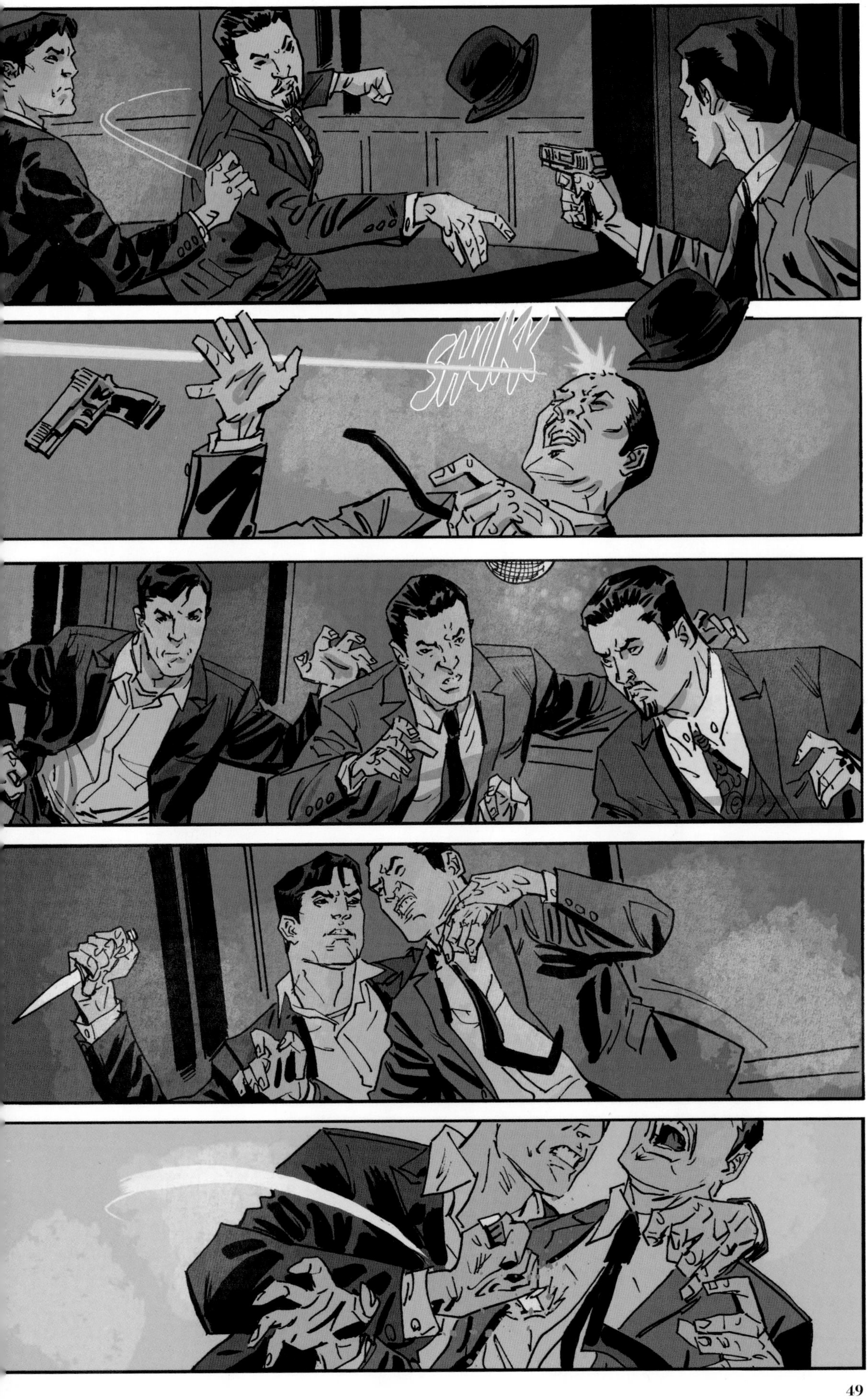
SHUKK

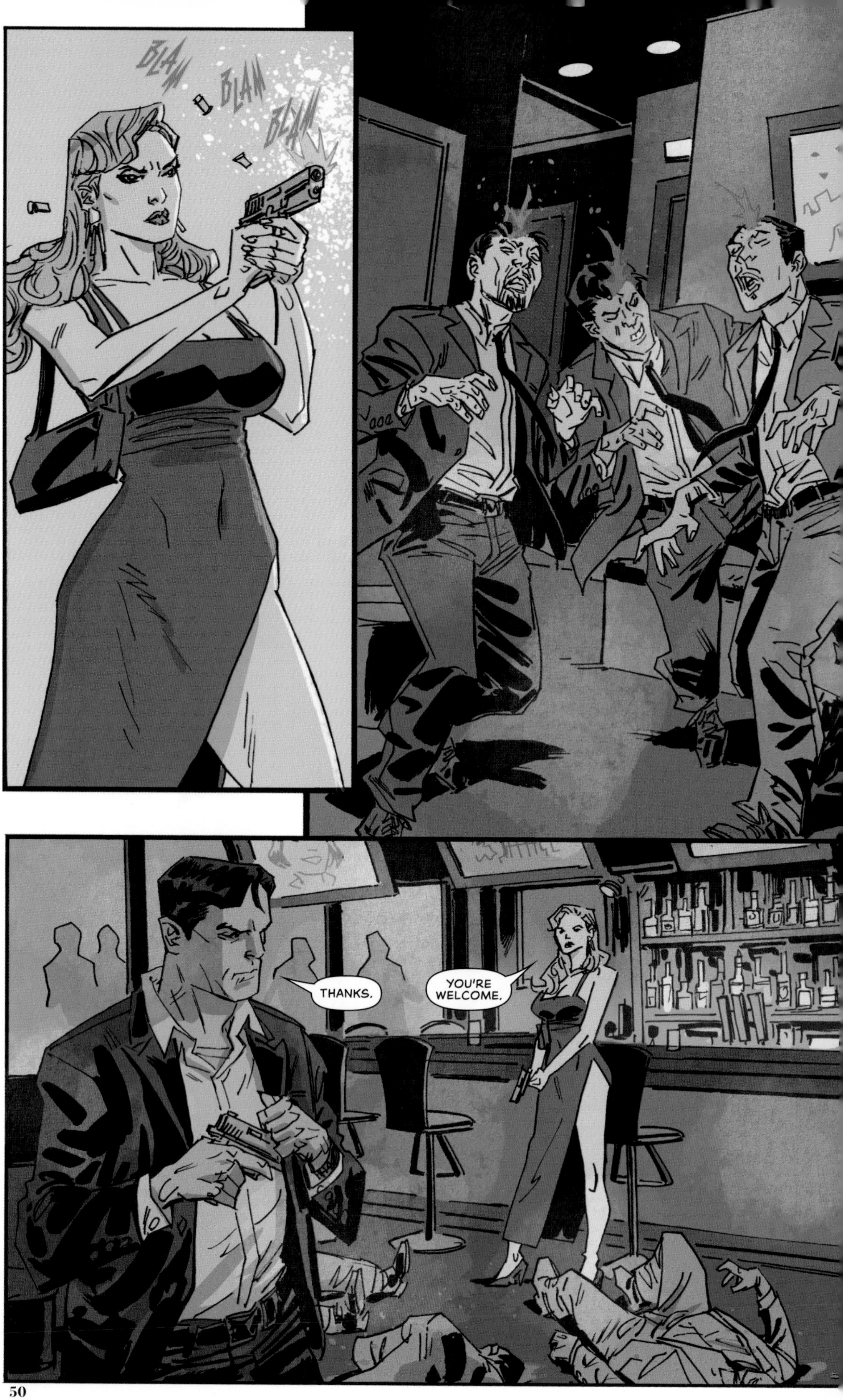
BLAM
BLAM
BLAM
THANKS.
YOU'RE WELCOME.

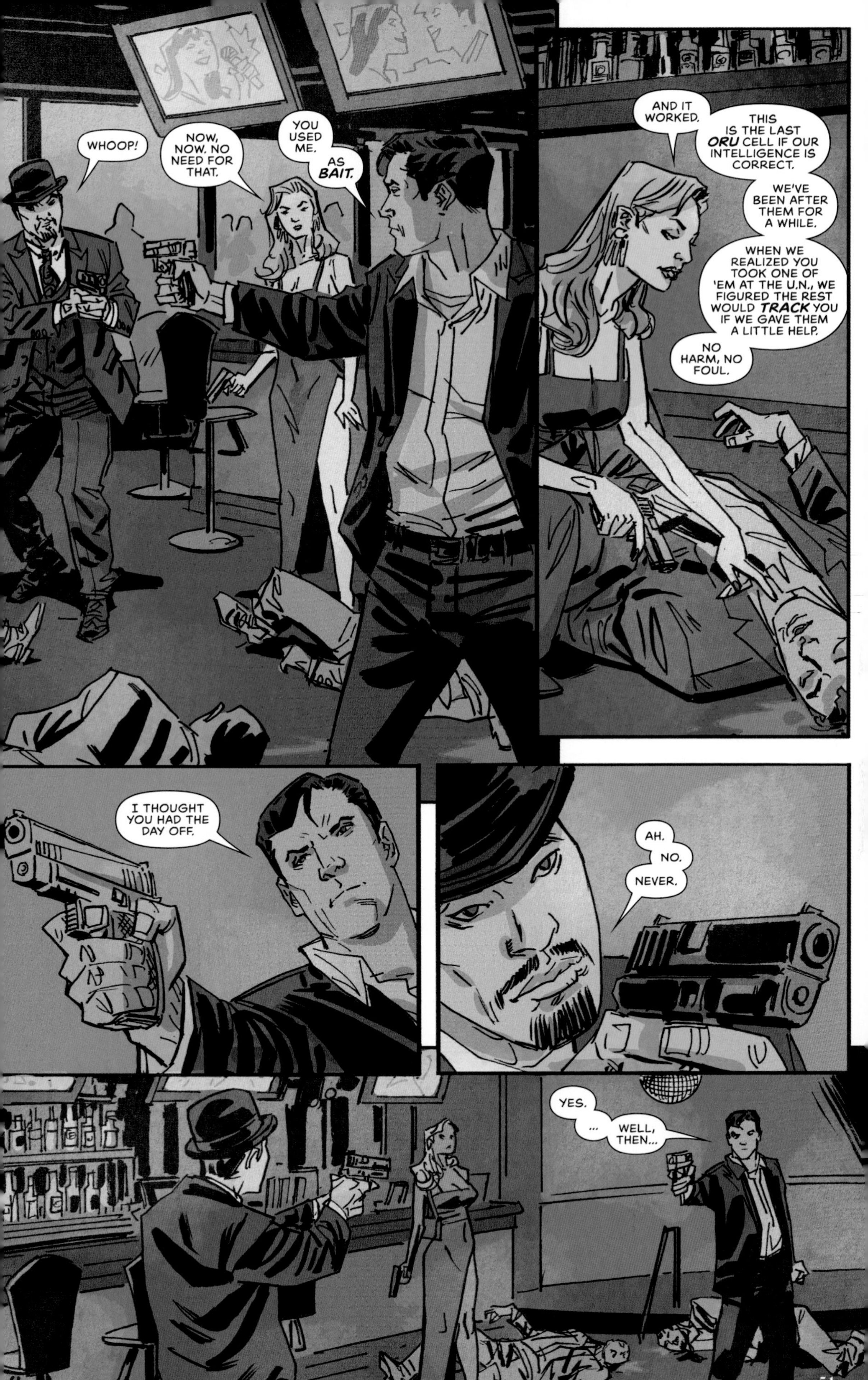

WHOOP!
NOW, NOW, NO NEED FOR THAT.
YOU USED ME.
AS BAIT.
AND IT WORKED.
THIS IS THE LAST ORU CELL IF OUR INTELLIGENCE IS CORRECT.
WE'VE BEEN AFTER THEM FOR A WHILE.
WHEN WE REALIZED YOU TOOK ONE OF 'EM AT THE U.N., WE FIGURED THE REST WOULD TRACK YOU IF WE GAVE THEM A LITTLE HELP.
NO HARM, NO FOUL.
I THOUGHT YOU HAD THE DAY OFF.
AH.
NO.
NEVER.
YES.
... WELL, THEN...

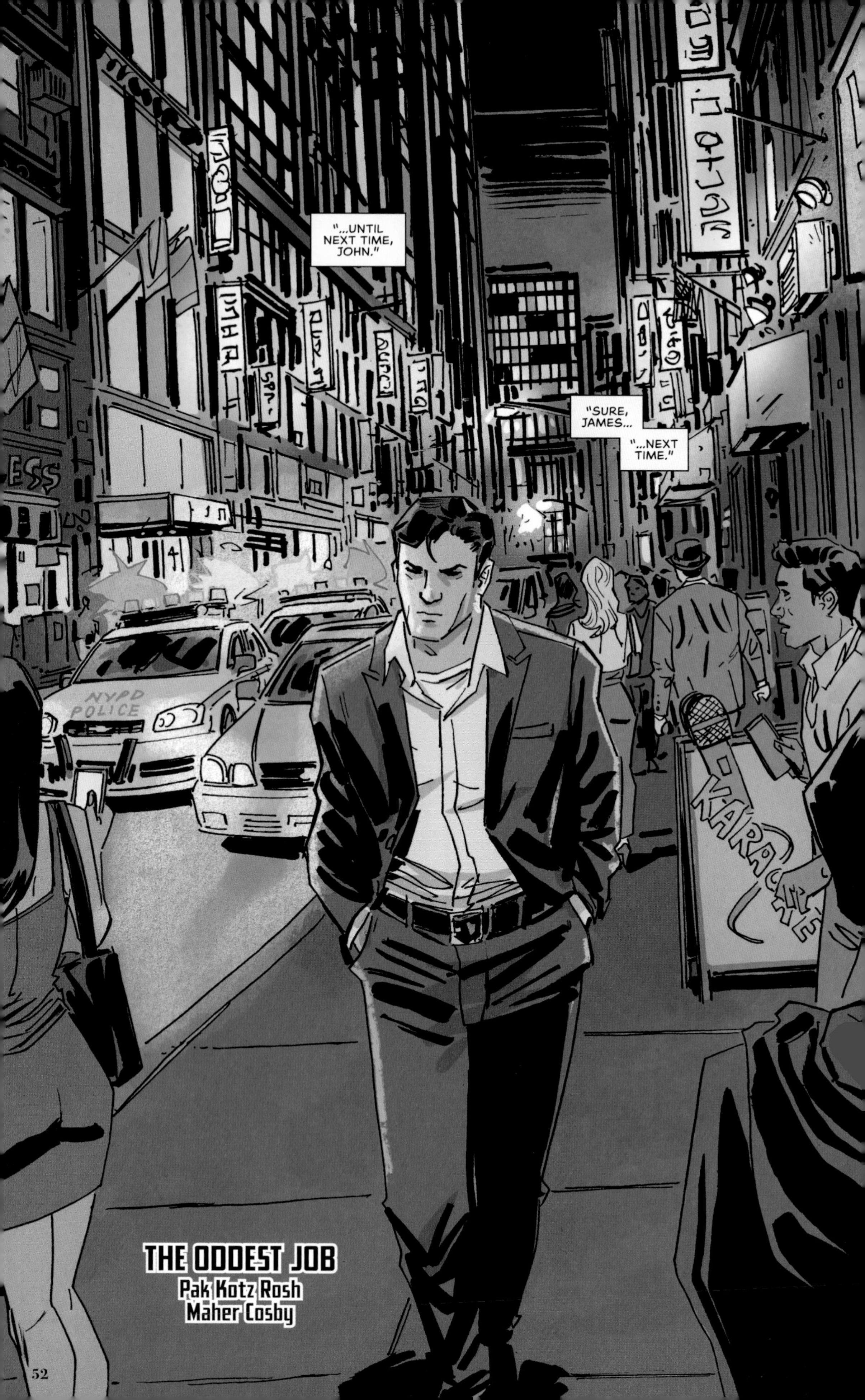
"...UNTIL NEXT TIME, JOHN."
"SURE, JAMES...
"...NEXT TIME."
NYPD POLICE
KARAOKE
THE ODDEST JOB
Pak Kotz Rosh
Maher Cosby

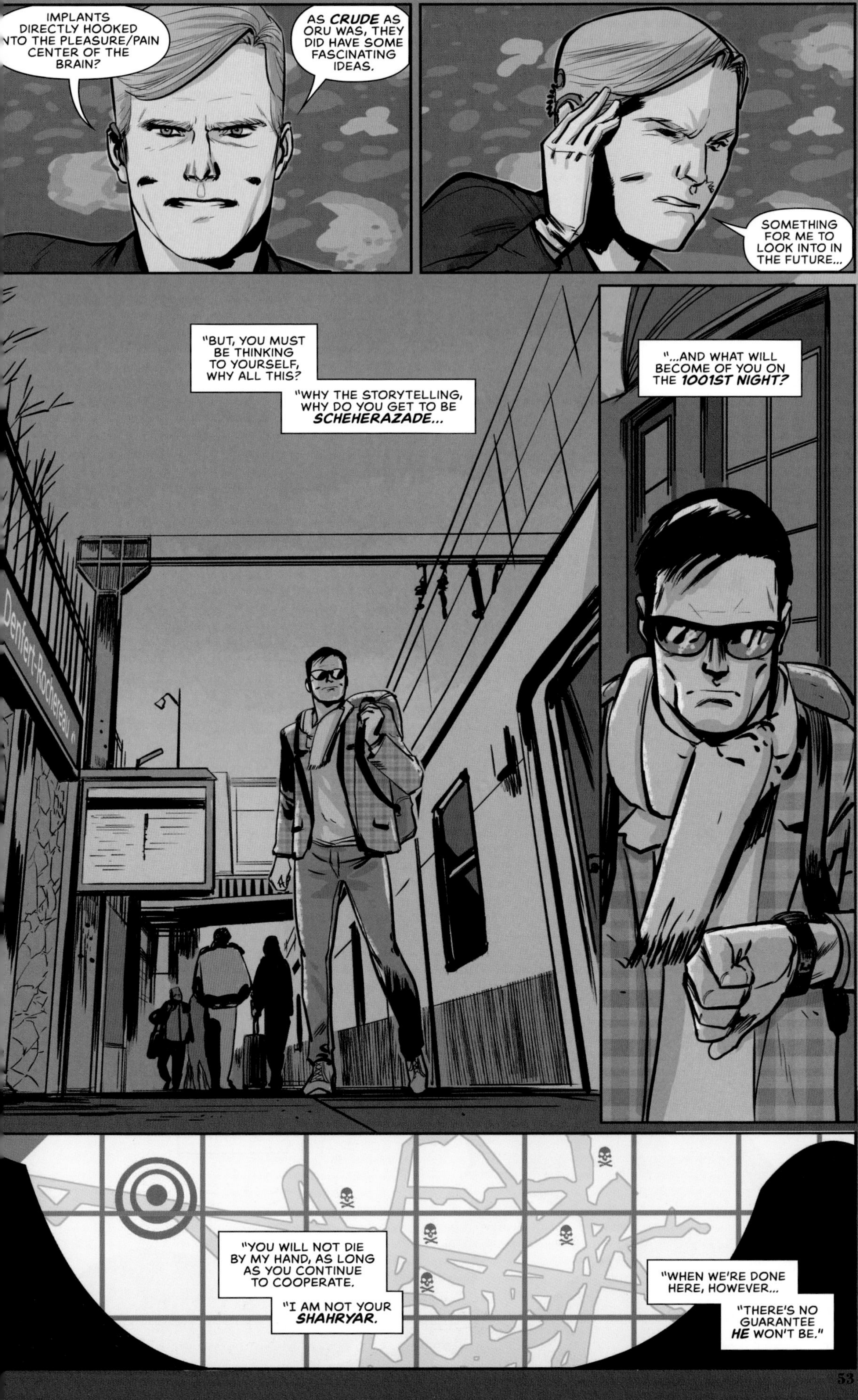

IMPLANTS DIRECTLY HOOKED INTO THE PLEASURE/PAIN CENTER OF THE BRAIN?
AS CRUDE AS ORU WAS, THEY DID HAVE SOME FASCINATING IDEAS.
SOMETHING FOR ME TO LOOK INTO IN THE FUTURE...
"BUT, YOU MUST BE THINKING TO YOURSELF, WHY ALL THIS?
"WHY THE STORYTELLING, WHY DO YOU GET TO BE SCHEHERAZADE...
Denfert-Rochereau
"...AND WHAT WILL BECOME OF YOU ON THE 1001ST NIGHT?
"YOU WILL NOT DIE BY MY HAND, AS LONG AS YOU CONTINUE TO COOPERATE.
"I AM NOT YOUR SHAHRYAR.
"WHEN WE'RE DONE HERE, HOWEVER...
"THERE'S NO GUARANTEE HE WON'T BE."

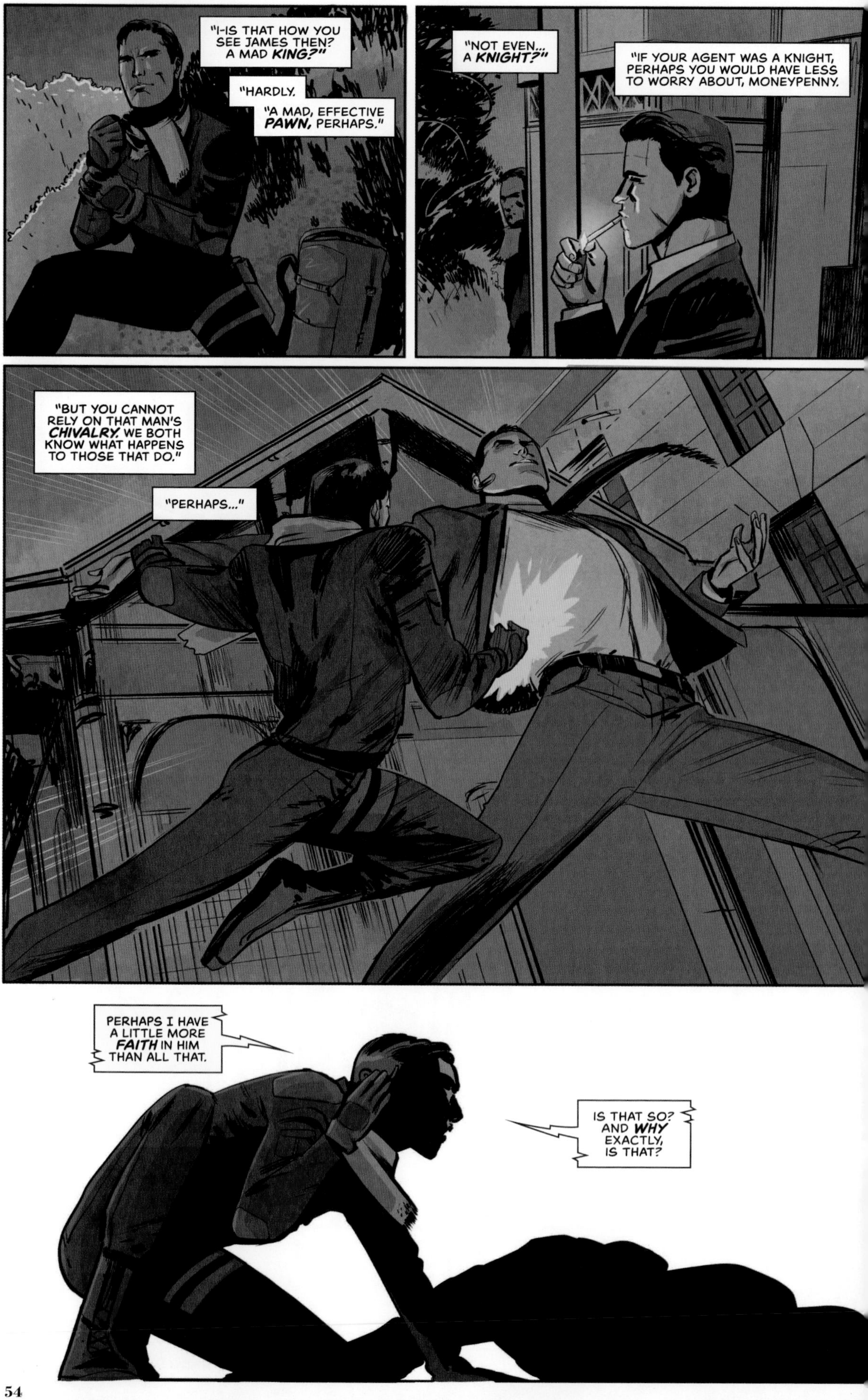
"I-IS THAT HOW YOU SEE JAMES THEN? A MAD KING?"
"HARDLY.
"A MAD, EFFECTIVE PAWN, PERHAPS."
"NOT EVEN... A KNIGHT?"
"IF YOUR AGENT WAS A KNIGHT, PERHAPS YOU WOULD HAVE LESS TO WORRY ABOUT, MONEYPENNY.
"BUT YOU CANNOT RELY ON THAT MAN'S CHIVALRY. WE BOTH KNOW WHAT HAPPENS TO THOSE THAT DO."
"PERHAPS..."
PERHAPS I HAVE A LITTLE MORE FAITH IN HIM THAN ALL THAT.
IS THAT SO? AND WHY EXACTLY, IS THAT?

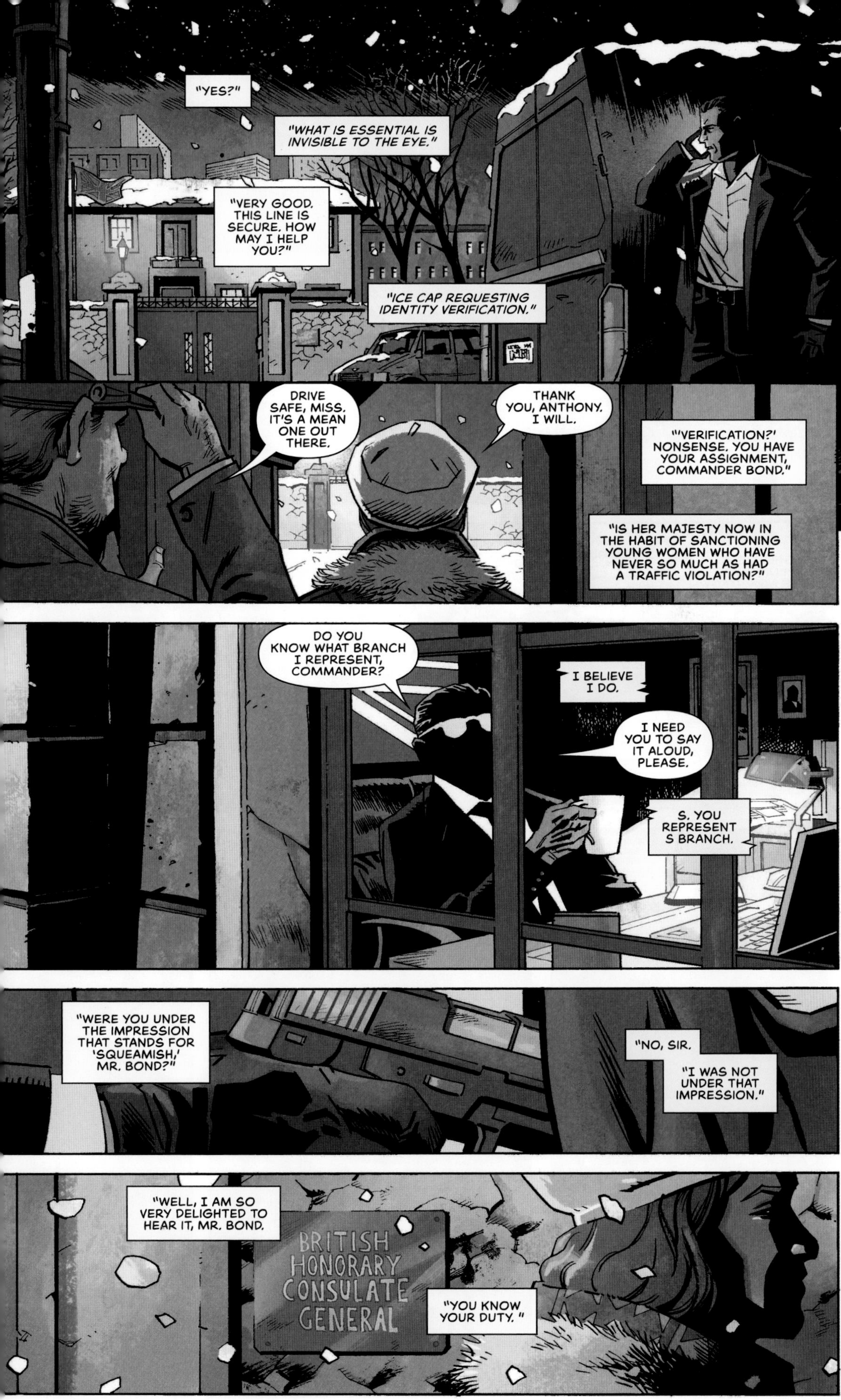
"YES?"
"WHAT IS ESSENTIAL IS INVISIBLE TO THE EYE."
"VERY GOOD. THIS LINE IS SECURE. HOW MAY I HELP YOU?"
"ICE CAP REQUESTING IDENTITY VERIFICATION."
DRIVE SAFE, MISS. IT'S A MEAN ONE OUT THERE.
THANK YOU, ANTHONY. I WILL.
"'VERIFICATION?' NONSENSE. YOU HAVE YOUR ASSIGNMENT, COMMANDER BOND."
"IS HER MAJESTY NOW IN THE HABIT OF SANCTIONING YOUNG WOMEN WHO HAVE NEVER SO MUCH AS HAD A TRAFFIC VIOLATION?"
DO YOU KNOW WHAT BRANCH I REPRESENT, COMMANDER?
I BELIEVE I DO.
I NEED YOU TO SAY IT ALOUD, PLEASE.
S. YOU REPRESENT S BRANCH.
"WERE YOU UNDER THE IMPRESSION THAT STANDS FOR 'SQUEAMISH,' MR. BOND?"
"NO, SIR.
"I WAS NOT UNDER THAT IMPRESSION."
"WELL, I AM SO VERY DELIGHTED TO HEAR IT, MR. BOND.
BRITISH HONORARY CONSULATE GENERAL
"YOU KNOW YOUR DUTY."

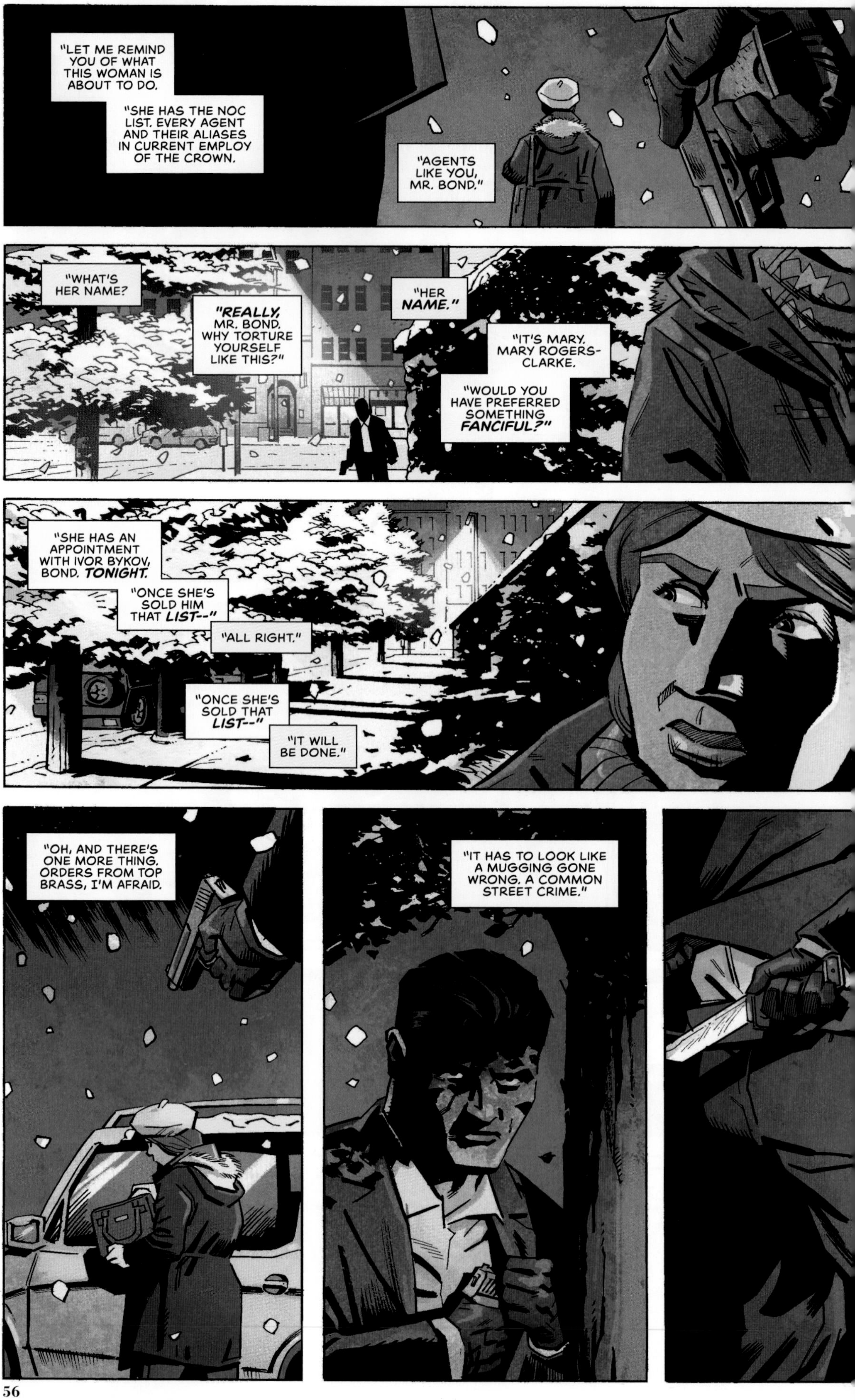
"LET ME REMIND YOU OF WHAT THIS WOMAN IS ABOUT TO DO.
"SHE HAS THE NOC LIST. EVERY AGENT AND THEIR ALIASES IN CURRENT EMPLOY OF THE CROWN.
"AGENTS LIKE YOU, MR. BOND."
"WHAT'S HER NAME?
"REALLY, MR. BOND. WHY TORTURE YOURSELF LIKE THIS?"
"HER NAME."
"IT'S MARY. MARY ROGERS-CLARKE.
"WOULD YOU HAVE PREFERRED SOMETHING FANCIFUL?"
"SHE HAS AN APPOINTMENT WITH IVOR BYKOV, BOND. TONIGHT.
"ONCE SHE'S SOLD HIM THAT LIST--"
"ALL RIGHT."
"ONCE SHE'S SOLD THAT LIST--"
"IT WILL BE DONE."
"OH, AND THERE'S ONE MORE THING. ORDERS FROM TOP BRASS, I'M AFRAID.
"IT HAS TO LOOK LIKE A MUGGING GONE WRONG. A COMMON STREET CRIME."

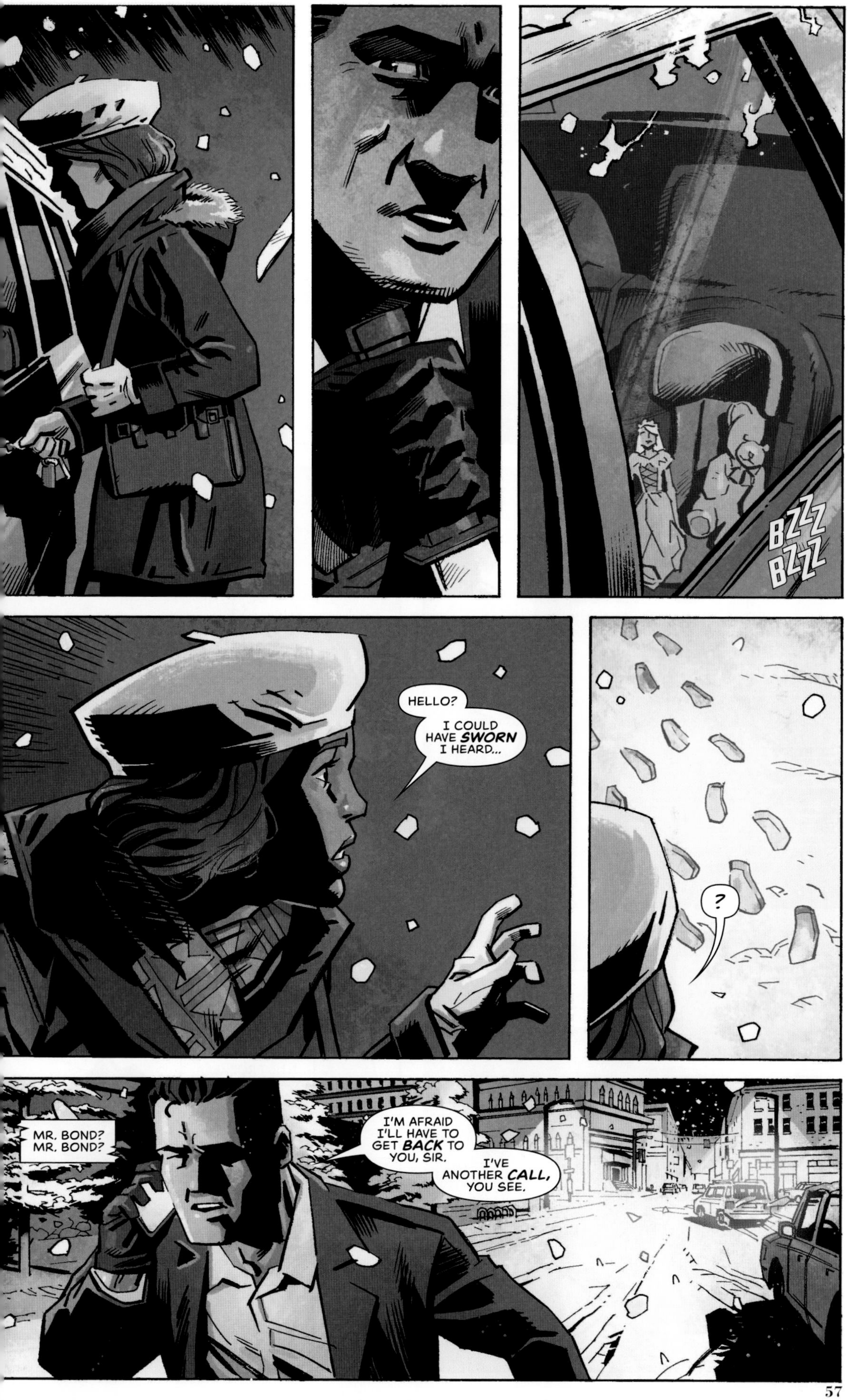
BZZZ
BZZZ
HELLO?
I COULD HAVE SWORN I HEARD...
?
MR. BOND? MR. BOND?
I'M AFRAID I'LL HAVE TO GET BACK TO YOU, SIR.
I'VE ANOTHER CALL, YOU SEE.

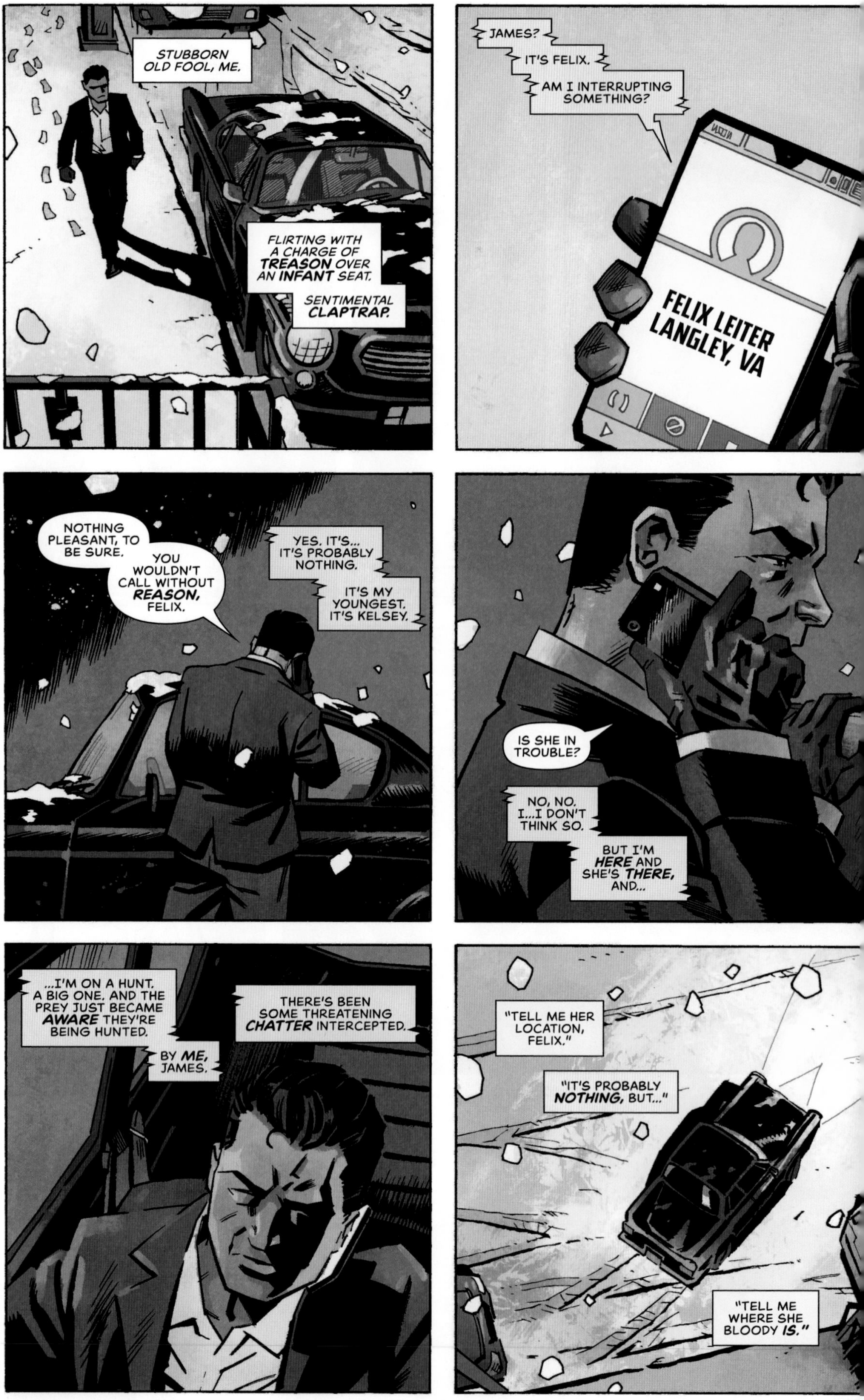

STUBBORN OLD FOOL, ME.
FLIRTING WITH A CHARGE OF TREASON OVER AN INFANT SEAT.
SENTIMENTAL CLAPTRAP.
JAMES?
IT'S FELIX.
AM I INTERRUPTING SOMETHING?
FELIX LEITER LANGLEY, VA
NOTHING PLEASANT, TO BE SURE.
YOU WOULDN'T CALL WITHOUT REASON, FELIX.
YES. IT'S... IT'S PROBABLY NOTHING.
IT'S MY YOUNGEST. IT'S KELSEY.
IS SHE IN TROUBLE?
NO, NO. I...I DON'T THINK SO.
BUT I'M HERE AND SHE'S THERE, AND...
...I'M ON A HUNT. A BIG ONE. AND THE PREY JUST BECAME AWARE THEY'RE BEING HUNTED.
BY ME, JAMES.
THERE'S BEEN SOME THREATENING CHATTER INTERCEPTED.
"TELL ME HER LOCATION, FELIX."
"IT'S PROBABLY NOTHING, BUT..."
"TELL ME WHERE SHE BLOODY IS."

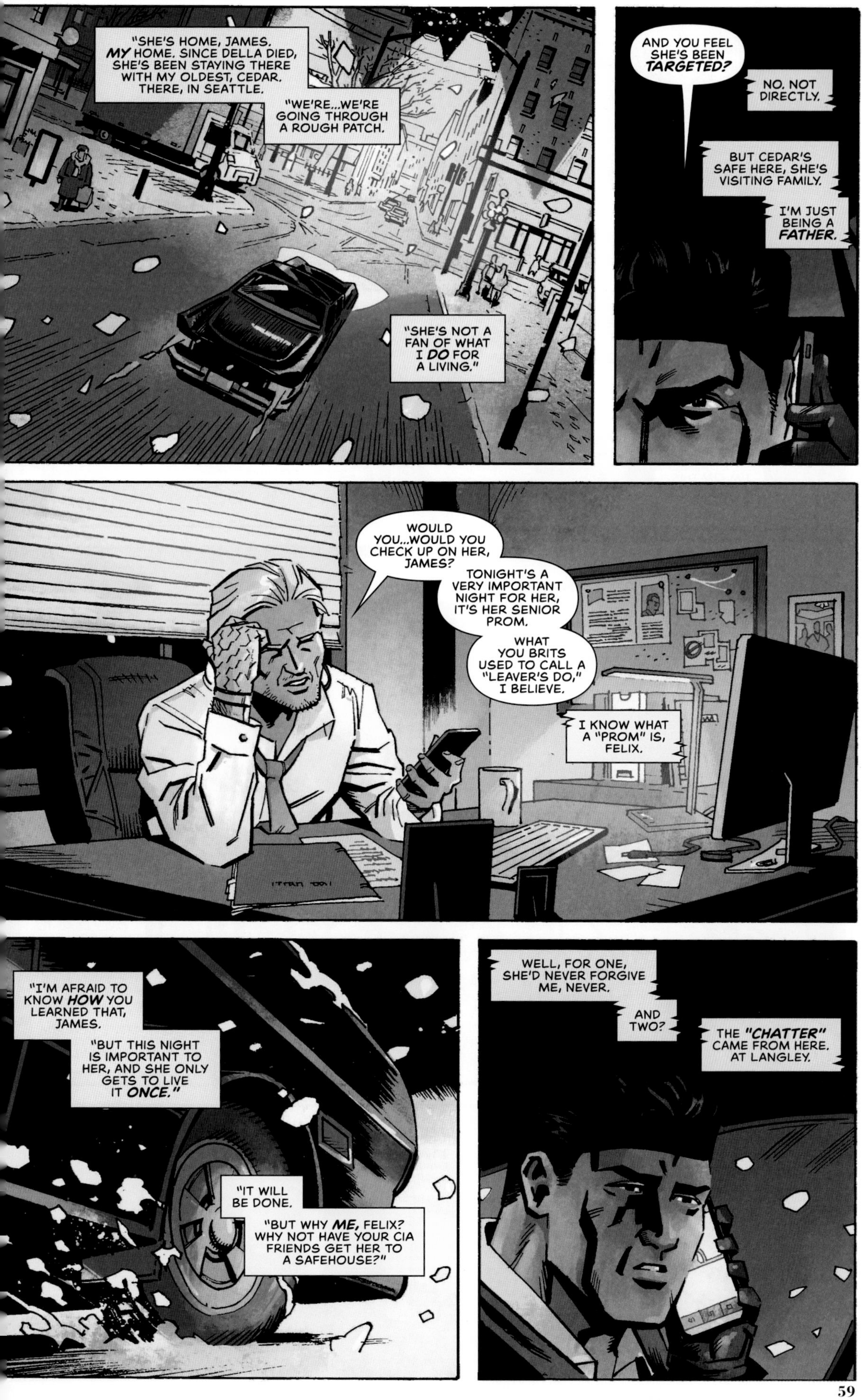
"SHE'S HOME, JAMES. MY HOME. SINCE DELLA DIED, SHE'S BEEN STAYING THERE WITH MY OLDEST, CEDAR. THERE, IN SEATTLE.
"WE'RE...WE'RE GOING THROUGH A ROUGH PATCH.
"SHE'S NOT A FAN OF WHAT I DO FOR A LIVING."
AND YOU FEEL SHE'S BEEN TARGETED?
NO. NOT DIRECTLY.
BUT CEDAR'S SAFE HERE, SHE'S VISITING FAMILY.
I'M JUST BEING A FATHER.
WOULD YOU...WOULD YOU CHECK UP ON HER, JAMES?
TONIGHT'S A VERY IMPORTANT NIGHT FOR HER, IT'S HER SENIOR PROM.
WHAT YOU BRITS USED TO CALL A "LEAVER'S DO," I BELIEVE.
I KNOW WHAT A "PROM" IS, FELIX.
"I'M AFRAID TO KNOW HOW YOU LEARNED THAT, JAMES.
"BUT THIS NIGHT IS IMPORTANT TO HER, AND SHE ONLY GETS TO LIVE IT ONCE."
"IT WILL BE DONE.
"BUT WHY ME, FELIX? WHY NOT HAVE YOUR CIA FRIENDS GET HER TO A SAFEHOUSE?"
WELL, FOR ONE, SHE'D NEVER FORGIVE ME, NEVER.
AND TWO?
THE "CHATTER" CAME FROM HERE. AT LANGLEY.

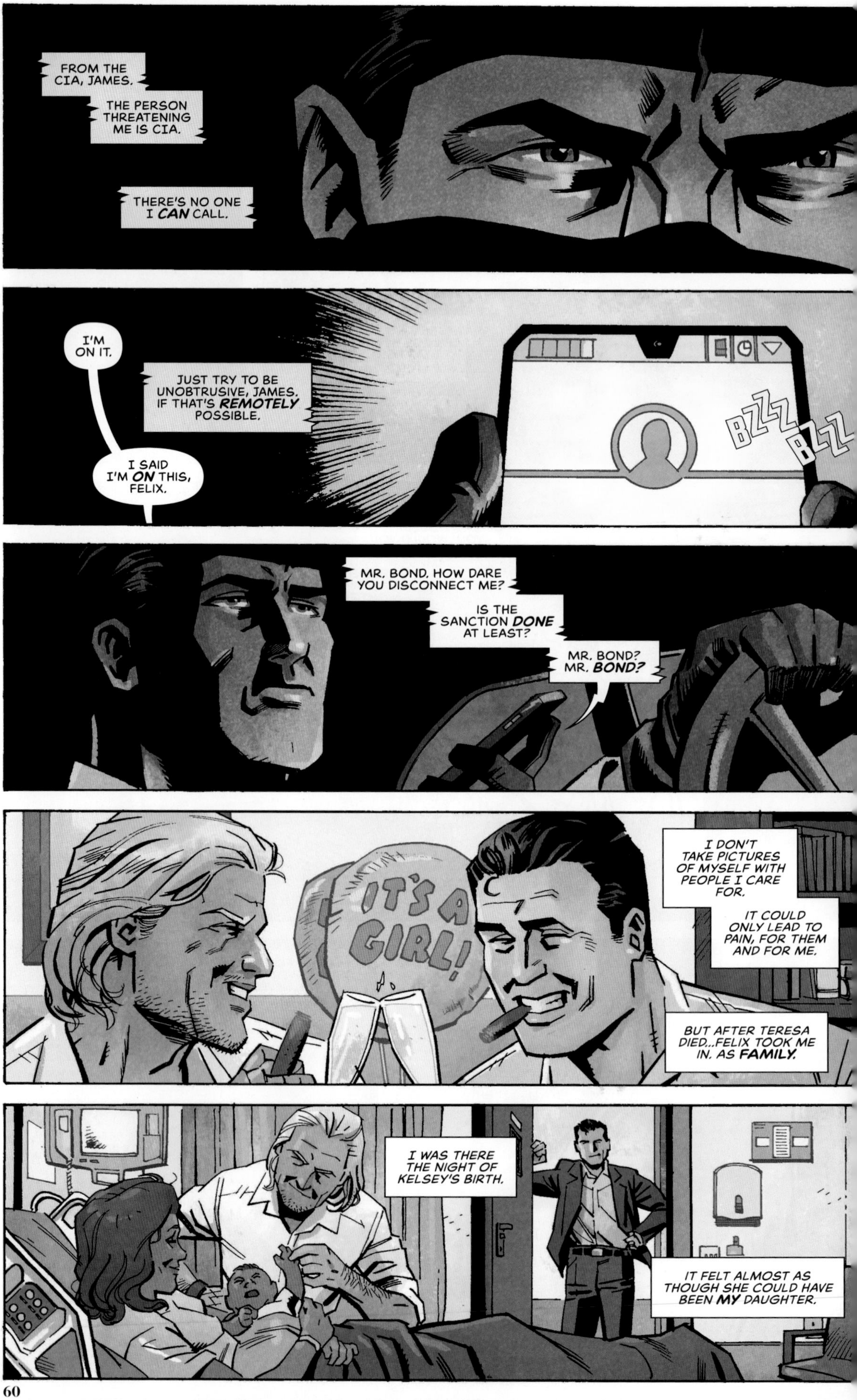

FROM THE CIA, JAMES.
THE PERSON THREATENING ME IS CIA.
THERE'S NO ONE I CAN CALL.
I'M ON IT.
JUST TRY TO BE UNOBTRUSIVE, JAMES. IF THAT'S REMOTELY POSSIBLE.
I SAID I'M ON THIS, FELIX.
BZZZ BZZZ
MR. BOND. HOW DARE YOU DISCONNECT ME?
IS THE SANCTION DONE AT LEAST?
MR. BOND? MR. BOND?
IT'S A GIRL!
I DON'T TAKE PICTURES OF MYSELF WITH PEOPLE I CARE FOR.
IT COULD ONLY LEAD TO PAIN, FOR THEM AND FOR ME.
BUT AFTER TERESA DIED...FELIX TOOK ME IN. AS FAMILY.
I WAS THERE THE NIGHT OF KELSEY'S BIRTH.
IT FELT ALMOST AS THOUGH SHE COULD HAVE BEEN MY DAUGHTER.

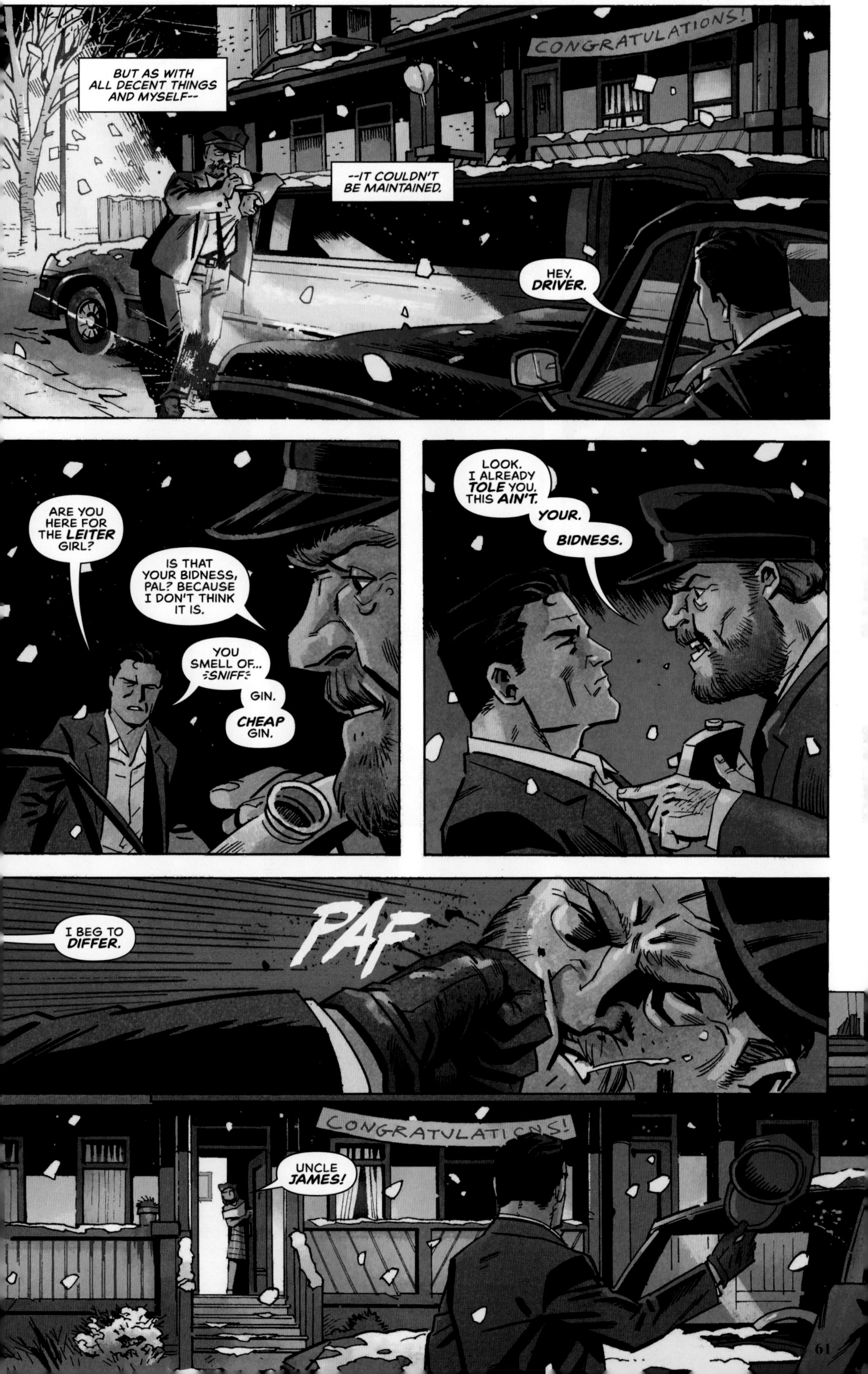
BUT AS WITH ALL DECENT THINGS AND MYSELF--
CONGRATULATIONS!
--IT COULDN'T BE MAINTAINED.
HEY. DRIVER.
ARE YOU HERE FOR THE LEITER GIRL?
IS THAT YOUR BIDNESS, PAL? BECAUSE I DON'T THINK IT IS.
YOU SMELL OF... SNIFF
GIN.
CHEAP GIN.
LOOK. I ALREADY TOLE YOU. THIS AIN'T.
YOUR.
BIDNESS.
I BEG TO DIFFER.
PAF
CONGRATULATIONS!
UNCLE JAMES!

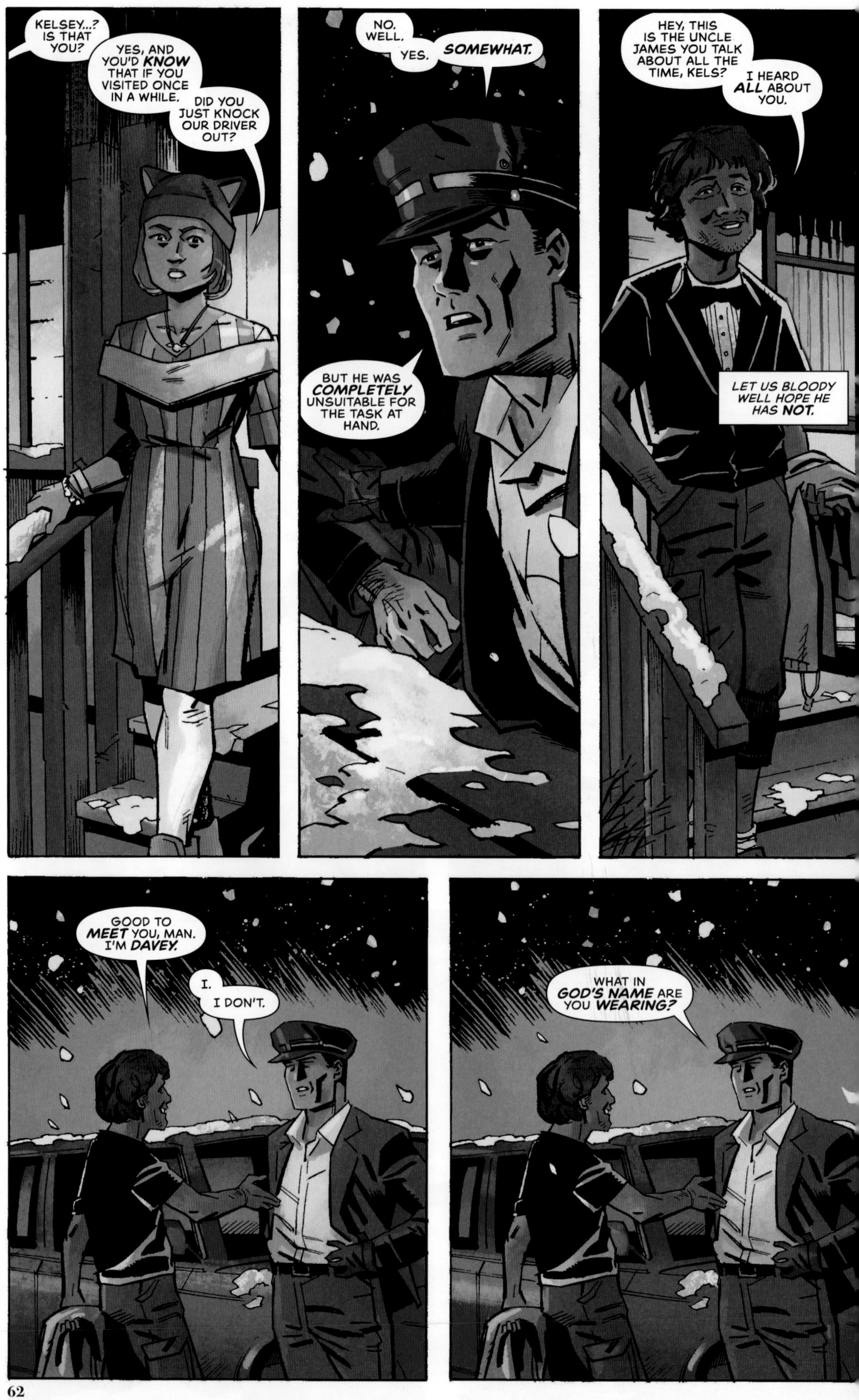
KELSEY...? IS THAT YOU?
YES, AND YOU'D KNOW THAT IF YOU VISITED ONCE IN A WHILE.
DID YOU JUST KNOCK OUR DRIVER OUT?
NO. WELL.
YES.
SOMEWHAT.
BUT HE WAS COMPLETELY UNSUITABLE FOR THE TASK AT HAND.
HEY, THIS IS THE UNCLE JAMES YOU TALK ABOUT ALL THE TIME, KELS?
I HEARD ALL ABOUT YOU.
LET US BLOODY WELL HOPE HE HAS NOT.
GOOD TO MEET YOU, MAN. I'M DAVEY.
I.
I DON'T.
WHAT IN GOD'S NAME ARE YOU WEARING?

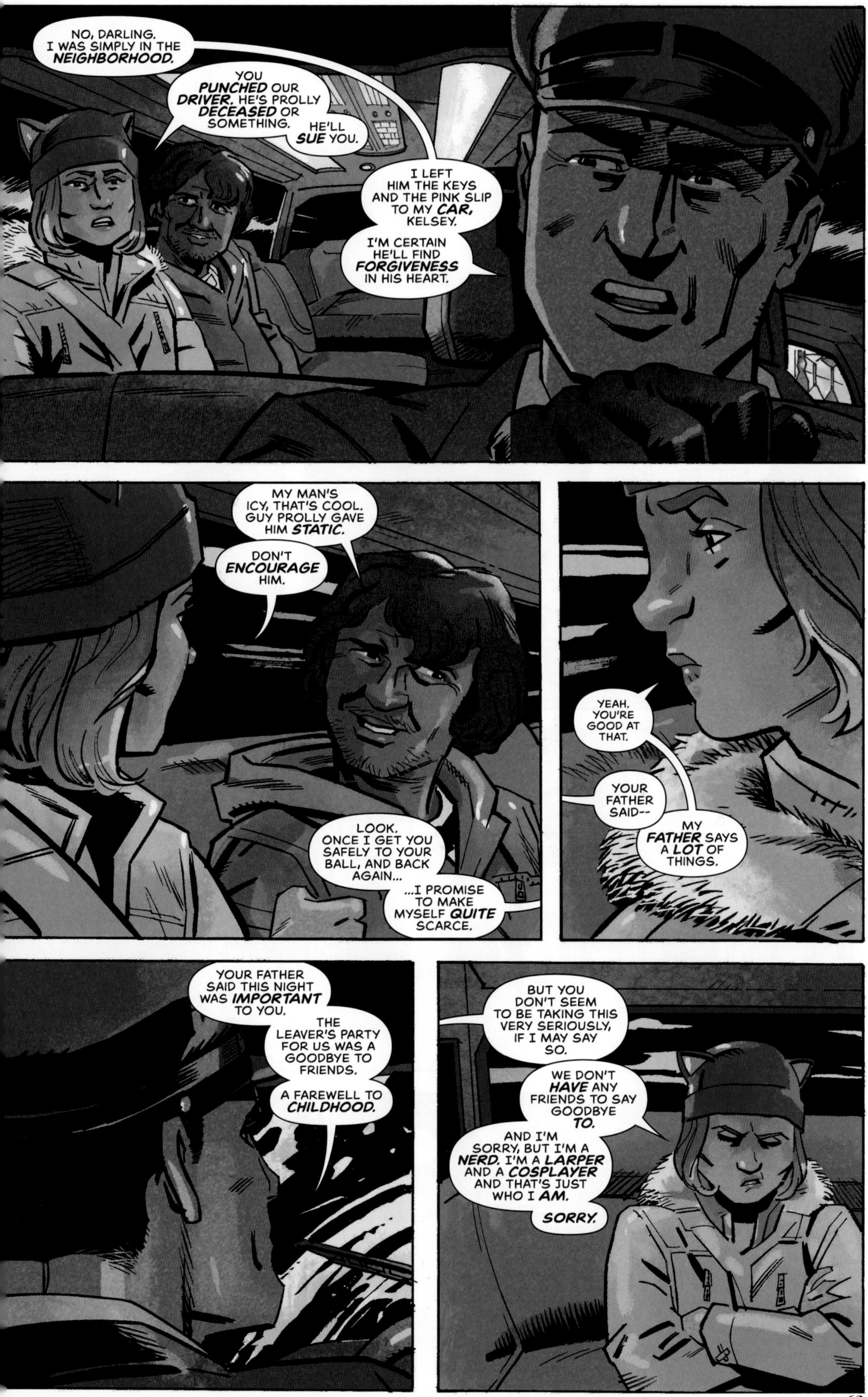

NO, DARLING. I WAS SIMPLY IN THE NEIGHBORHOOD.
YOU PUNCHED OUR DRIVER. HE'S PROLLY DECEASED OR SOMETHING.
HE'LL SUE YOU.
I LEFT HIM THE KEYS AND THE PINK SLIP TO MY CAR, KELSEY.
I'M CERTAIN HE'LL FIND FORGIVENESS IN HIS HEART.
MY MAN'S ICY, THAT'S COOL. GUY PROLLY GAVE HIM STATIC.
DON'T ENCOURAGE HIM.
LOOK. ONCE I GET YOU SAFELY TO YOUR BALL, AND BACK AGAIN...
...I PROMISE TO MAKE MYSELF QUITE SCARCE.
YEAH. YOU'RE GOOD AT THAT.
YOUR FATHER SAID--
MY FATHER SAYS A LOT OF THINGS.
YOUR FATHER SAID THIS NIGHT WAS IMPORTANT TO YOU.
THE LEAVER'S PARTY FOR US WAS A GOODBYE TO FRIENDS.
A FAREWELL TO CHILDHOOD.
BUT YOU DON'T SEEM TO BE TAKING THIS VERY SERIOUSLY, IF I MAY SAY SO.
WE DON'T HAVE ANY FRIENDS TO SAY GOODBYE TO.
AND I'M SORRY, BUT I'M A NERD, I'M A LARPER AND A COSPLAYER AND THAT'S JUST WHO I AM.
SORRY.

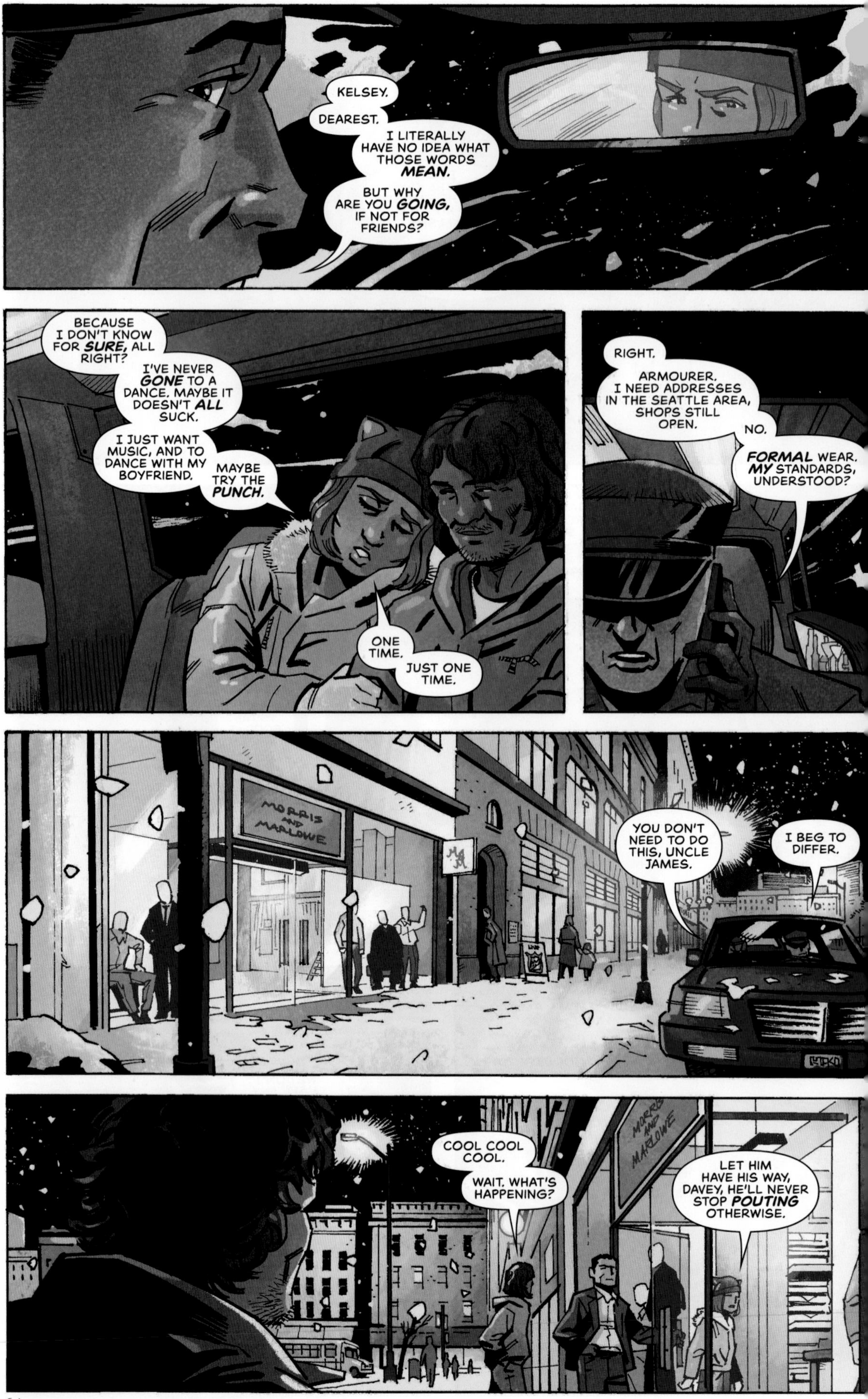
KELSEY.
DEAREST.
I LITERALLY HAVE NO IDEA WHAT THOSE WORDS MEAN.
BUT WHY ARE YOU GOING, IF NOT FOR FRIENDS?
BECAUSE I DON'T KNOW FOR SURE, ALL RIGHT?
I'VE NEVER GONE TO A DANCE. MAYBE IT DOESN'T ALL SUCK.
I JUST WANT MUSIC, AND TO DANCE WITH MY BOYFRIEND.
MAYBE TRY THE PUNCH.
ONE TIME.
JUST ONE TIME.
RIGHT.
ARMOURER. I NEED ADDRESSES IN THE SEATTLE AREA, SHOPS STILL OPEN.
NO.
FORMAL WEAR. MY STANDARDS, UNDERSTOOD?
MORRIS AND MARLOWE
YOU DON'T NEED TO DO THIS, UNCLE JAMES.
I BEG TO DIFFER.
COOL COOL COOL.
WAIT. WHAT'S HAPPENING?
MORRIS AND MARLOWE
LET HIM HAVE HIS WAY, DAVEY, HE'LL NEVER STOP POUTING OTHERWISE.

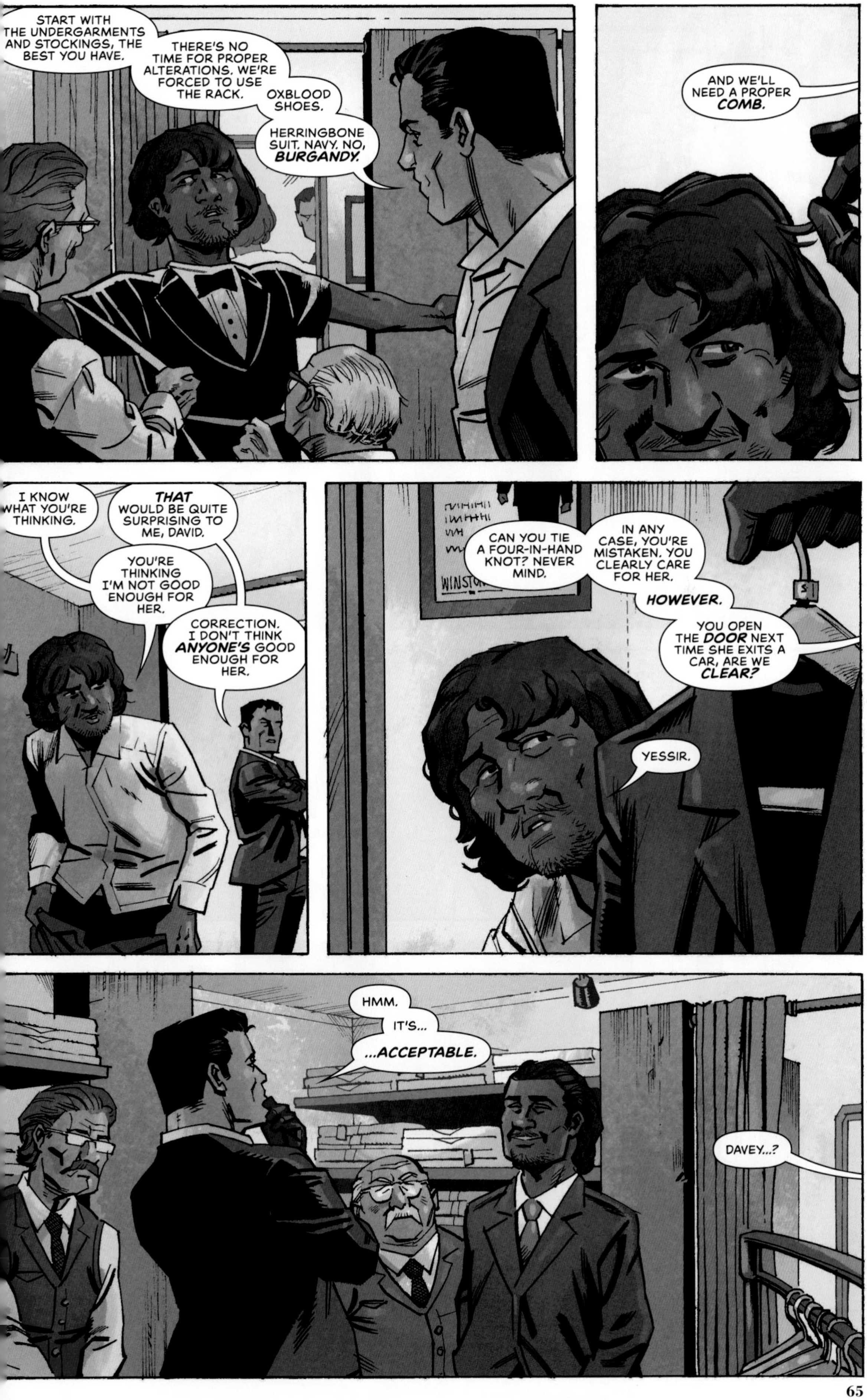
START WITH THE UNDERGARMENTS AND STOCKINGS, THE BEST YOU HAVE.
THERE'S NO TIME FOR PROPER ALTERATIONS. WE'RE FORCED TO USE THE RACK.
OXBLOOD SHOES.
HERRINGBONE SUIT. NAVY. NO, BURGANDY.
AND WE'LL NEED A PROPER COMB.
I KNOW WHAT YOU'RE THINKING.
THAT WOULD BE QUITE SURPRISING TO ME, DAVID.
YOU'RE THINKING I'M NOT GOOD ENOUGH FOR HER.
CORRECTION. I DON'T THINK ANYONE'S GOOD ENOUGH FOR HER.
CAN YOU TIE A FOUR-IN-HAND KNOT? NEVER MIND.
IN ANY CASE, YOU'RE MISTAKEN. YOU CLEARLY CARE FOR HER.
HOWEVER.
YOU OPEN THE DOOR NEXT TIME SHE EXITS A CAR, ARE WE CLEAR?
YESSIR.
HMM.
IT'S...
...ACCEPTABLE.
DAVEY...?

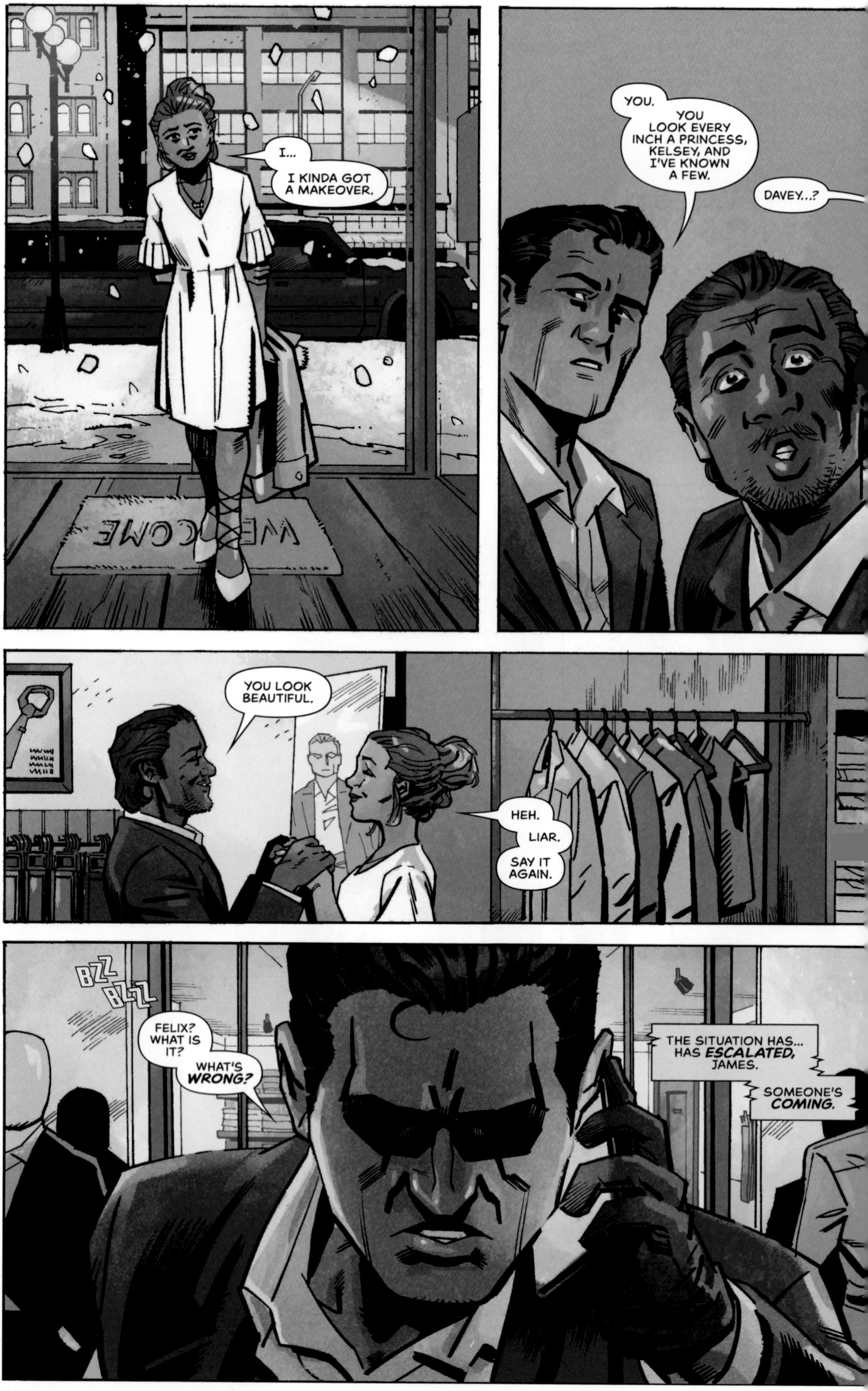
I...
I KINDA GOT A MAKEOVER.
WELCOME
YOU.
YOU LOOK EVERY INCH A PRINCESS, KELSEY, AND I'VE KNOWN A FEW.
DAVEY...?
YOU LOOK BEAUTIFUL.
HEH.
LIAR.
SAY IT AGAIN.
BZZ BZZZ
FELIX? WHAT IS IT?
WHAT'S **WRONG?**
THE SITUATION HAS... HAS **ESCALATED,** JAMES.
SOMEONE'S **COMING.**

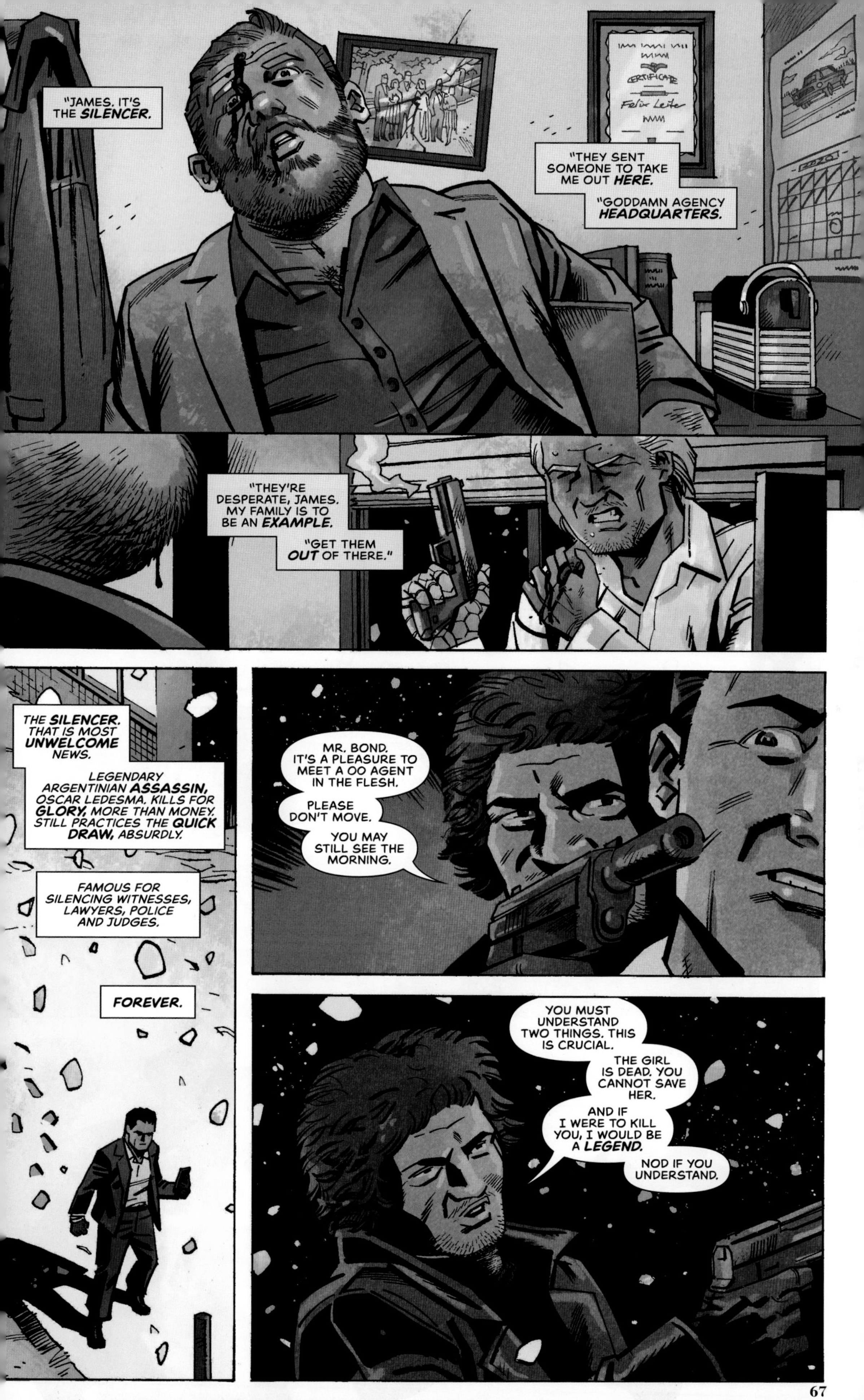
"JAMES. IT'S THE **SILENCER.**
Felix Leiter
"THEY SENT SOMEONE TO TAKE ME OUT **HERE.**
"GODDAMN AGENCY **HEADQUARTERS.**
"THEY'RE DESPERATE, JAMES. MY FAMILY IS TO BE AN **EXAMPLE.**
"GET THEM **OUT** OF THERE."
*THE **SILENCER.** THAT IS MOST **UNWELCOME** NEWS.*
*LEGENDARY ARGENTINIAN **ASSASSIN,** OSCAR LEDESMA. KILLS FOR **GLORY,** MORE THAN MONEY. STILL PRACTICES THE **QUICK DRAW,** ABSURDLY.*
FAMOUS FOR SILENCING WITNESSES, LAWYERS, POLICE AND JUDGES.
FOREVER.
MR. BOND. IT'S A PLEASURE TO MEET A 00 AGENT IN THE FLESH.
PLEASE DON'T MOVE.
YOU MAY STILL SEE THE MORNING.
YOU MUST UNDERSTAND TWO THINGS. THIS IS CRUCIAL.
THE GIRL IS DEAD. YOU CANNOT SAVE HER.
AND IF I WERE TO KILL YOU, I WOULD BE A **LEGEND.**
NOD IF YOU UNDERSTAND.

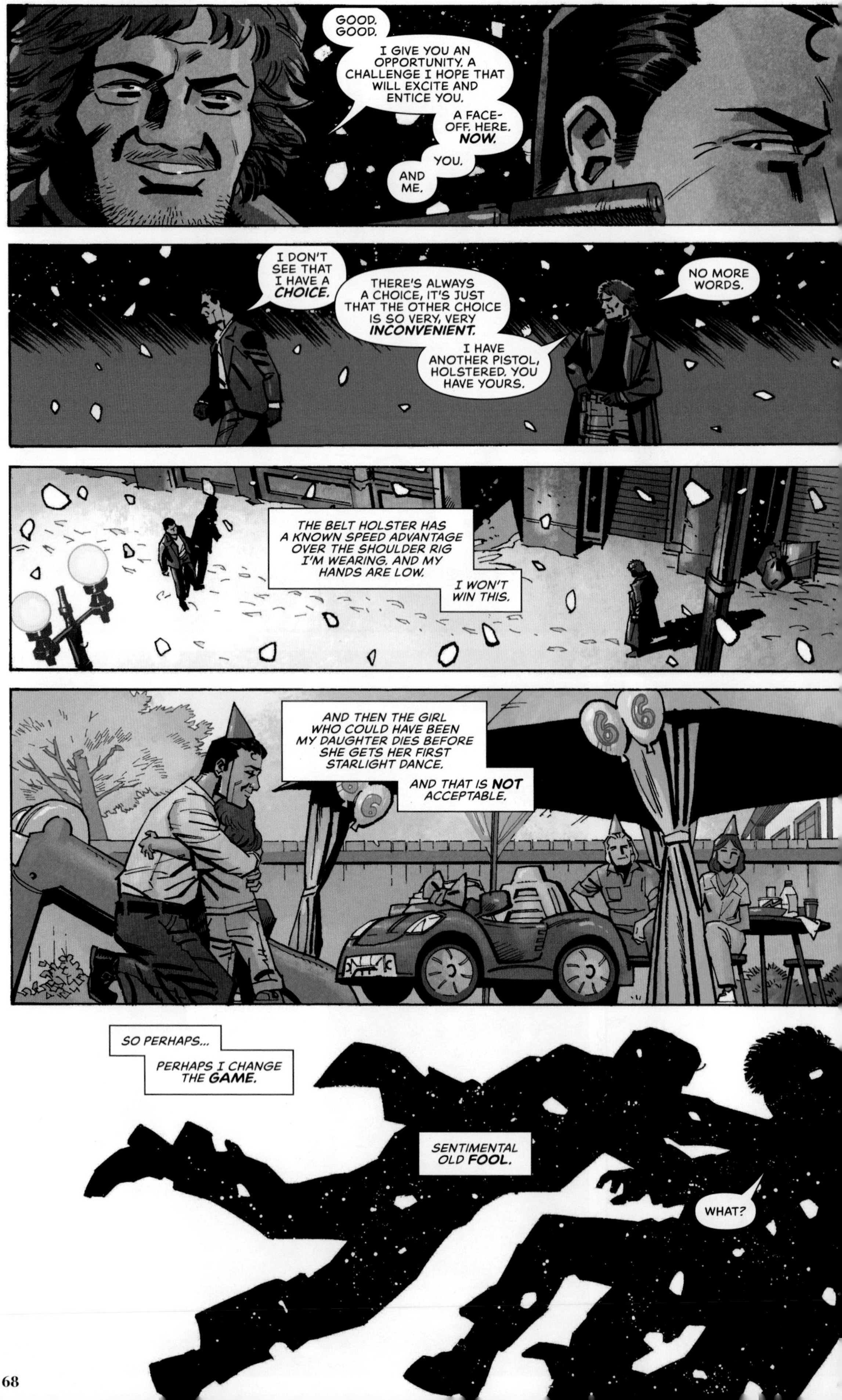
GOOD. GOOD.
I GIVE YOU AN OPPORTUNITY. A CHALLENGE I HOPE THAT WILL EXCITE AND ENTICE YOU.
A FACE-OFF. HERE. **NOW.**
YOU.
AND ME.
I DON'T SEE THAT I HAVE A *CHOICE.*
THERE'S ALWAYS A CHOICE, IT'S JUST THAT THE OTHER CHOICE IS SO VERY, VERY *INCONVENIENT.*
I HAVE ANOTHER PISTOL, HOLSTERED. YOU HAVE YOURS.
NO MORE WORDS.
THE BELT HOLSTER HAS A KNOWN SPEED ADVANTAGE OVER THE SHOULDER RIG I'M WEARING. AND MY HANDS ARE LOW.
I WON'T WIN THIS.
AND THEN THE GIRL WHO COULD HAVE BEEN MY DAUGHTER DIES BEFORE SHE GETS HER FIRST STARLIGHT DANCE.
*AND THAT IS **NOT** ACCEPTABLE.*
SO PERHAPS...
*PERHAPS I CHANGE THE **GAME.***
*SENTIMENTAL OLD **FOOL.***
WHAT?

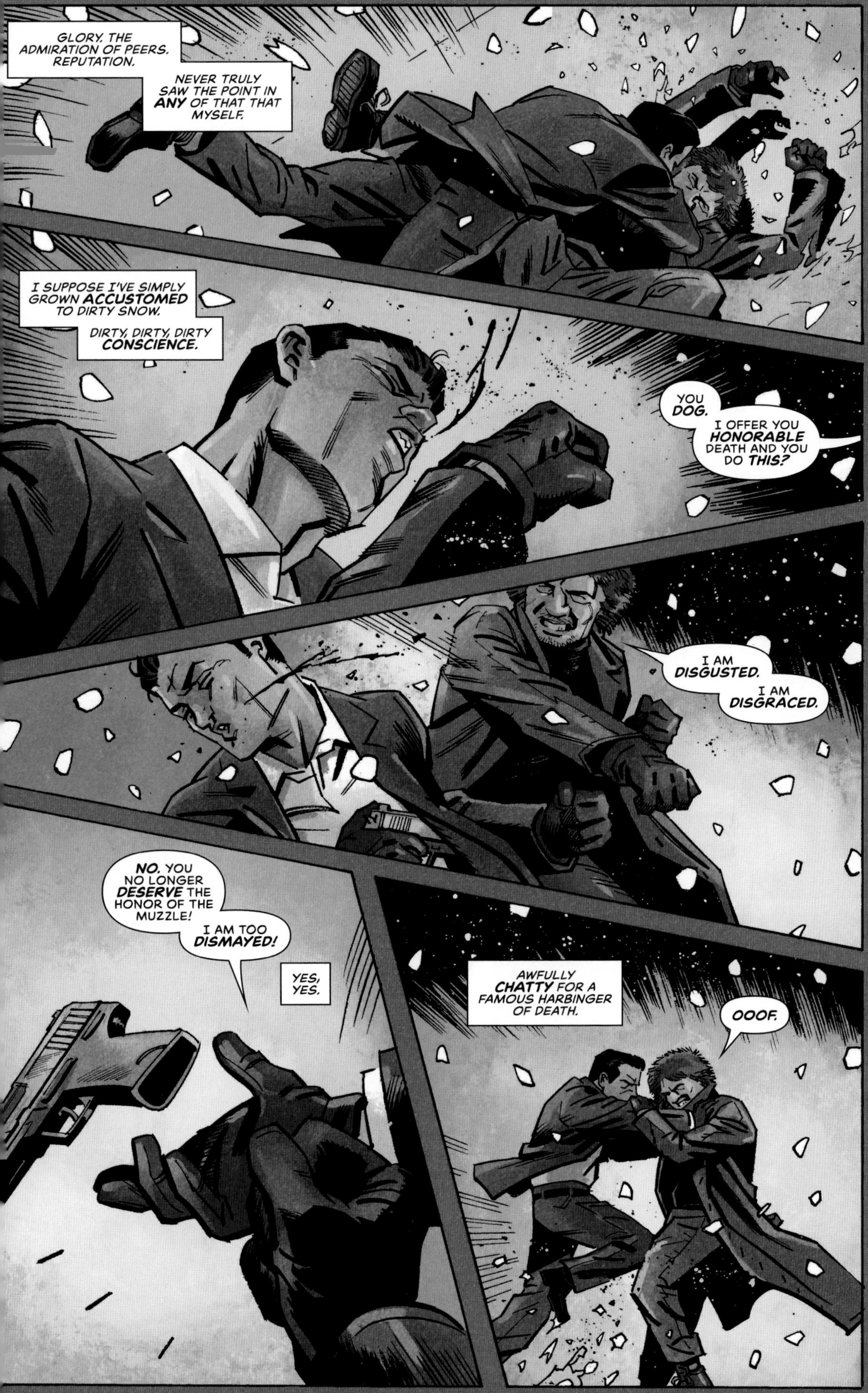
GLORY, THE ADMIRATION OF PEERS. REPUTATION.
NEVER TRULY SAW THE POINT IN ANY OF THAT THAT MYSELF.
I SUPPOSE I'VE SIMPLY GROWN ACCUSTOMED TO DIRTY SNOW.
DIRTY, DIRTY, DIRTY CONSCIENCE.
YOU DOG.
I OFFER YOU HONORABLE DEATH AND YOU DO THIS?
I AM DISGUSTED.
I AM DISGRACED.
NO. YOU NO LONGER DESERVE THE HONOR OF THE MUZZLE!
I AM TOO DISMAYED!
YES, YES.
AWFULLY CHATTY FOR A FAMOUS HARBINGER OF DEATH.
OOOF.

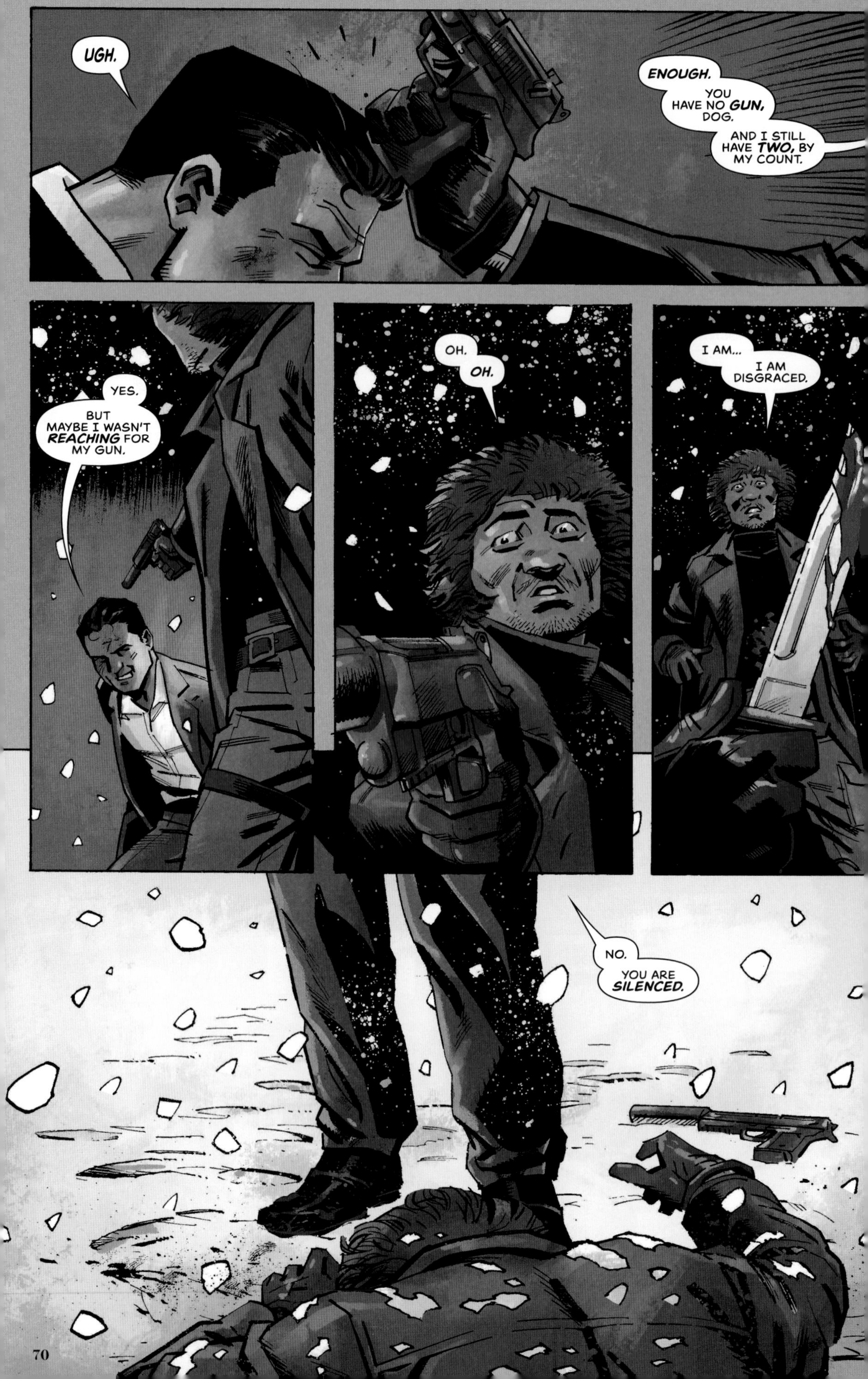
UGH.
ENOUGH.
YOU HAVE NO GUN, DOG.
AND I STILL HAVE TWO, BY MY COUNT.
YES.
BUT MAYBE I WASN'T REACHING FOR MY GUN.
OH.
OH.
I AM...
I AM DISGRACED.
NO.
YOU ARE SILENCED.

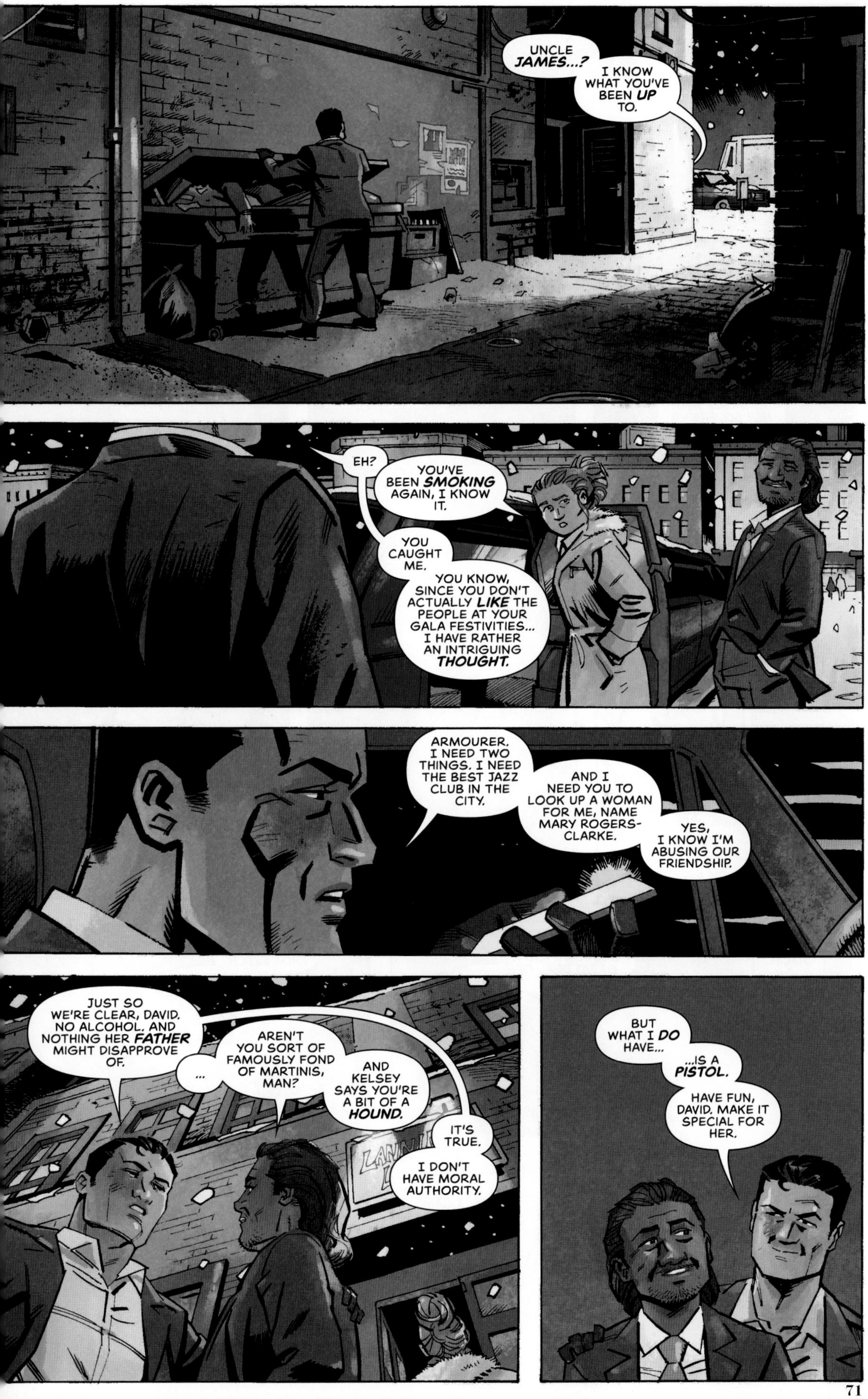
UNCLE JAMES...?
I KNOW WHAT YOU'VE BEEN UP TO.
EH?
YOU'VE BEEN SMOKING AGAIN, I KNOW IT.
YOU CAUGHT ME.
YOU KNOW, SINCE YOU DON'T ACTUALLY LIKE THE PEOPLE AT YOUR GALA FESTIVITIES... I HAVE RATHER AN INTRIGUING THOUGHT.
ARMOURER. I NEED TWO THINGS. I NEED THE BEST JAZZ CLUB IN THE CITY.
AND I NEED YOU TO LOOK UP A WOMAN FOR ME, NAME MARY ROGERS-CLARKE.
YES, I KNOW I'M ABUSING OUR FRIENDSHIP.
JUST SO WE'RE CLEAR, DAVID. NO ALCOHOL. AND NOTHING HER FATHER MIGHT DISAPPROVE OF.
...
AREN'T YOU SORT OF FAMOUSLY FOND OF MARTINIS, MAN?
AND KELSEY SAYS YOU'RE A BIT OF A HOUND.
IT'S TRUE.
I DON'T HAVE MORAL AUTHORITY.
BUT WHAT I DO HAVE...
...IS A PISTOL.
HAVE FUN, DAVID. MAKE IT SPECIAL FOR HER.

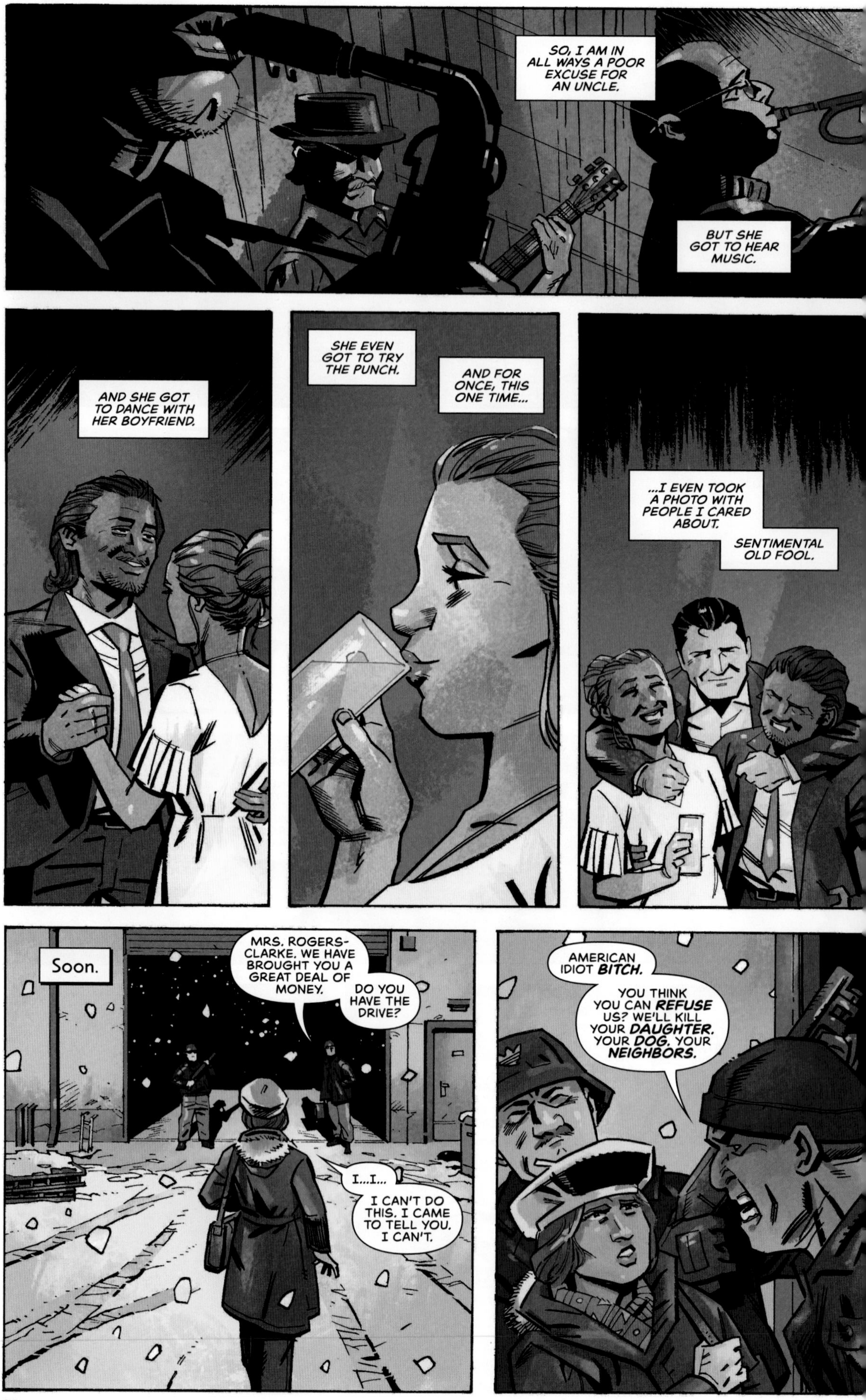
SO, I AM IN ALL WAYS A POOR EXCUSE FOR AN UNCLE.
BUT SHE GOT TO HEAR MUSIC.
AND SHE GOT TO DANCE WITH HER BOYFRIEND.
SHE EVEN GOT TO TRY THE PUNCH.
AND FOR ONCE, THIS ONE TIME...
...I EVEN TOOK A PHOTO WITH PEOPLE I CARED ABOUT.
SENTIMENTAL OLD FOOL.
Soon.
MRS. ROGERS-CLARKE. WE HAVE BROUGHT YOU A GREAT DEAL OF MONEY.
DO YOU HAVE THE DRIVE?
I...I...
I CAN'T DO THIS. I CAME TO TELL YOU. I CAN'T.
AMERICAN IDIOT BITCH.
YOU THINK YOU CAN REFUSE US? WE'LL KILL YOUR DAUGHTER. YOUR DOG. YOUR NEIGHBORS.

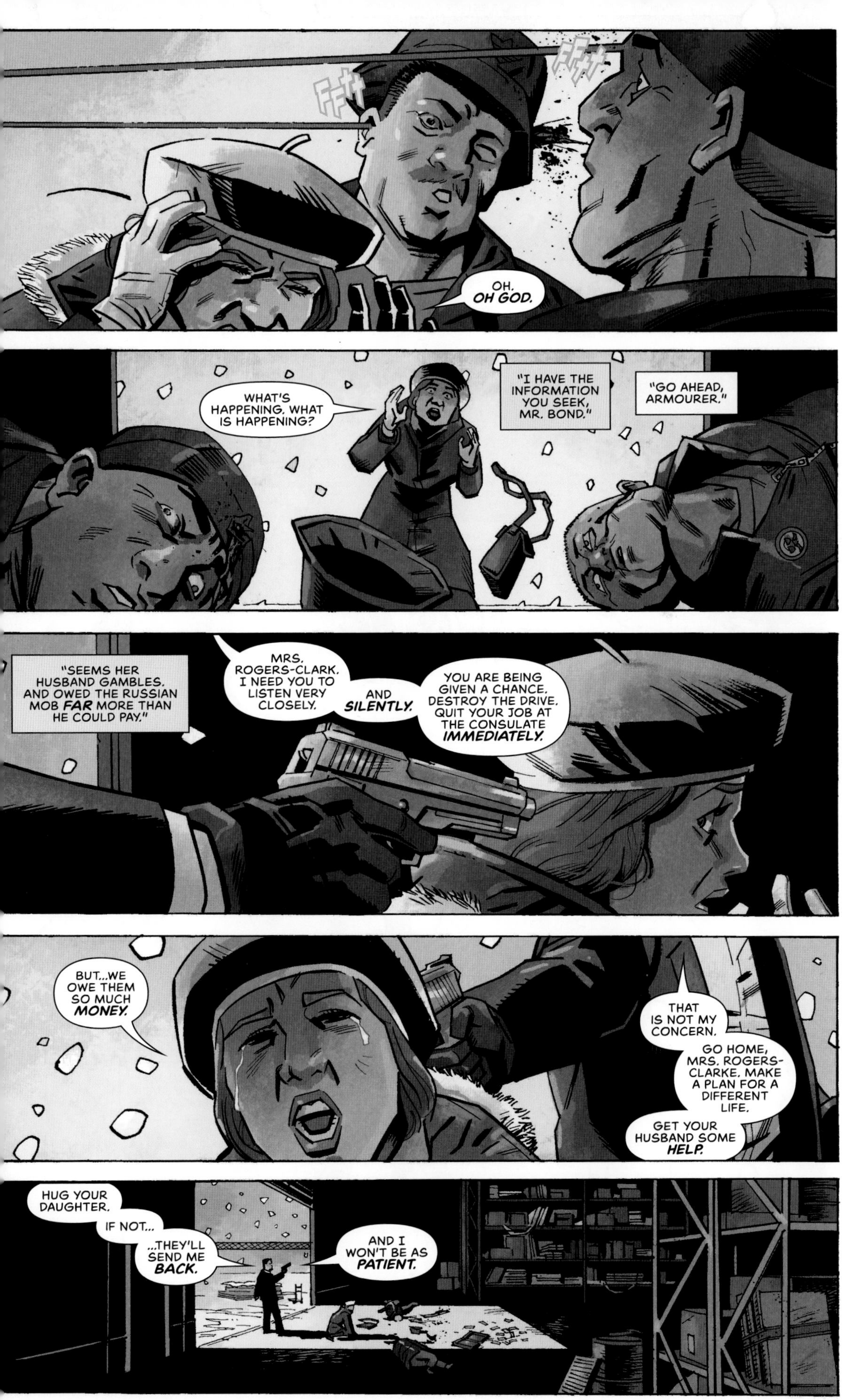
FFT
FFT
OH. OH GOD.
WHAT'S HAPPENING. WHAT IS HAPPENING?
"I HAVE THE INFORMATION YOU SEEK, MR. BOND."
"GO AHEAD, ARMOURER."
"SEEMS HER HUSBAND GAMBLES. AND OWED THE RUSSIAN MOB FAR MORE THAN HE COULD PAY."
MRS. ROGERS-CLARK. I NEED YOU TO LISTEN VERY CLOSELY.
AND SILENTLY.
YOU ARE BEING GIVEN A CHANCE. DESTROY THE DRIVE. QUIT YOUR JOB AT THE CONSULATE IMMEDIATELY.
BUT...WE OWE THEM SO MUCH MONEY.
THAT IS NOT MY CONCERN.
GO HOME, MRS. ROGERS-CLARKE. MAKE A PLAN FOR A DIFFERENT LIFE.
GET YOUR HUSBAND SOME HELP.
HUG YOUR DAUGHTER.
IF NOT...
...THEY'LL SEND ME BACK.
AND I WON'T BE AS PATIENT.

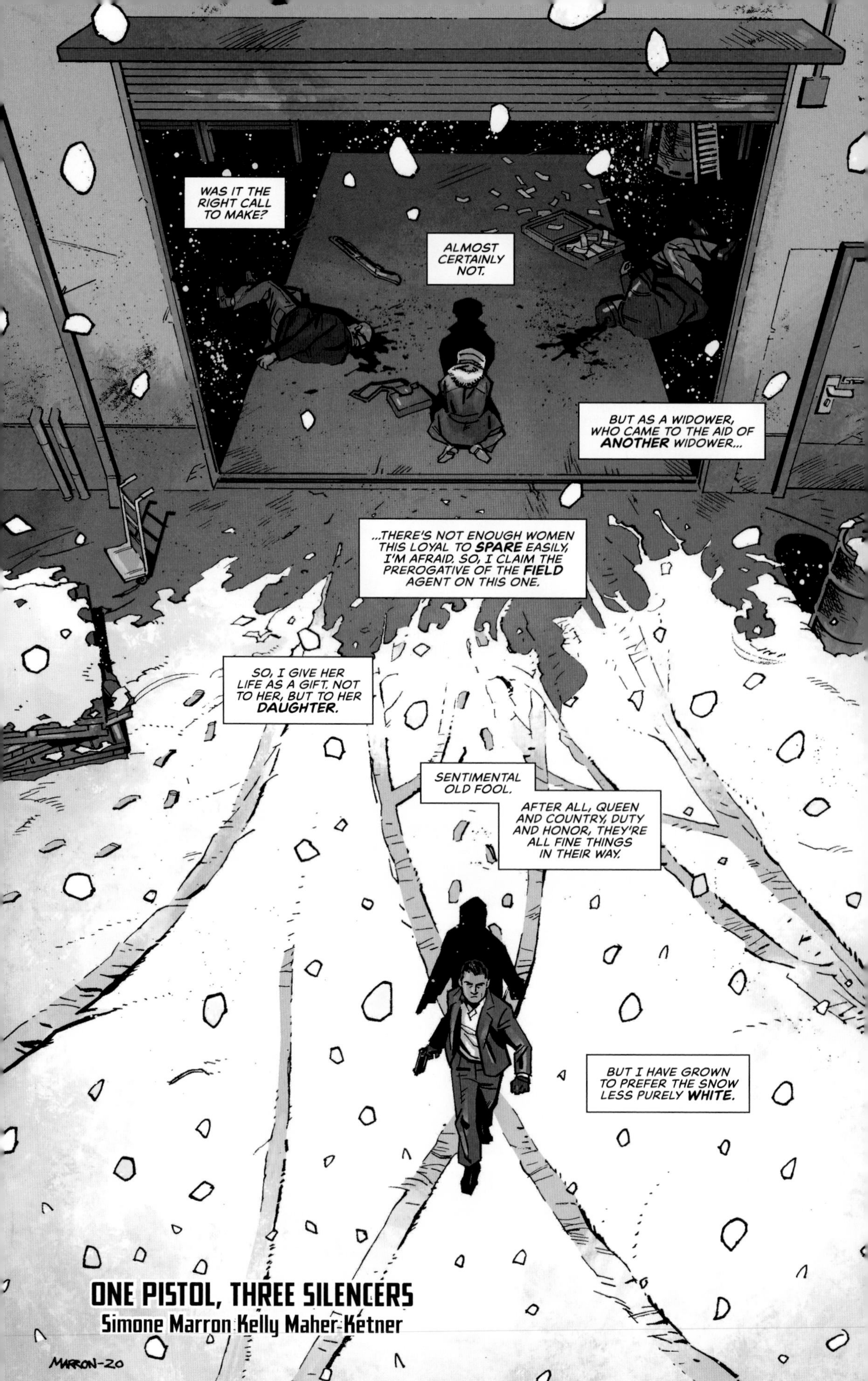

WAS IT THE RIGHT CALL TO MAKE?
ALMOST CERTAINLY NOT.
BUT AS A WIDOWER, WHO CAME TO THE AID OF ANOTHER WIDOWER...
...THERE'S NOT ENOUGH WOMEN THIS LOYAL TO SPARE EASILY, I'M AFRAID. SO, I CLAIM THE PREROGATIVE OF THE FIELD AGENT ON THIS ONE.
SO, I GIVE HER LIFE AS A GIFT, NOT TO HER, BUT TO HER DAUGHTER.
SENTIMENTAL OLD FOOL.
AFTER ALL, QUEEN AND COUNTRY, DUTY AND HONOR, THEY'RE ALL FINE THINGS IN THEIR WAY.
BUT I HAVE GROWN TO PREFER THE SNOW LESS PURELY WHITE.
MARRON-20

ONE PISTOL, THREE SILENCERS

Simone Marron Kelly Maher-Ketner

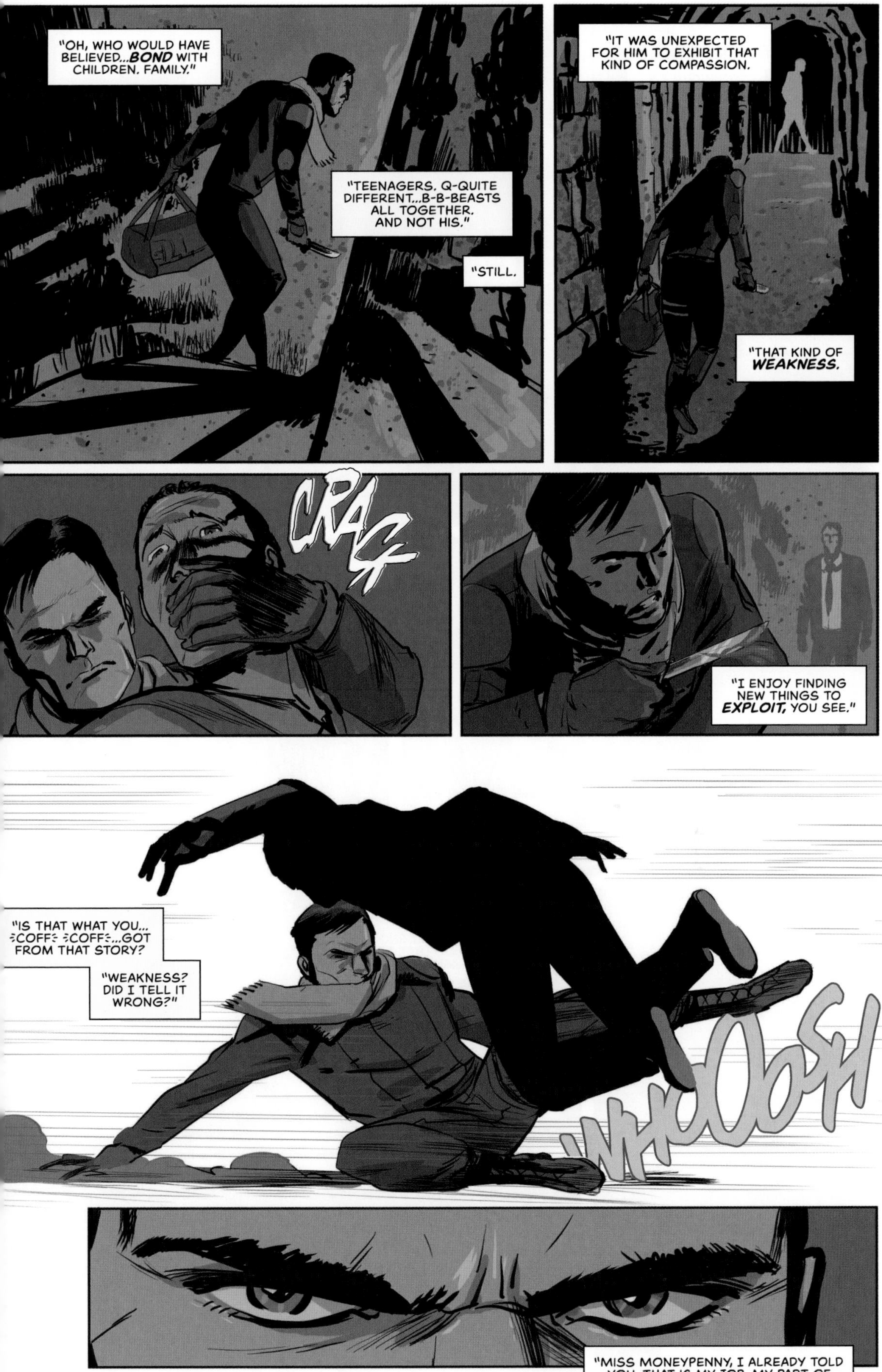
"OH, WHO WOULD HAVE BELIEVED...BOND WITH CHILDREN. FAMILY."
"TEENAGERS. Q-QUITE DIFFERENT...B-B-BEASTS ALL TOGETHER. AND NOT HIS."
"STILL.
"IT WAS UNEXPECTED FOR HIM TO EXHIBIT THAT KIND OF COMPASSION.
"THAT KIND OF WEAKNESS.
CRACK
"I ENJOY FINDING NEW THINGS TO EXPLOIT, YOU SEE."
"IS THAT WHAT YOU... COFF COFF...GOT FROM THAT STORY?
"WEAKNESS? DID I TELL IT WRONG?"
WHOOOSH
"MISS MONEYPENNY, I ALREADY TOLD YOU...THAT IS MY JOB. MY PART OF THIS SYMBIOTIC RELATIONSHIP."

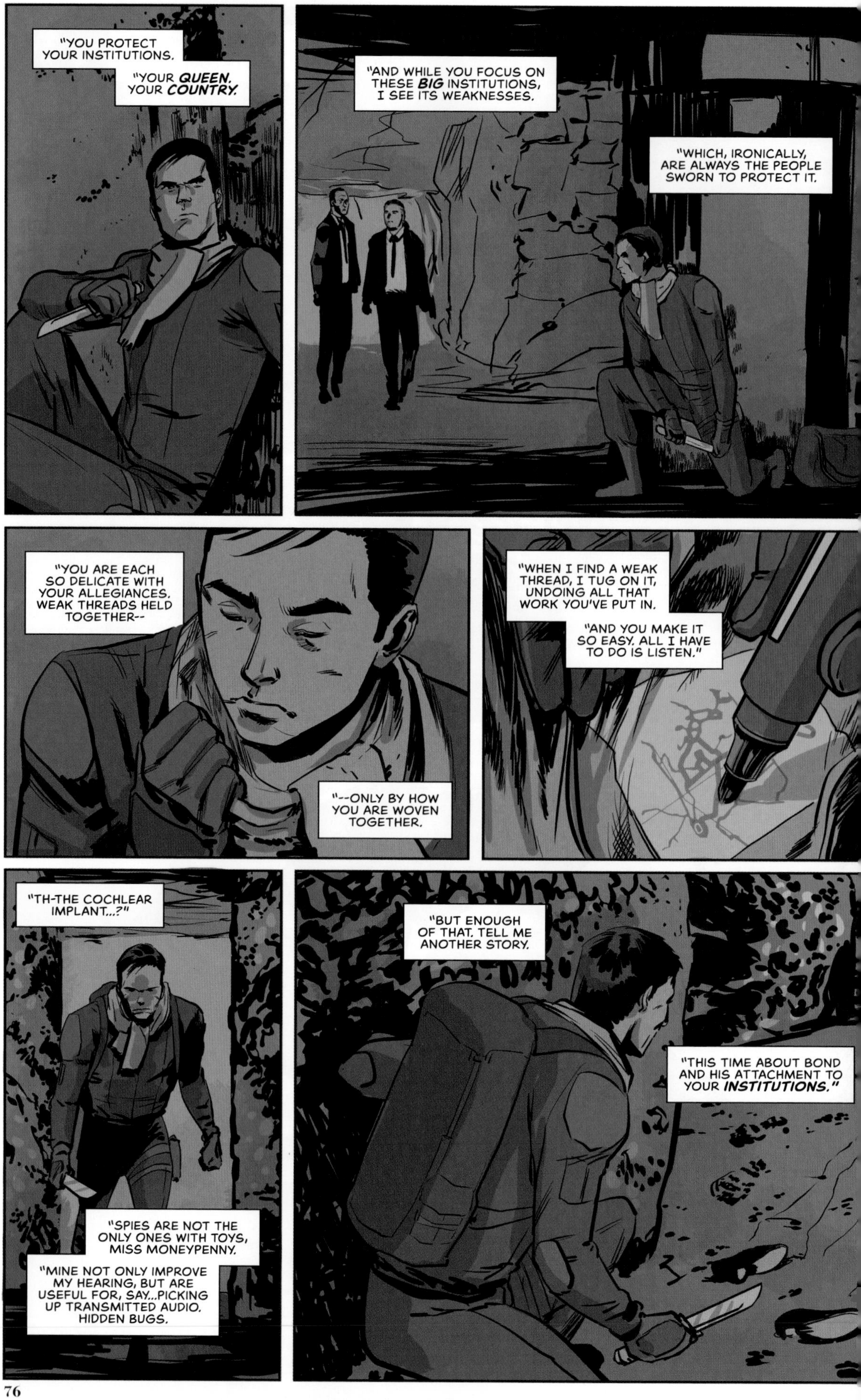
"YOU PROTECT YOUR INSTITUTIONS.
"YOUR QUEEN. YOUR COUNTRY.
"AND WHILE YOU FOCUS ON THESE BIG INSTITUTIONS, I SEE ITS WEAKNESSES.
"WHICH, IRONICALLY, ARE ALWAYS THE PEOPLE SWORN TO PROTECT IT.
"YOU ARE EACH SO DELICATE WITH YOUR ALLEGIANCES. WEAK THREADS HELD TOGETHER--
"--ONLY BY HOW YOU ARE WOVEN TOGETHER.
"WHEN I FIND A WEAK THREAD, I TUG ON IT, UNDOING ALL THAT WORK YOU'VE PUT IN.
"AND YOU MAKE IT SO EASY. ALL I HAVE TO DO IS LISTEN."
"TH-THE COCHLEAR IMPLANT...?"
"SPIES ARE NOT THE ONLY ONES WITH TOYS, MISS MONEYPENNY.
"MINE NOT ONLY IMPROVE MY HEARING, BUT ARE USEFUL FOR, SAY...PICKING UP TRANSMITTED AUDIO. HIDDEN BUGS.
"BUT ENOUGH OF THAT. TELL ME ANOTHER STORY.
"THIS TIME ABOUT BOND AND HIS ATTACHMENT TO YOUR INSTITUTIONS."

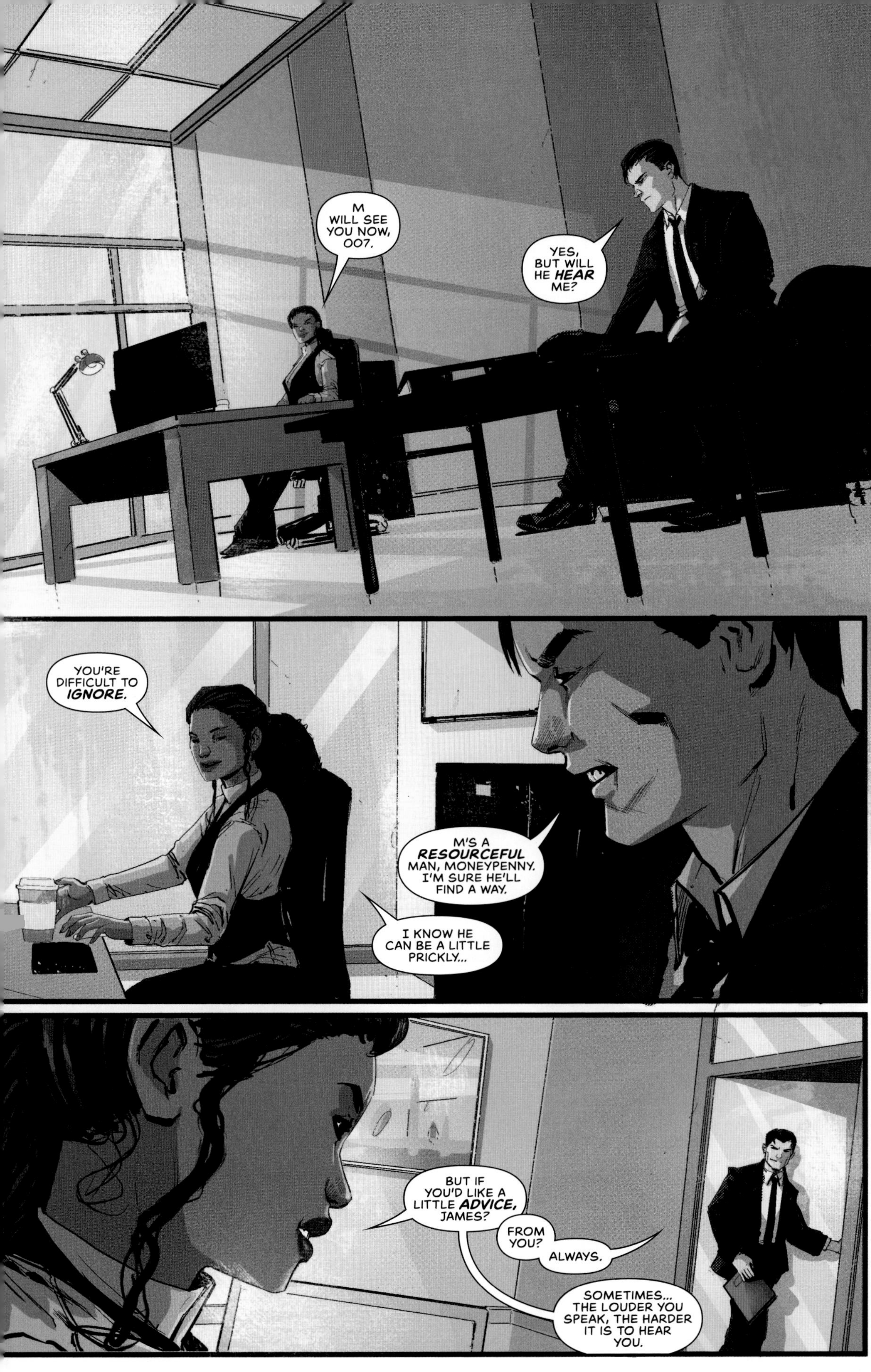
M WILL SEE YOU NOW, 007.
YES, BUT WILL HE HEAR ME?
YOU'RE DIFFICULT TO IGNORE.
M'S A RESOURCEFUL MAN, MONEYPENNY. I'M SURE HE'LL FIND A WAY.
I KNOW HE CAN BE A LITTLE PRICKLY...
BUT IF YOU'D LIKE A LITTLE ADVICE, JAMES?
FROM YOU?
ALWAYS.
SOMETIMES... THE LOUDER YOU SPEAK, THE HARDER IT IS TO HEAR YOU.

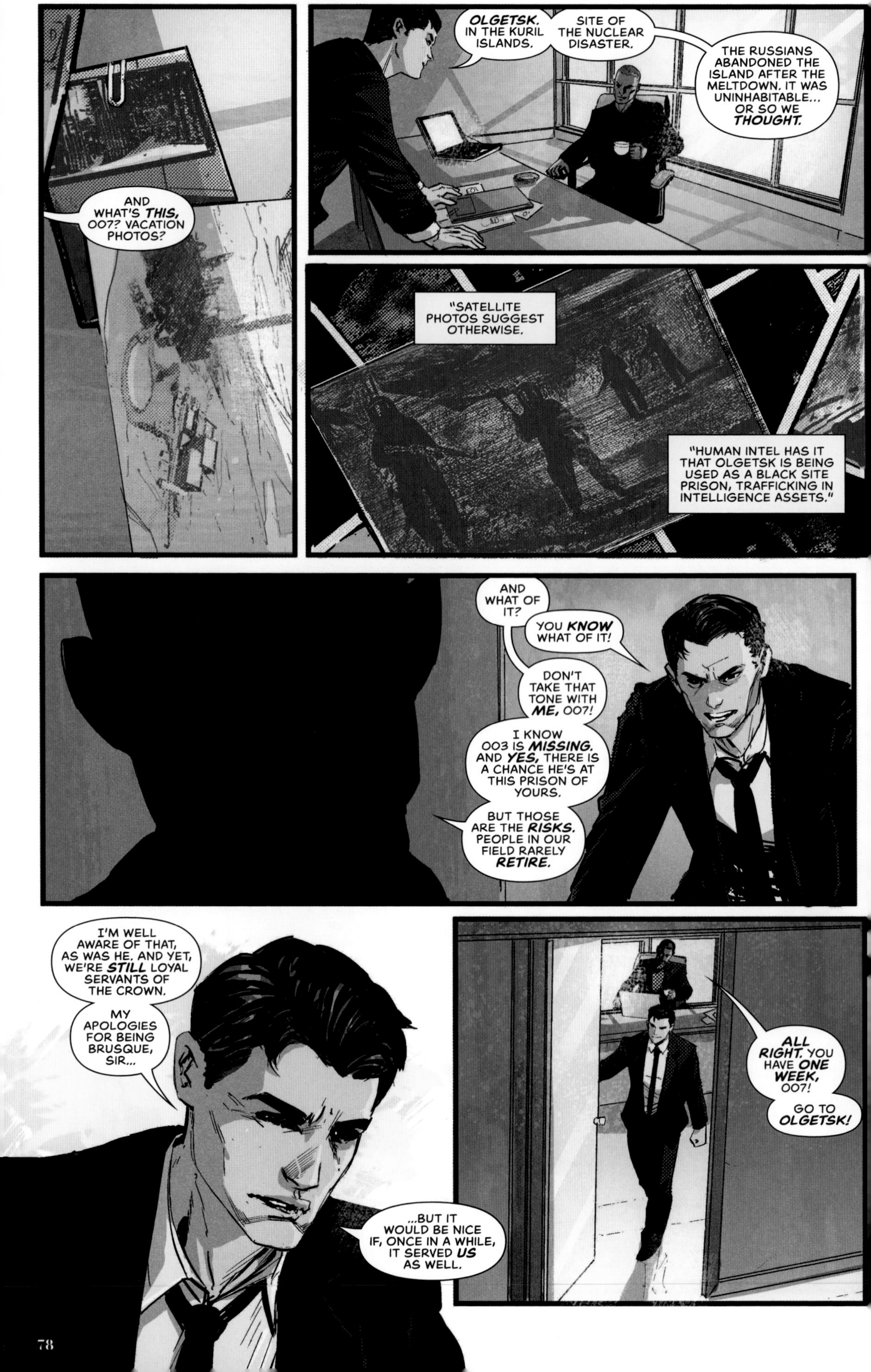
AND WHAT'S THIS, 007? VACATION PHOTOS?
OLGETSK. IN THE KURIL ISLANDS.
SITE OF THE NUCLEAR DISASTER.
THE RUSSIANS ABANDONED THE ISLAND AFTER THE MELTDOWN. IT WAS UNINHABITABLE... OR SO WE THOUGHT.
"SATELLITE PHOTOS SUGGEST OTHERWISE.
"HUMAN INTEL HAS IT THAT OLGETSK IS BEING USED AS A BLACK SITE PRISON, TRAFFICKING IN INTELLIGENCE ASSETS."
AND WHAT OF IT?
YOU KNOW WHAT OF IT!
DON'T TAKE THAT TONE WITH ME, 007!
I KNOW 003 IS MISSING. AND YES, THERE IS A CHANCE HE'S AT THIS PRISON OF YOURS.
BUT THOSE ARE THE RISKS. PEOPLE IN OUR FIELD RARELY RETIRE.
I'M WELL AWARE OF THAT, AS WAS HE. AND YET, WE'RE STILL LOYAL SERVANTS OF THE CROWN.
MY APOLOGIES FOR BEING BRUSQUE, SIR...
...BUT IT WOULD BE NICE IF, ONCE IN A WHILE, IT SERVED US AS WELL.
ALL RIGHT. YOU HAVE ONE WEEK, 007!
GO TO OLGETSK!

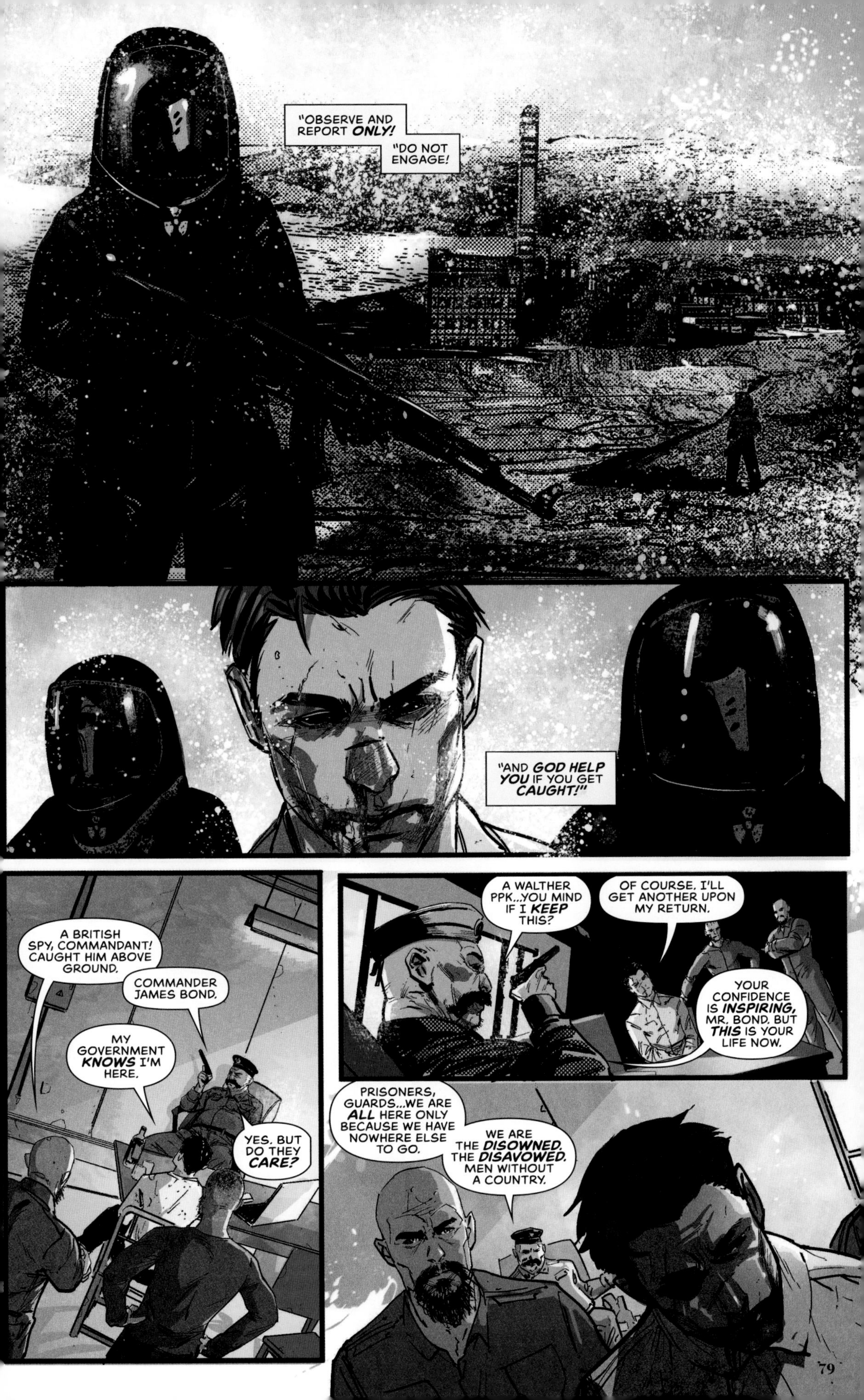
"OBSERVE AND REPORT ONLY!
"DO NOT ENGAGE!
"AND GOD HELP YOU IF YOU GET CAUGHT!"
A BRITISH SPY, COMMANDANT! CAUGHT HIM ABOVE GROUND.
COMMANDER JAMES BOND.
MY GOVERNMENT KNOWS I'M HERE.
YES, BUT DO THEY CARE?
A WALTHER PPK...YOU MIND IF I KEEP THIS?
OF COURSE. I'LL GET ANOTHER UPON MY RETURN.
YOUR CONFIDENCE IS INSPIRING, MR. BOND, BUT THIS IS YOUR LIFE NOW.
PRISONERS, GUARDS...WE ARE ALL HERE ONLY BECAUSE WE HAVE NOWHERE ELSE TO GO.
WE ARE THE DISOWNED. THE DISAVOWED. MEN WITHOUT A COUNTRY.

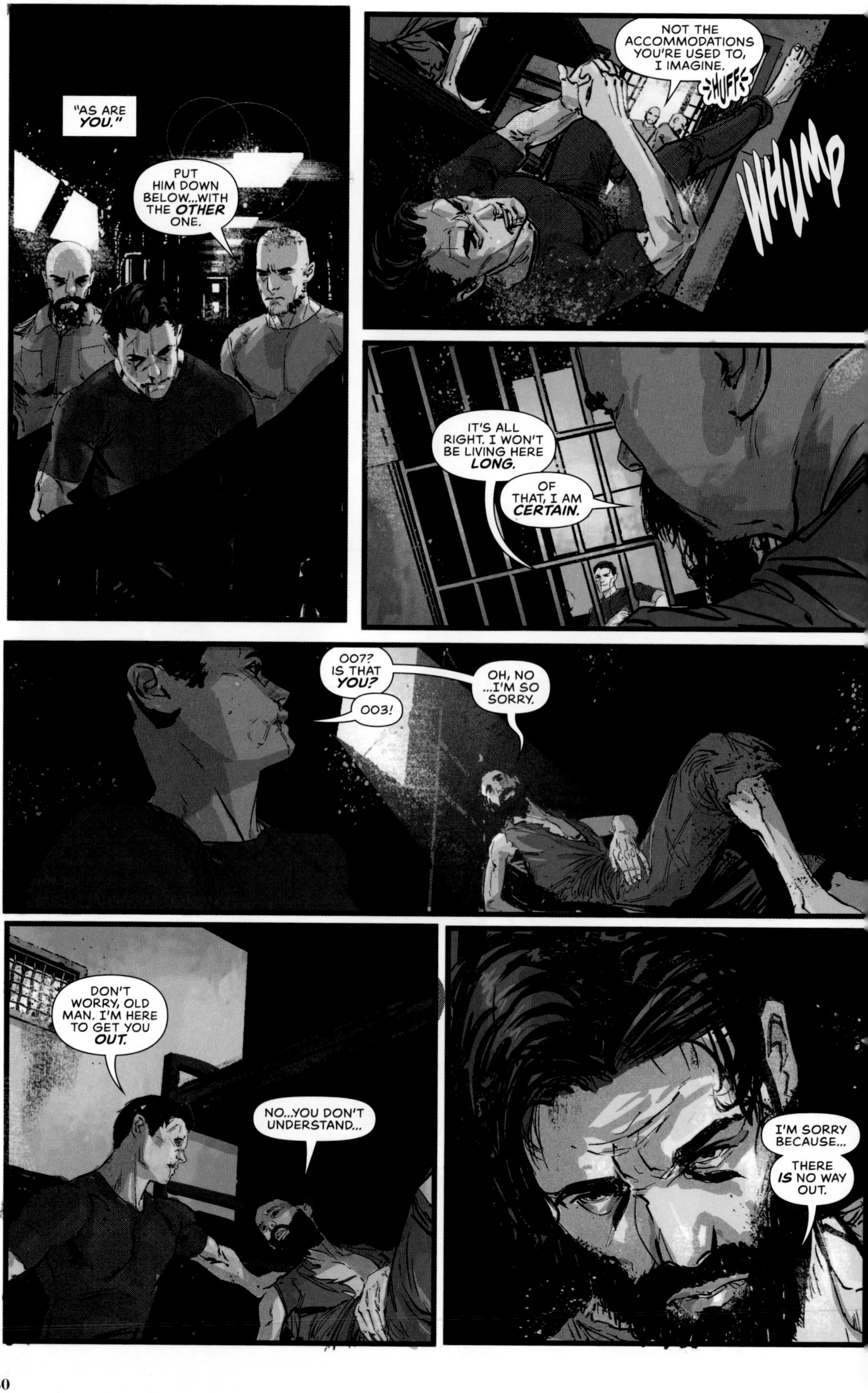
"AS ARE *YOU.*"
PUT HIM DOWN BELOW...WITH THE *OTHER* ONE.
NOT THE ACCOMMODATIONS YOU'RE USED TO, I IMAGINE.
HUFF
WHUMP
IT'S ALL RIGHT. I WON'T BE LIVING HERE *LONG.*
OF THAT, I AM *CERTAIN.*
007? IS THAT *YOU?*
003!
OH, NO ...I'M SO SORRY.
DON'T WORRY, OLD MAN. I'M HERE TO GET YOU *OUT.*
NO...YOU DON'T UNDERSTAND...
I'M SORRY BECAUSE...
THERE *IS* NO WAY OUT.

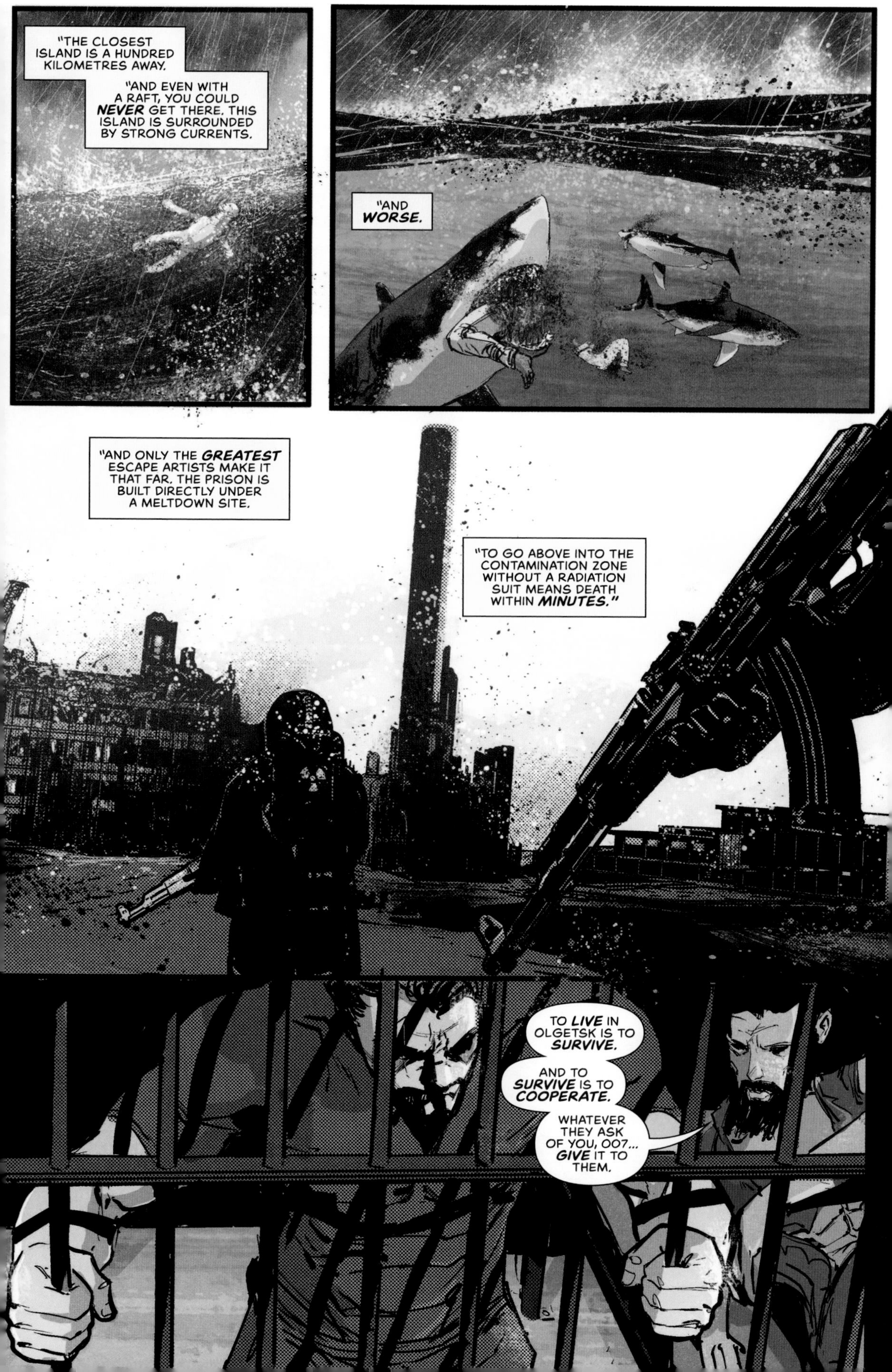
"THE CLOSEST ISLAND IS A HUNDRED KILOMETRES AWAY.
"AND EVEN WITH A RAFT, YOU COULD NEVER GET THERE. THIS ISLAND IS SURROUNDED BY STRONG CURRENTS.
"AND WORSE.
"AND ONLY THE GREATEST ESCAPE ARTISTS MAKE IT THAT FAR. THE PRISON IS BUILT DIRECTLY UNDER A MELTDOWN SITE.
"TO GO ABOVE INTO THE CONTAMINATION ZONE WITHOUT A RADIATION SUIT MEANS DEATH WITHIN MINUTES."
TO LIVE IN OLGETSK IS TO SURVIVE.
AND TO SURVIVE IS TO COOPERATE.
WHATEVER THEY ASK OF YOU, 007... GIVE IT TO THEM.

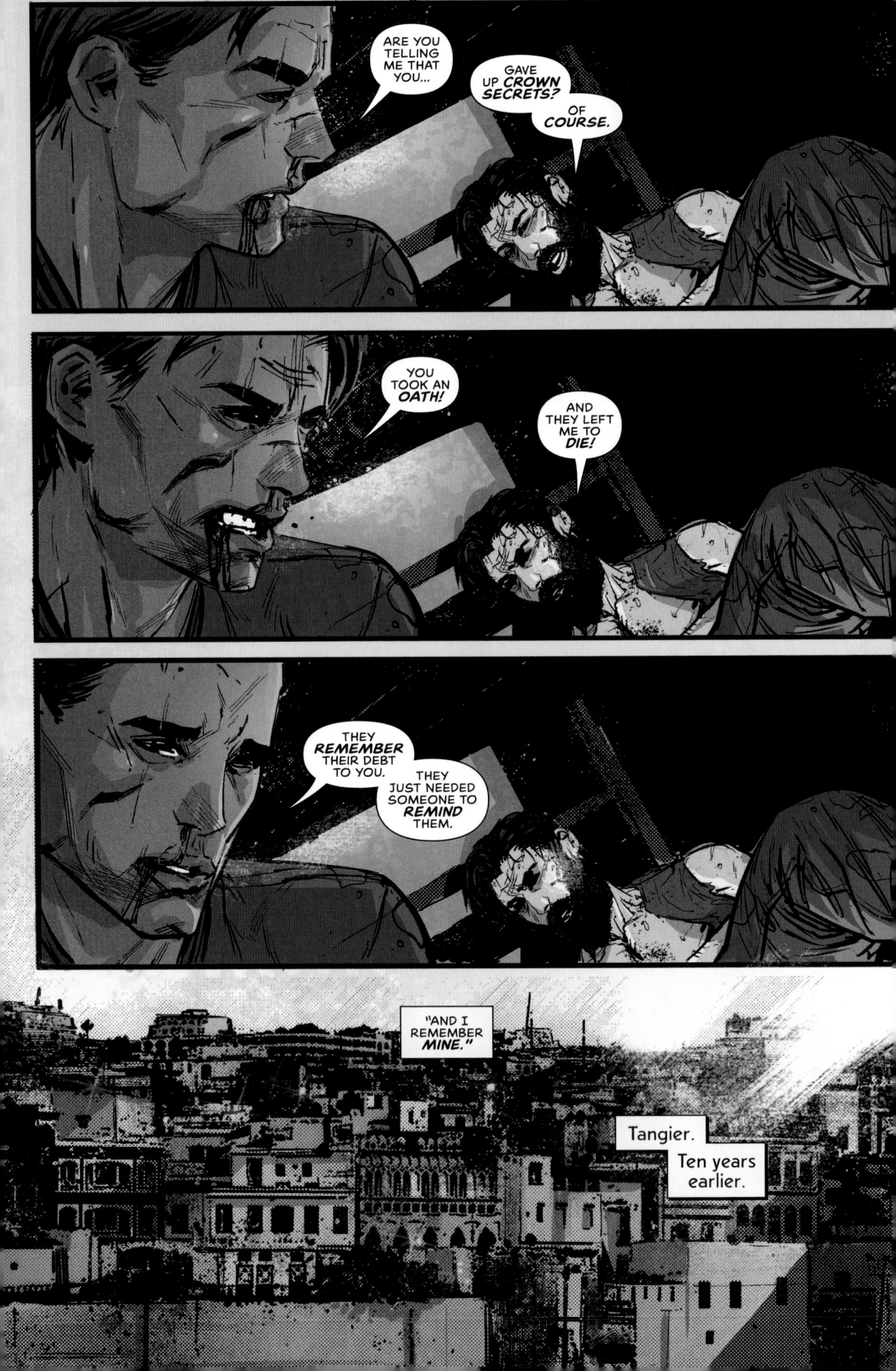

ARE YOU TELLING ME THAT YOU...
GAVE UP CROWN SECRETS?
OF COURSE.
YOU TOOK AN OATH!
AND THEY LEFT ME TO DIE!
THEY REMEMBER THEIR DEBT TO YOU.
THEY JUST NEEDED SOMEONE TO REMIND THEM.
"AND I REMEMBER MINE."
Tangier.
Ten years earlier.

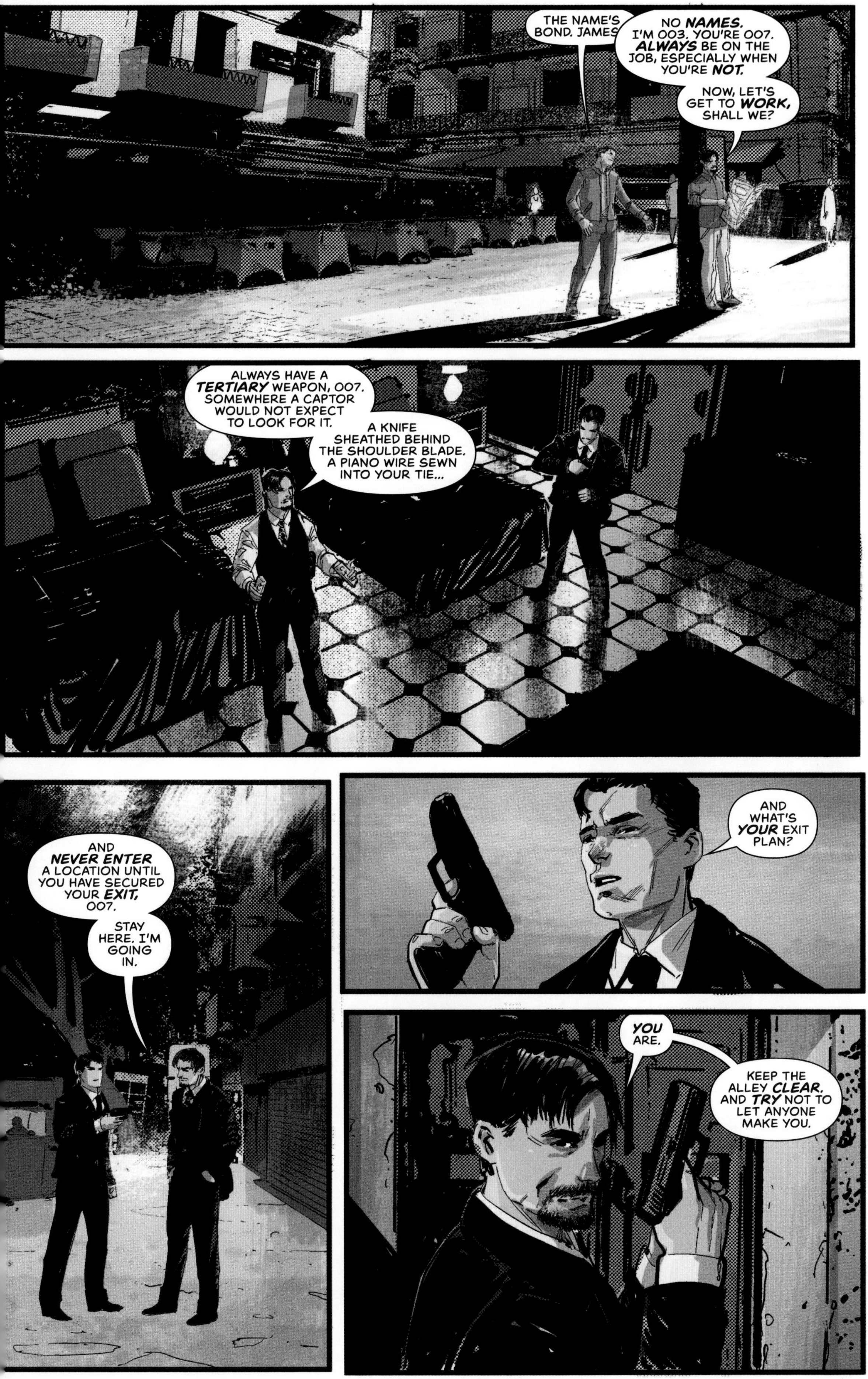
THE NAME'S BOND. JAMES
NO NAMES. I'M 003. YOU'RE 007. ALWAYS BE ON THE JOB, ESPECIALLY WHEN YOU'RE NOT.
NOW, LET'S GET TO WORK, SHALL WE?
ALWAYS HAVE A TERTIARY WEAPON, 007. SOMEWHERE A CAPTOR WOULD NOT EXPECT TO LOOK FOR IT.
A KNIFE SHEATHED BEHIND THE SHOULDER BLADE. A PIANO WIRE SEWN INTO YOUR TIE...
AND NEVER ENTER A LOCATION UNTIL YOU HAVE SECURED YOUR EXIT, 007.
STAY HERE. I'M GOING IN.
AND WHAT'S YOUR EXIT PLAN?
YOU ARE.
KEEP THE ALLEY CLEAR. AND TRY NOT TO LET ANYONE MAKE YOU.

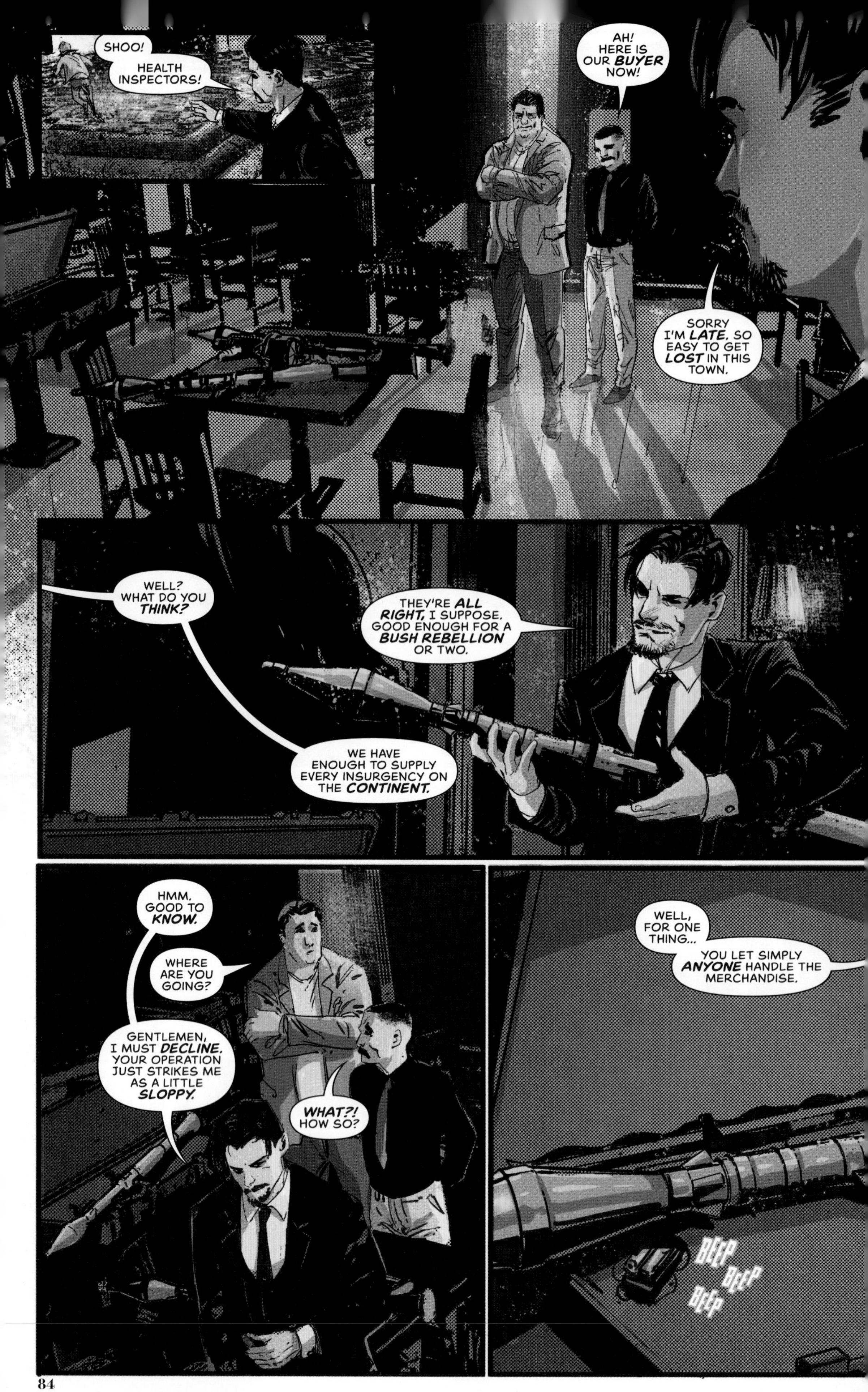
SHOO!
HEALTH INSPECTORS!
AH! HERE IS OUR BUYER NOW!
SORRY I'M LATE. SO EASY TO GET LOST IN THIS TOWN.
WELL? WHAT DO YOU THINK?
THEY'RE ALL RIGHT, I SUPPOSE. GOOD ENOUGH FOR A BUSH REBELLION OR TWO.
WE HAVE ENOUGH TO SUPPLY EVERY INSURGENCY ON THE CONTINENT.
HMM. GOOD TO KNOW.
WHERE ARE YOU GOING?
GENTLEMEN, I MUST DECLINE. YOUR OPERATION JUST STRIKES ME AS A LITTLE SLOPPY.
WHAT?! HOW SO?
WELL, FOR ONE THING...
YOU LET SIMPLY ANYONE HANDLE THE MERCHANDISE.
BEEP BEEP BEEP

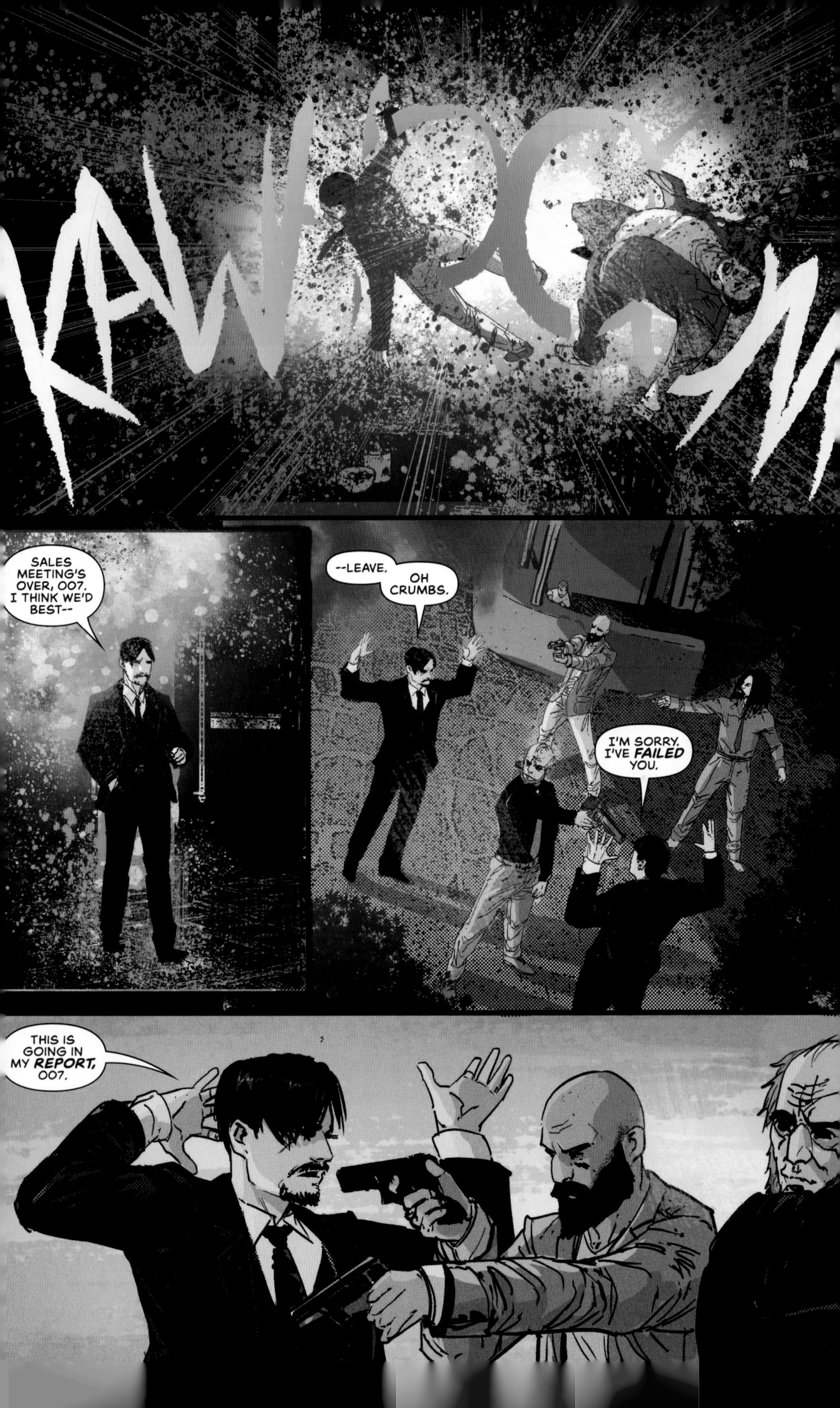
SALES MEETING'S OVER, 007. I THINK WE'D BEST--
--LEAVE.
OH CRUMBS.
I'M SORRY. I'VE **FAILED** YOU.
THIS IS GOING IN MY **REPORT,** 007.

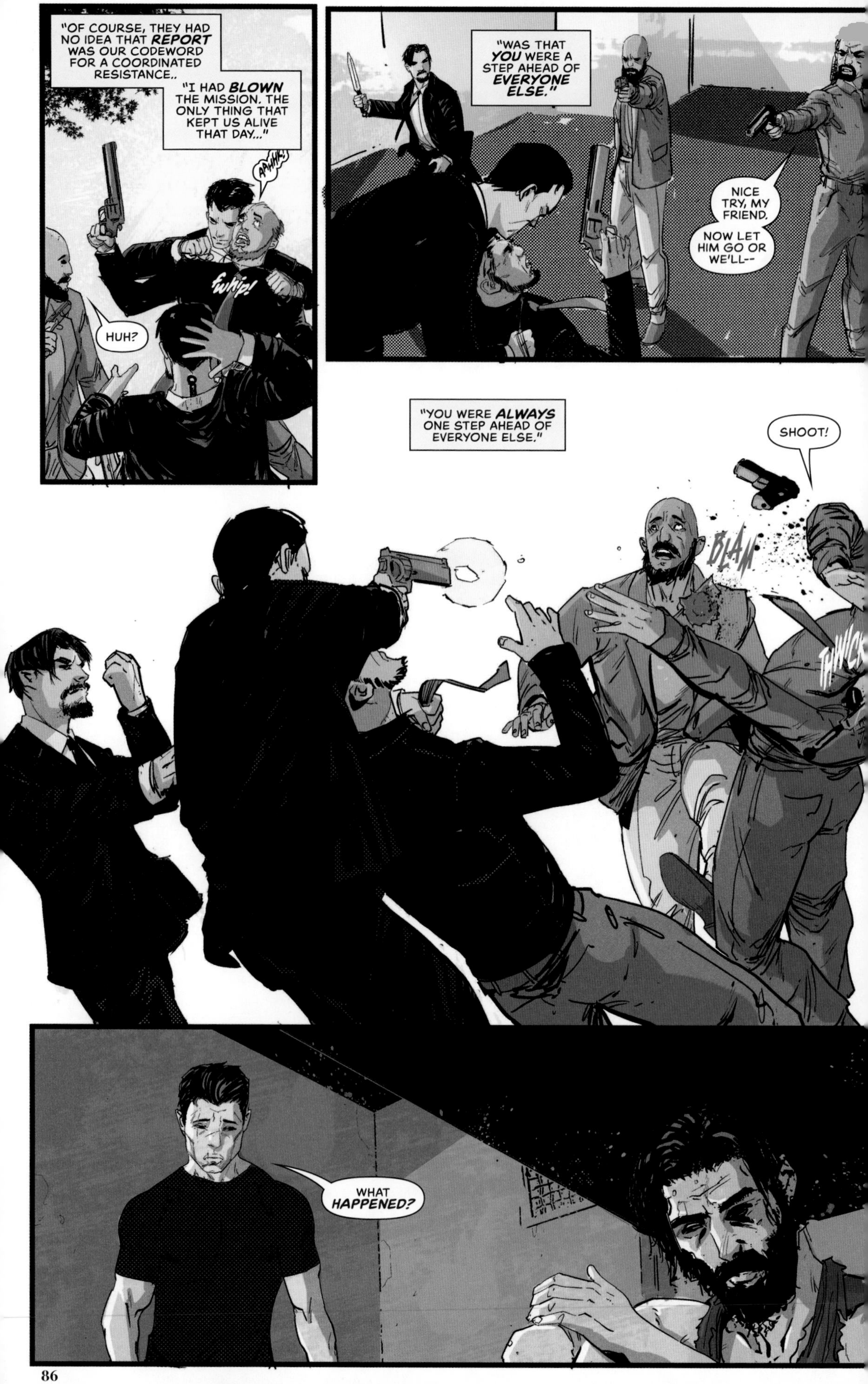
"OF COURSE, THEY HAD NO IDEA THAT REPORT WAS OUR CODEWORD FOR A COORDINATED RESISTANCE..
"I HAD BLOWN THE MISSION. THE ONLY THING THAT KEPT US ALIVE THAT DAY..."
AAHHK!
fwhip!
HUH?
"WAS THAT YOU WERE A STEP AHEAD OF EVERYONE ELSE."
NICE TRY, MY FRIEND.
NOW LET HIM GO OR WE'LL--
"YOU WERE ALWAYS ONE STEP AHEAD OF EVERYONE ELSE."
SHOOT!
BLAM
THWICK
WHAT HAPPENED?

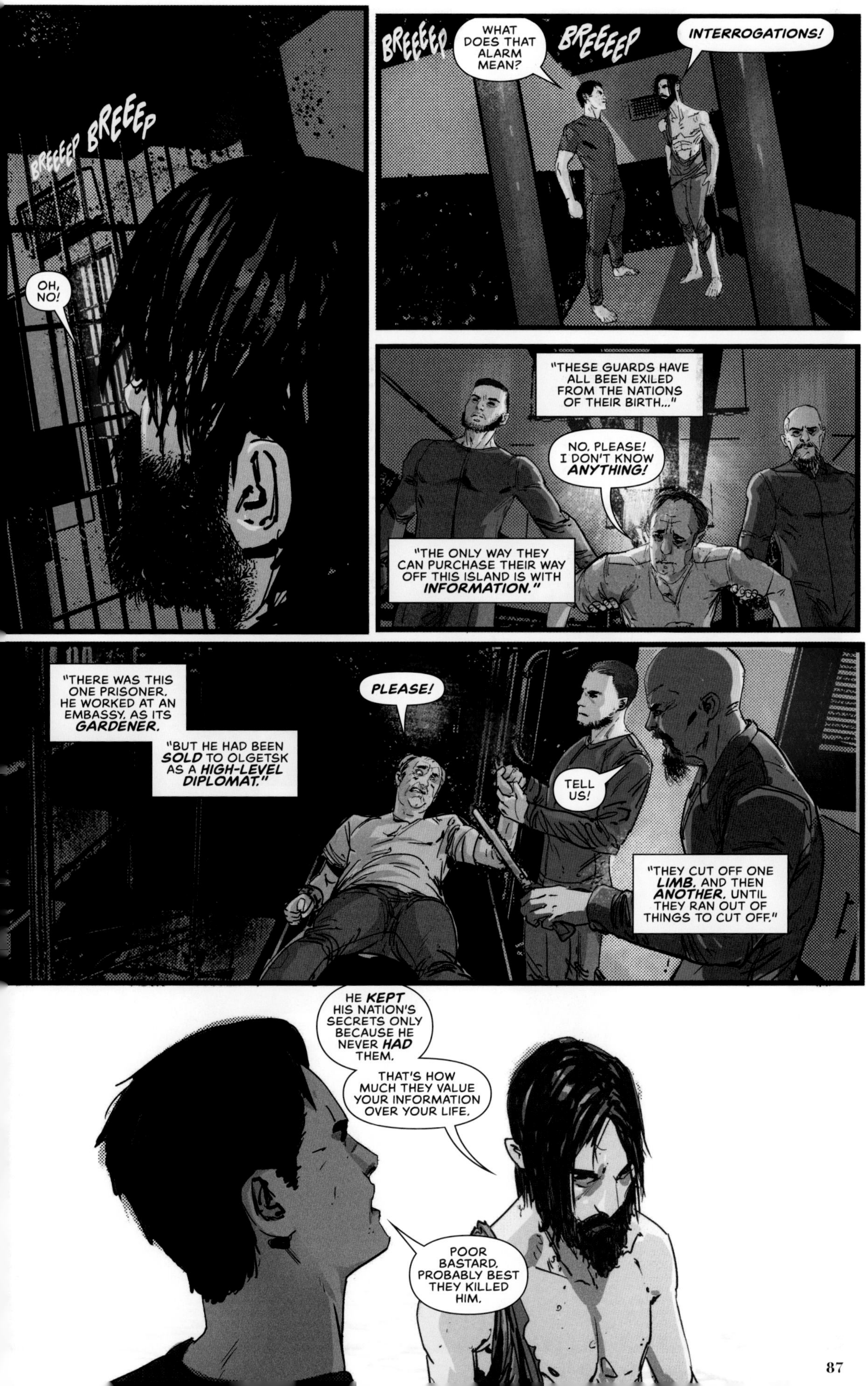
BREEEEP BREEEEP
OH, NO!
BREEEEP
WHAT DOES THAT ALARM MEAN?
BREEEEP
INTERROGATIONS!
"THESE GUARDS HAVE ALL BEEN EXILED FROM THE NATIONS OF THEIR BIRTH..."
NO, PLEASE! I DON'T KNOW ANYTHING!
"THE ONLY WAY THEY CAN PURCHASE THEIR WAY OFF THIS ISLAND IS WITH INFORMATION."
"THERE WAS THIS ONE PRISONER. HE WORKED AT AN EMBASSY, AS ITS GARDENER.
"BUT HE HAD BEEN SOLD TO OLGETSK AS A HIGH-LEVEL DIPLOMAT."
PLEASE!
TELL US!
"THEY CUT OFF ONE LIMB, AND THEN ANOTHER, UNTIL THEY RAN OUT OF THINGS TO CUT OFF."
HE KEPT HIS NATION'S SECRETS ONLY BECAUSE HE NEVER HAD THEM.
THAT'S HOW MUCH THEY VALUE YOUR INFORMATION OVER YOUR LIFE.
POOR BASTARD. PROBABLY BEST THEY KILLED HIM.

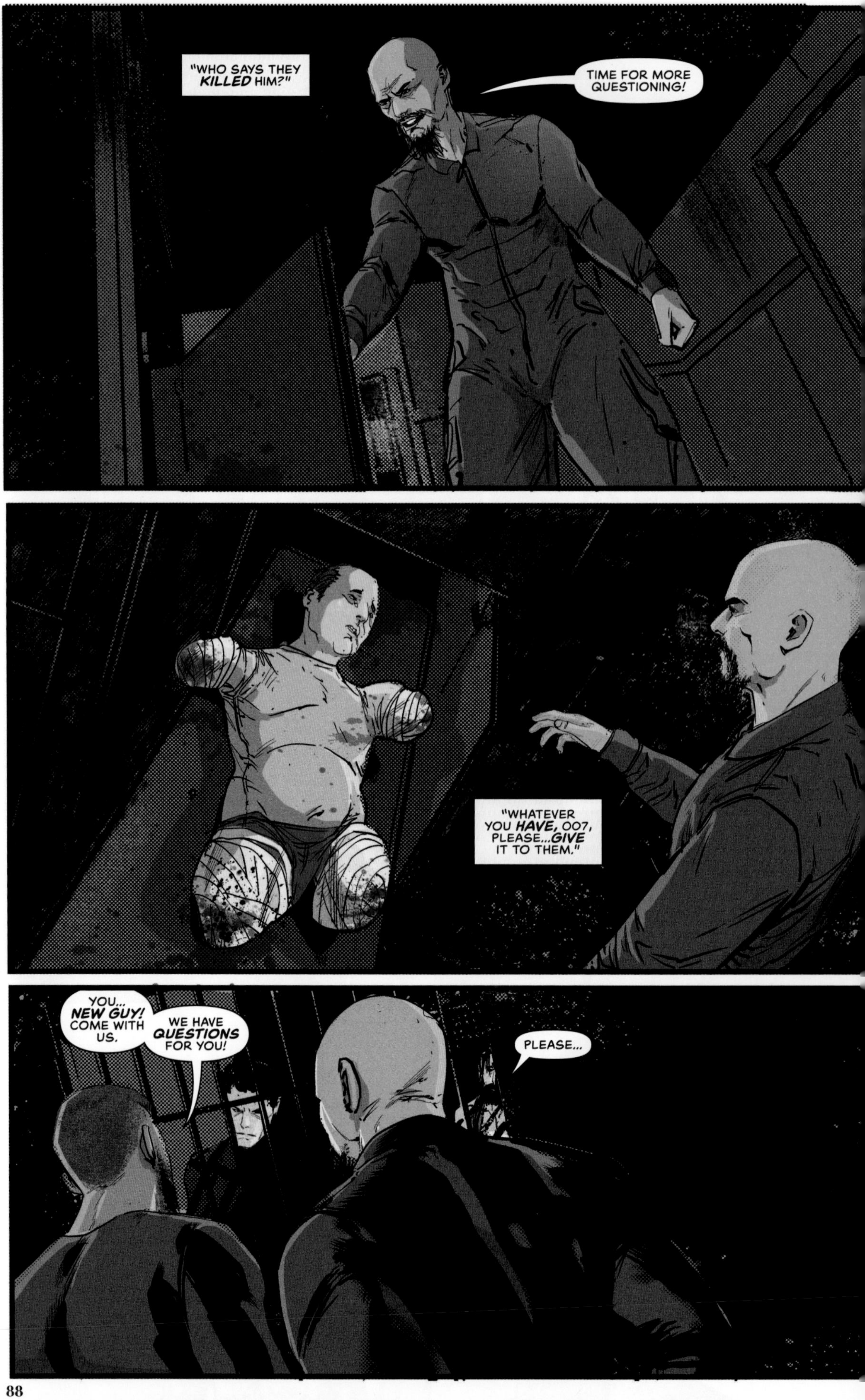
"WHO SAYS THEY KILLED HIM?"
TIME FOR MORE QUESTIONING!
"WHATEVER YOU HAVE, 007, PLEASE...GIVE IT TO THEM."
YOU... NEW GUY! COME WITH US.
WE HAVE QUESTIONS FOR YOU!
PLEASE...

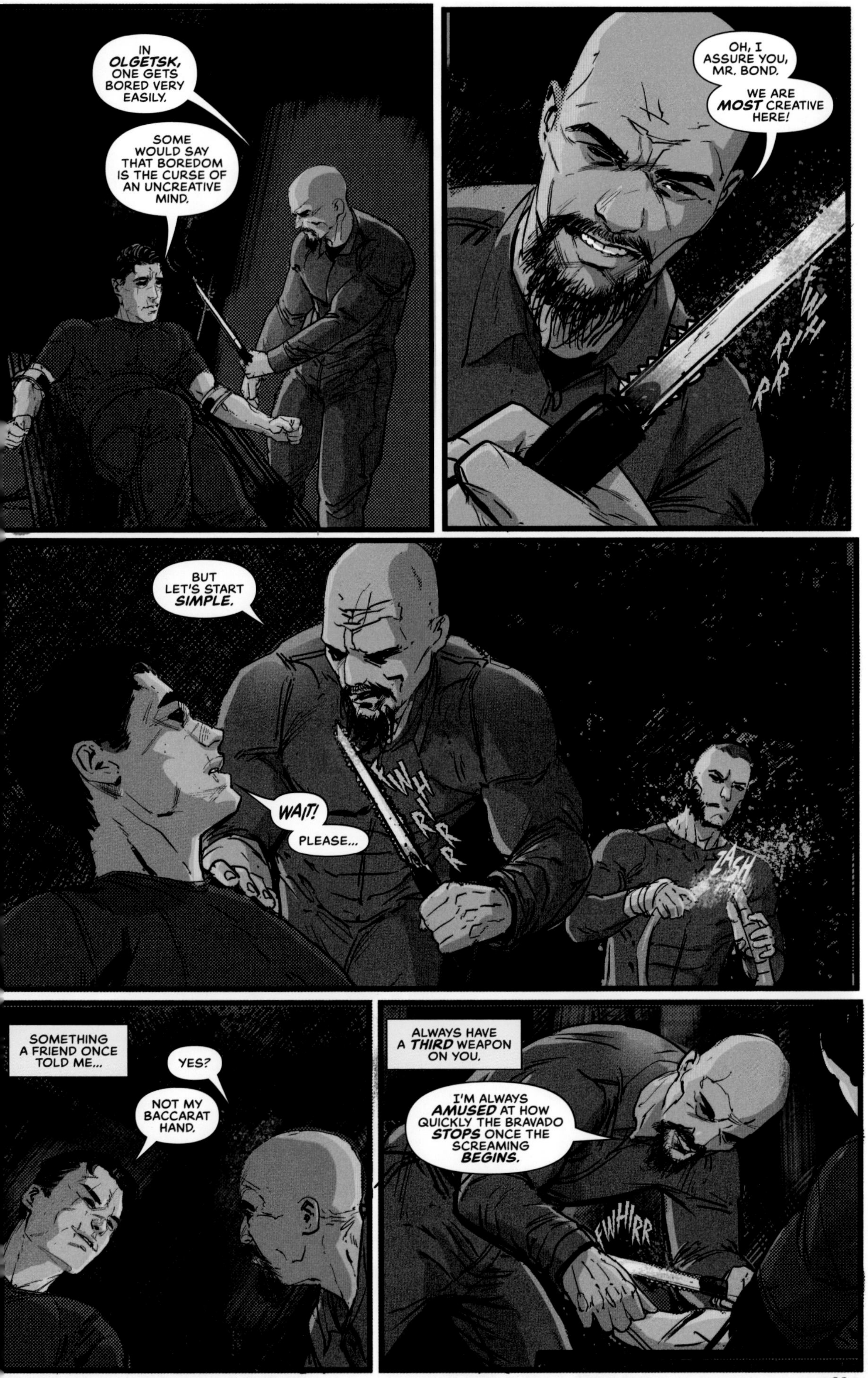

IN OLGETSK, ONE GETS BORED VERY EASILY.
SOME WOULD SAY THAT BOREDOM IS THE CURSE OF AN UNCREATIVE MIND.
OH, I ASSURE YOU, MR. BOND.
WE ARE MOST CREATIVE HERE!
FWHIRR
BUT LET'S START SIMPLE.
WAIT!
PLEASE...
FWHIRR
ZASH
SOMETHING A FRIEND ONCE TOLD ME...
YES?
NOT MY BACCARAT HAND.
ALWAYS HAVE A THIRD WEAPON ON YOU.
I'M ALWAYS AMUSED AT HOW QUICKLY THE BRAVADO STOPS ONCE THE SCREAMING BEGINS.
FWHIRR

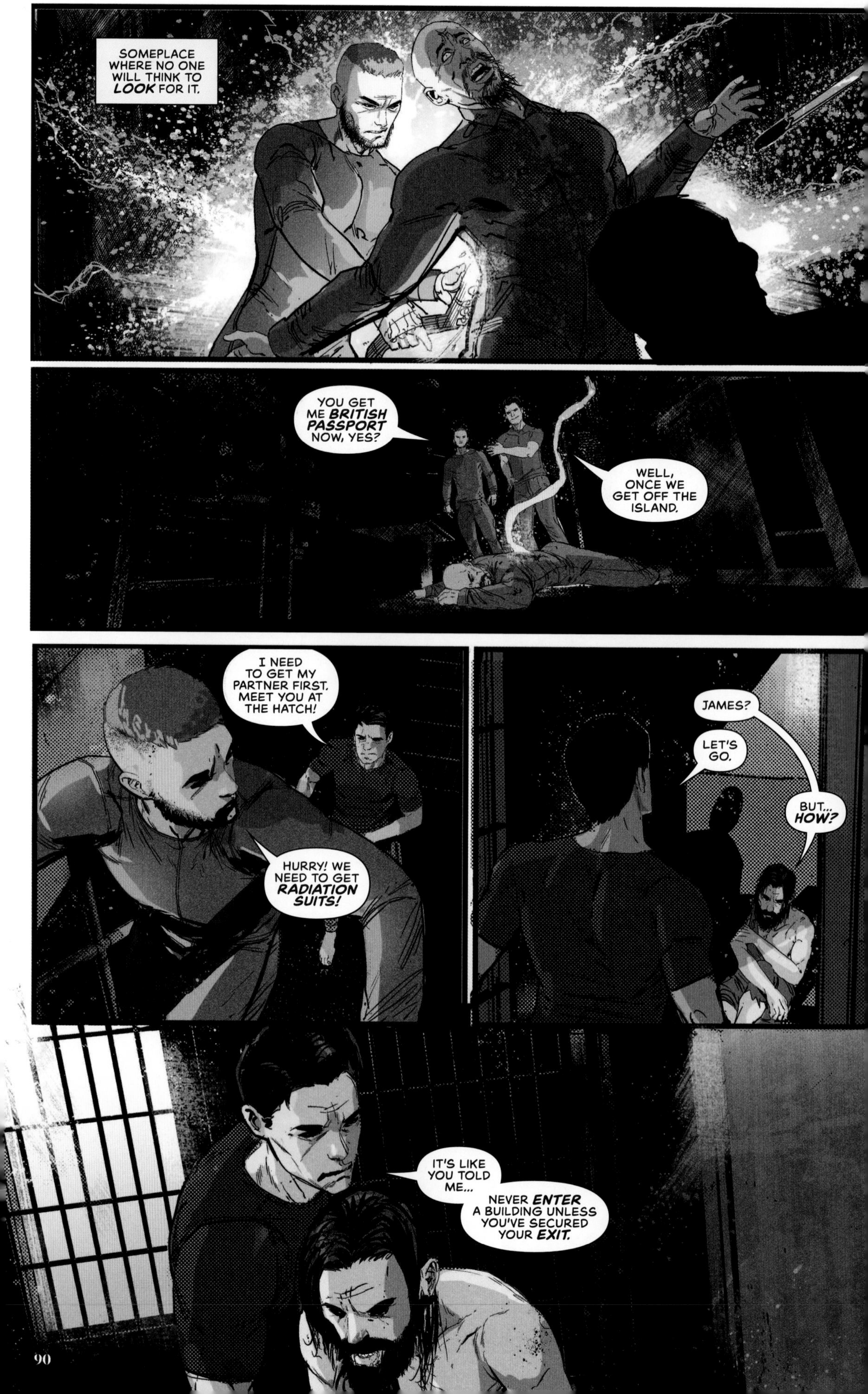
SOMEPLACE WHERE NO ONE WILL THINK TO **LOOK** FOR IT.
YOU GET ME **BRITISH PASSPORT** NOW, YES?
WELL, ONCE WE GET OFF THE ISLAND.
I NEED TO GET MY PARTNER FIRST. MEET YOU AT THE HATCH!
HURRY! WE NEED TO GET **RADIATION SUITS!**
JAMES?
LET'S GO.
BUT... **HOW?**
IT'S LIKE YOU TOLD ME...
NEVER **ENTER** A BUILDING UNLESS YOU'VE SECURED YOUR **EXIT.**

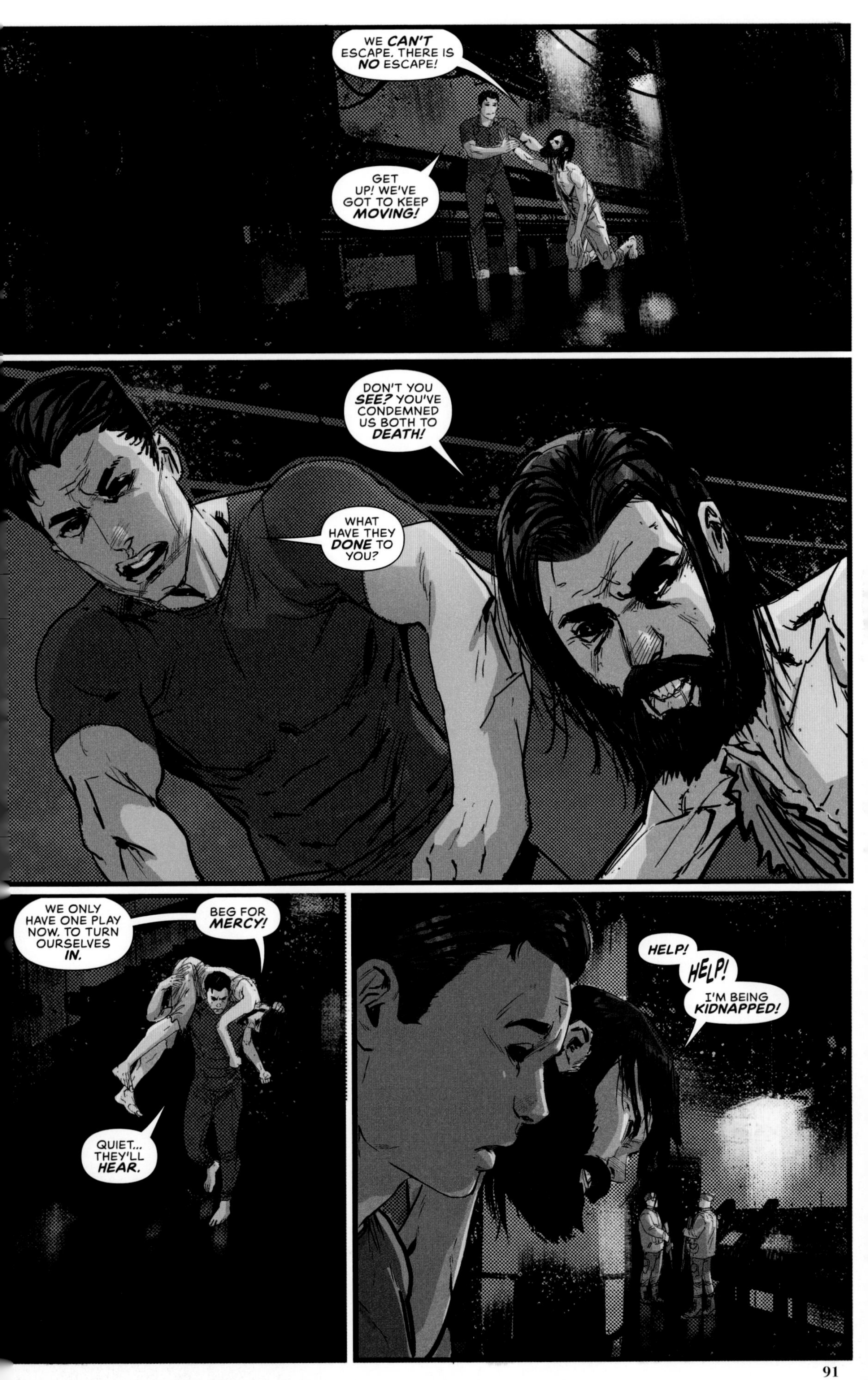
WE CAN'T ESCAPE. THERE IS NO ESCAPE!
GET UP! WE'VE GOT TO KEEP MOVING!
DON'T YOU SEE? YOU'VE CONDEMNED US BOTH TO DEATH!
WHAT HAVE THEY DONE TO YOU?
WE ONLY HAVE ONE PLAY NOW, TO TURN OURSELVES IN.
BEG FOR MERCY!
QUIET... THEY'LL HEAR.
HELP!
HELP!
I'M BEING KIDNAPPED!

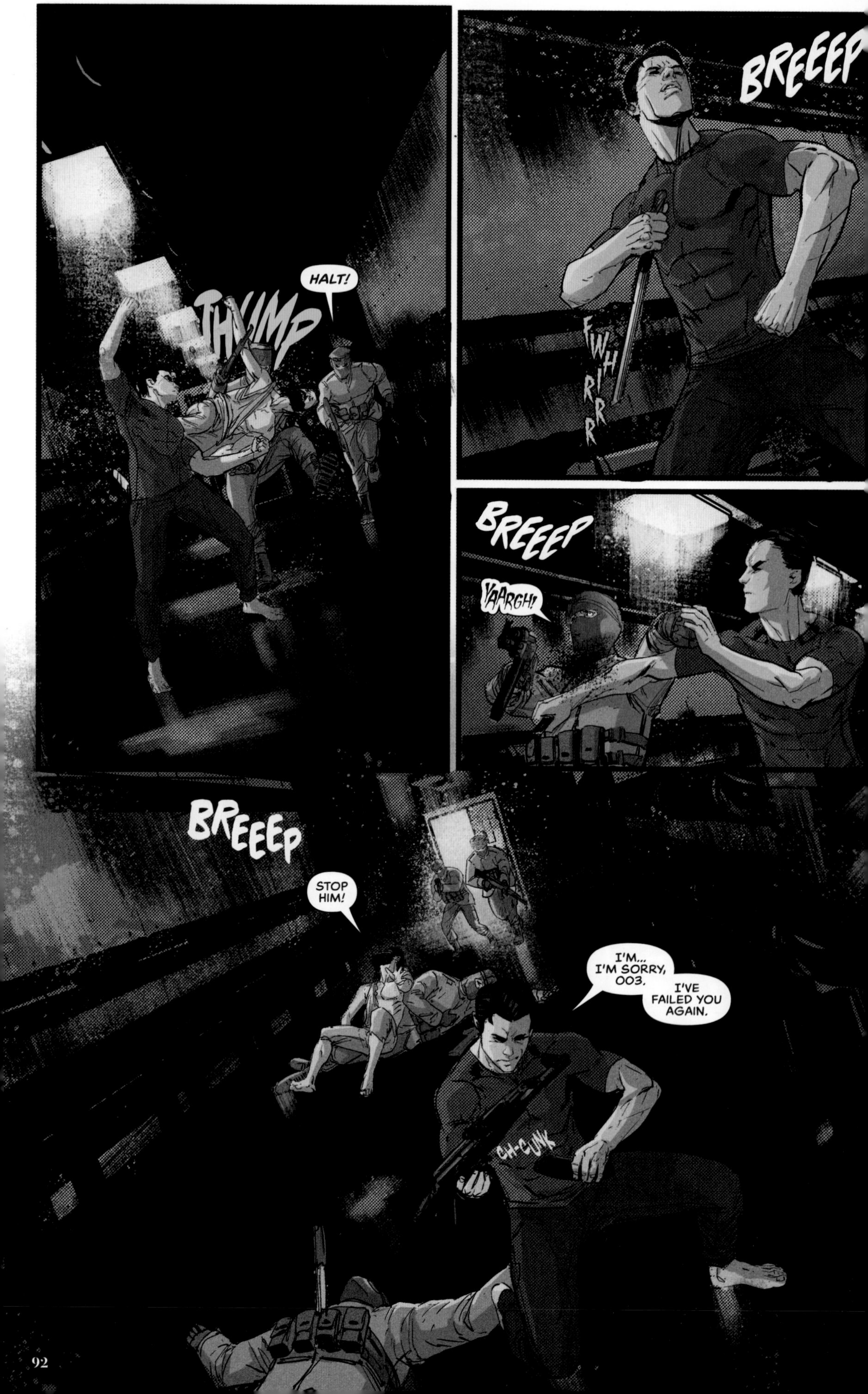
HALT!
THUMP
BREEEP
FWHIRRR
BREEEP
YAARGH!
BREEEP
STOP HIM!
I'M... I'M SORRY, 003.
I'VE FAILED YOU AGAIN.
CH-CUNK

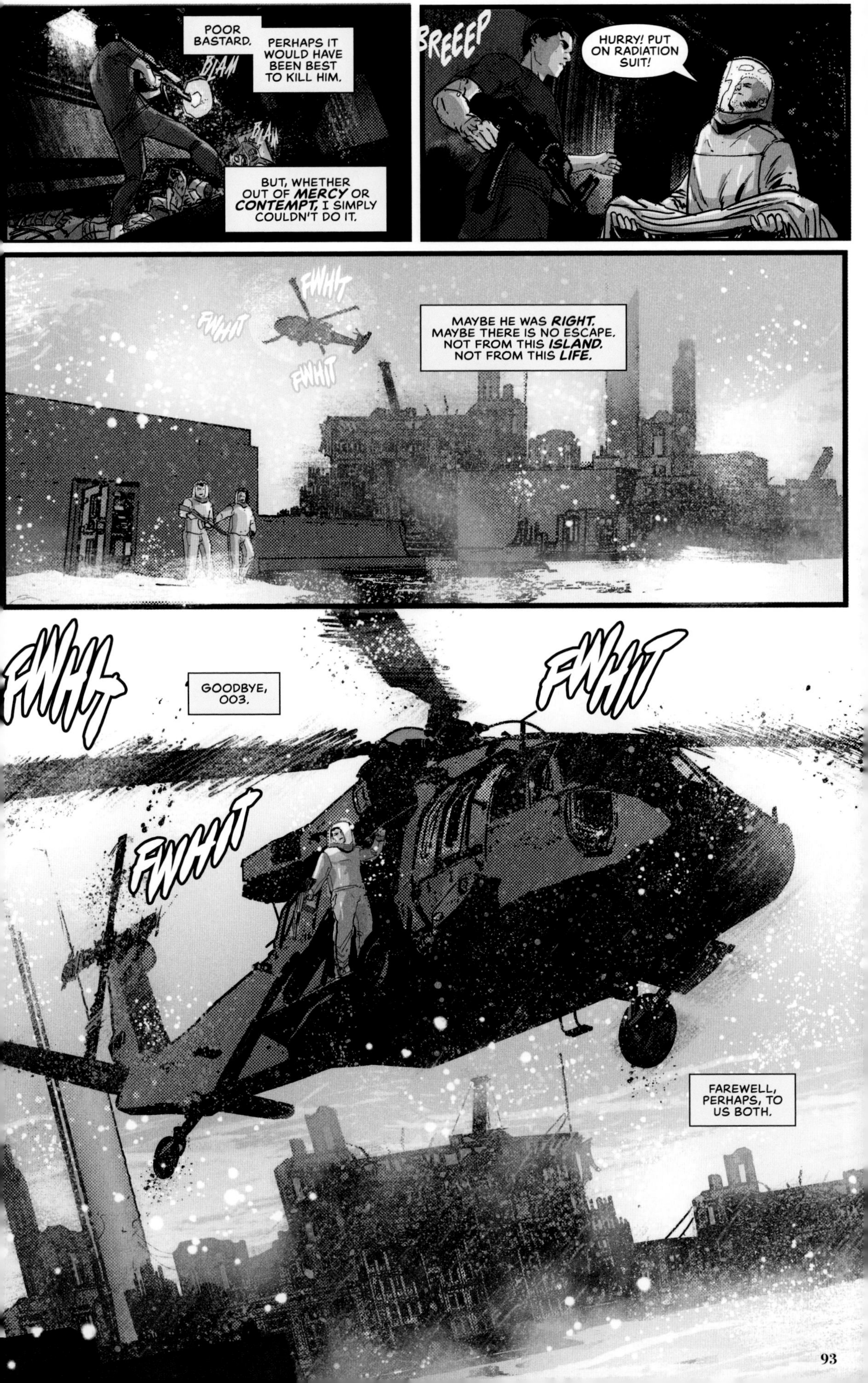
POOR BASTARD.
PERHAPS IT WOULD HAVE BEEN BEST TO KILL HIM.
BLAM
BLAM
BUT, WHETHER OUT OF MERCY OR CONTEMPT, I SIMPLY COULDN'T DO IT.
BREEEP
HURRY! PUT ON RADIATION SUIT!
FWHIT
FWHIT
FWHIT
MAYBE HE WAS RIGHT. MAYBE THERE IS NO ESCAPE. NOT FROM THIS ISLAND. NOT FROM THIS LIFE.
FWHIT
GOODBYE, 003.
FWHIT
FWHIT
FAREWELL, PERHAPS, TO US BOTH.

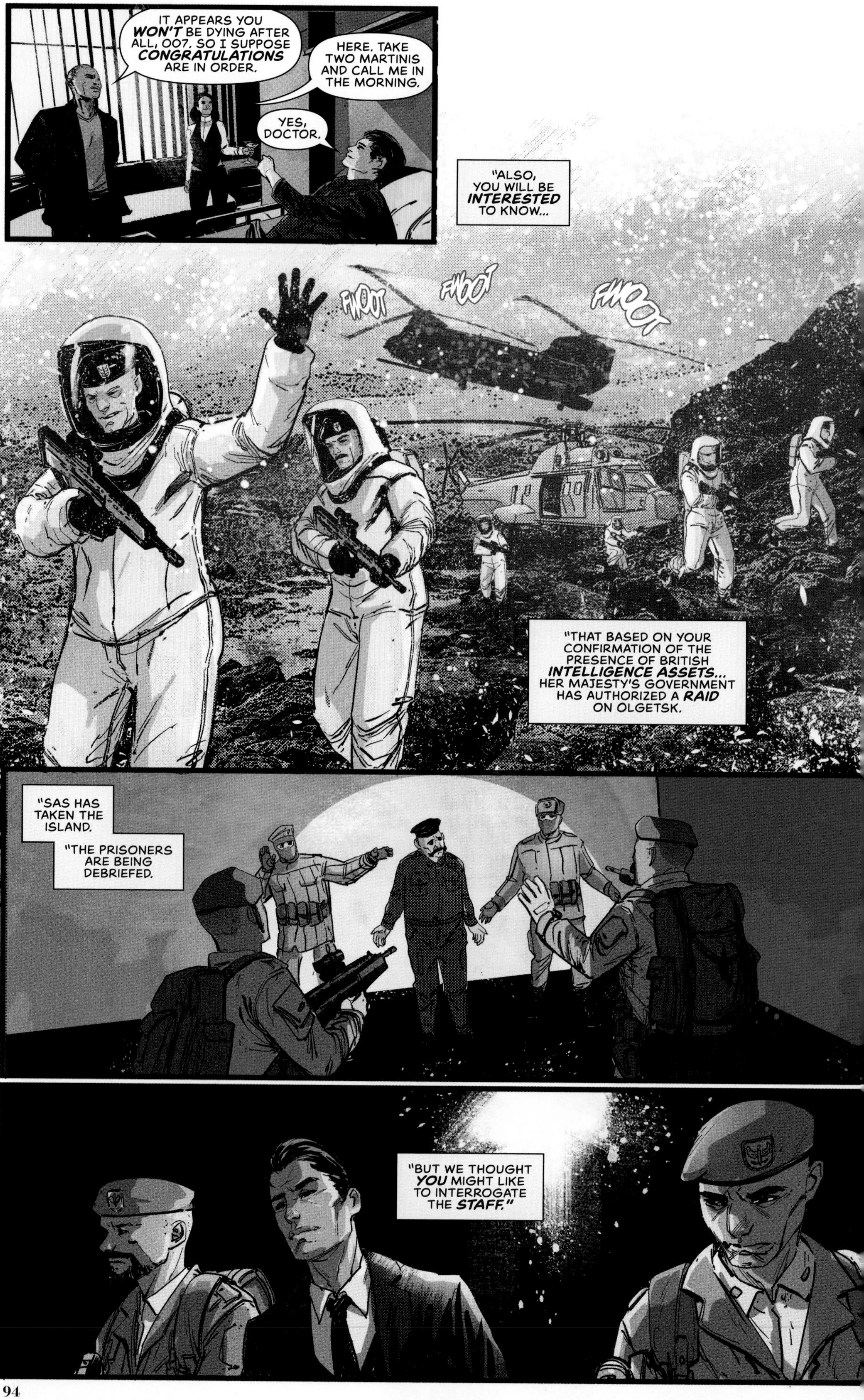
IT APPEARS YOU WON'T BE DYING AFTER ALL, 007. SO I SUPPOSE CONGRATULATIONS ARE IN ORDER.
HERE, TAKE TWO MARTINIS AND CALL ME IN THE MORNING.
YES, DOCTOR.
"ALSO, YOU WILL BE INTERESTED TO KNOW...
FWOOT
FWOOT
FWOOT
"THAT BASED ON YOUR CONFIRMATION OF THE PRESENCE OF BRITISH INTELLIGENCE ASSETS... HER MAJESTY'S GOVERNMENT HAS AUTHORIZED A RAID ON OLGETSK.
"SAS HAS TAKEN THE ISLAND.
"THE PRISONERS ARE BEING DEBRIEFED.
"BUT WE THOUGHT YOU MIGHT LIKE TO INTERROGATE THE STAFF."

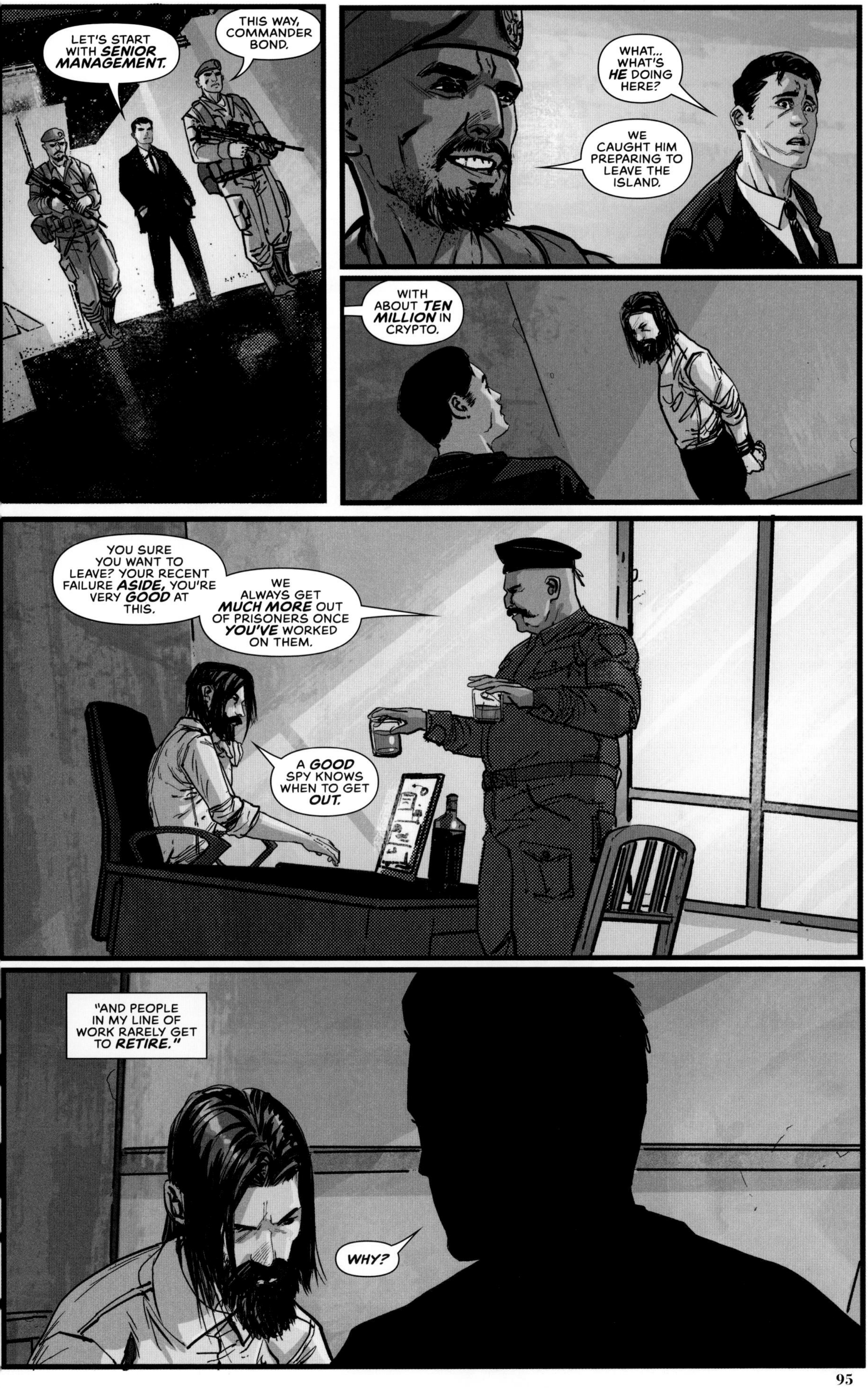
LET'S START WITH SENIOR MANAGEMENT.
THIS WAY, COMMANDER BOND.
WHAT... WHAT'S HE DOING HERE?
WE CAUGHT HIM PREPARING TO LEAVE THE ISLAND.
WITH ABOUT TEN MILLION IN CRYPTO.
YOU SURE YOU WANT TO LEAVE? YOUR RECENT FAILURE ASIDE, YOU'RE VERY GOOD AT THIS.
WE ALWAYS GET MUCH MORE OUT OF PRISONERS ONCE YOU'VE WORKED ON THEM.
A GOOD SPY KNOWS WHEN TO GET OUT.
"AND PEOPLE IN MY LINE OF WORK RARELY GET TO RETIRE."
WHY?

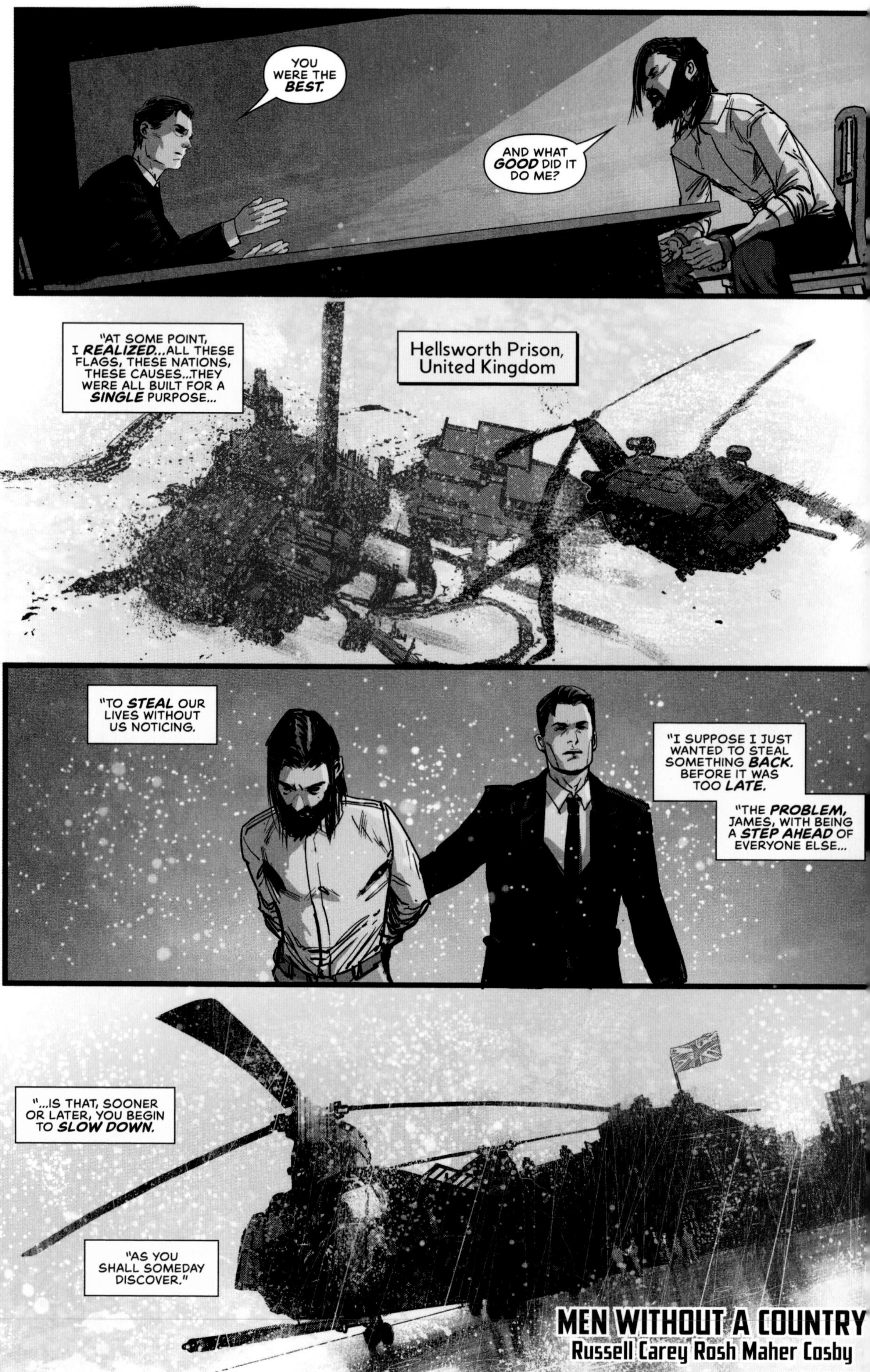

YOU WERE THE BEST.
AND WHAT GOOD DID IT DO ME?
"AT SOME POINT, I REALIZED...ALL THESE FLAGS, THESE NATIONS, THESE CAUSES...THEY WERE ALL BUILT FOR A SINGLE PURPOSE...
Hellsworth Prison, United Kingdom
"TO STEAL OUR LIVES WITHOUT US NOTICING.
"I SUPPOSE I JUST WANTED TO STEAL SOMETHING BACK. BEFORE IT WAS TOO LATE.
"THE PROBLEM, JAMES, WITH BEING A STEP AHEAD OF EVERYONE ELSE...
"...IS THAT, SOONER OR LATER, YOU BEGIN TO SLOW DOWN.
"AS YOU SHALL SOMEDAY DISCOVER."
MEN WITHOUT A COUNTRY
Russell Carey Rosh Maher Cosby

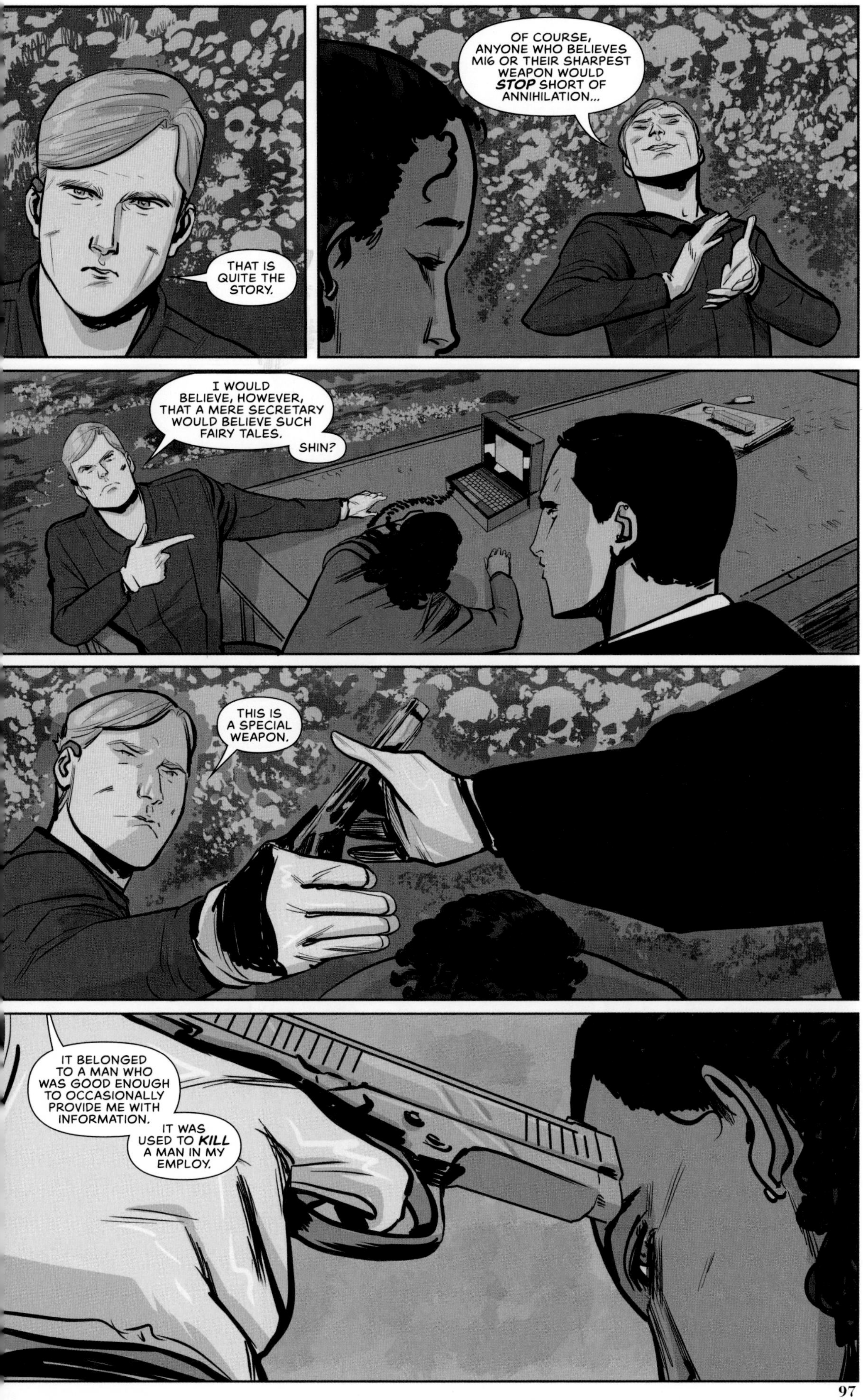
THAT IS QUITE THE STORY.
OF COURSE, ANYONE WHO BELIEVES MI6 OR THEIR SHARPEST WEAPON WOULD STOP SHORT OF ANNIHILATION...
I WOULD BELIEVE, HOWEVER, THAT A MERE SECRETARY WOULD BELIEVE SUCH FAIRY TALES.
SHIN?
THIS IS A SPECIAL WEAPON.
IT BELONGED TO A MAN WHO WAS GOOD ENOUGH TO OCCASIONALLY PROVIDE ME WITH INFORMATION.
IT WAS USED TO KILL A MAN IN MY EMPLOY.

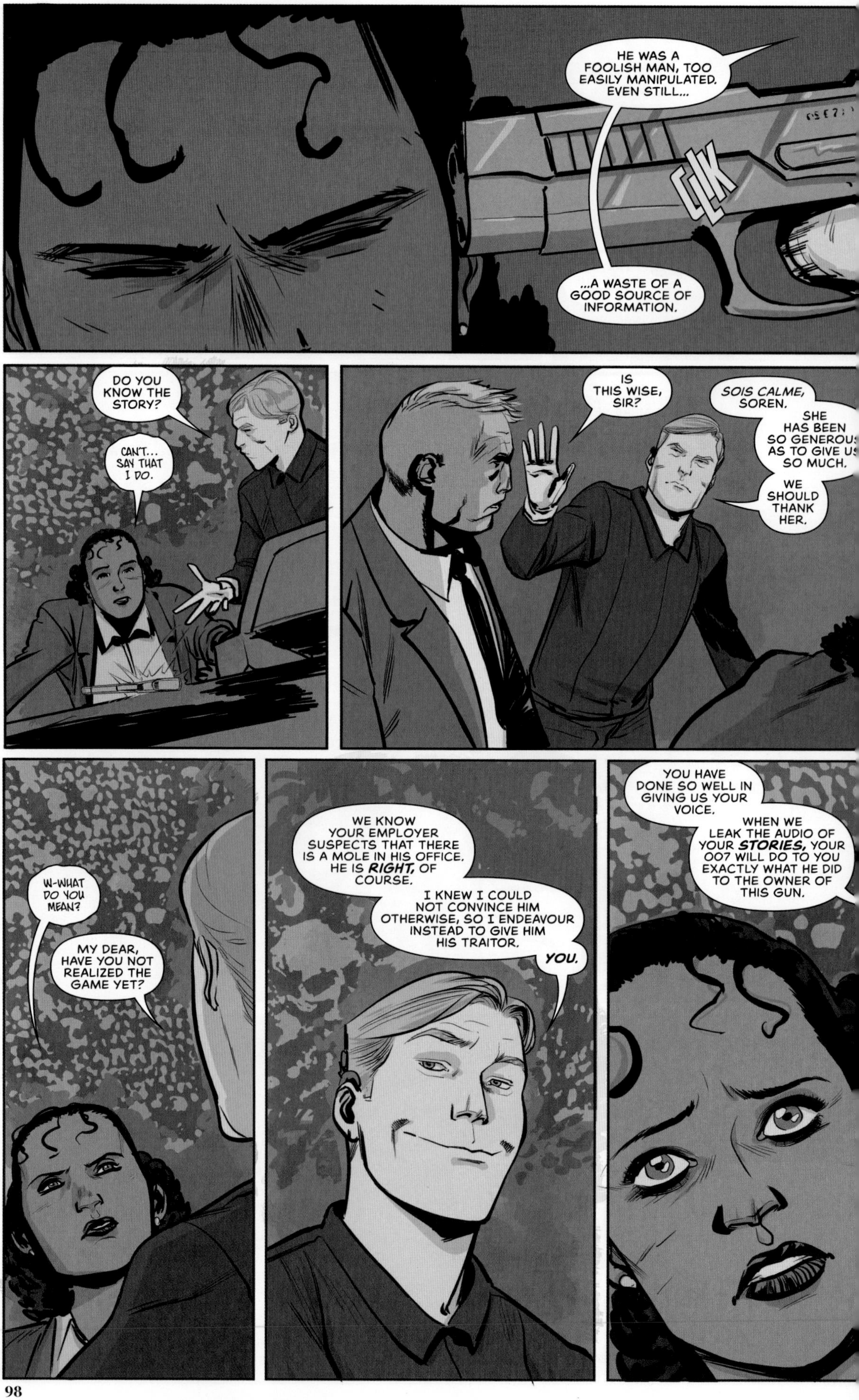
HE WAS A FOOLISH MAN, TOO EASILY MANIPULATED. EVEN STILL...
CLIK
...A WASTE OF A GOOD SOURCE OF INFORMATION.
DO YOU KNOW THE STORY?
CAN'T... SAY THAT I DO.
IS THIS WISE, SIR?
SOIS CALME, SOREN.
SHE HAS BEEN SO GENEROUS AS TO GIVE US SO MUCH.
WE SHOULD THANK HER.
W-WHAT DO YOU MEAN?
MY DEAR, HAVE YOU NOT REALIZED THE GAME YET?
WE KNOW YOUR EMPLOYER SUSPECTS THAT THERE IS A MOLE IN HIS OFFICE. HE IS RIGHT, OF COURSE.
I KNEW I COULD NOT CONVINCE HIM OTHERWISE, SO I ENDEAVOUR INSTEAD TO GIVE HIM HIS TRAITOR.
YOU.
YOU HAVE DONE SO WELL IN GIVING US YOUR VOICE.
WHEN WE LEAK THE AUDIO OF YOUR STORIES, YOUR 007 WILL DO TO YOU EXACTLY WHAT HE DID TO THE OWNER OF THIS GUN.

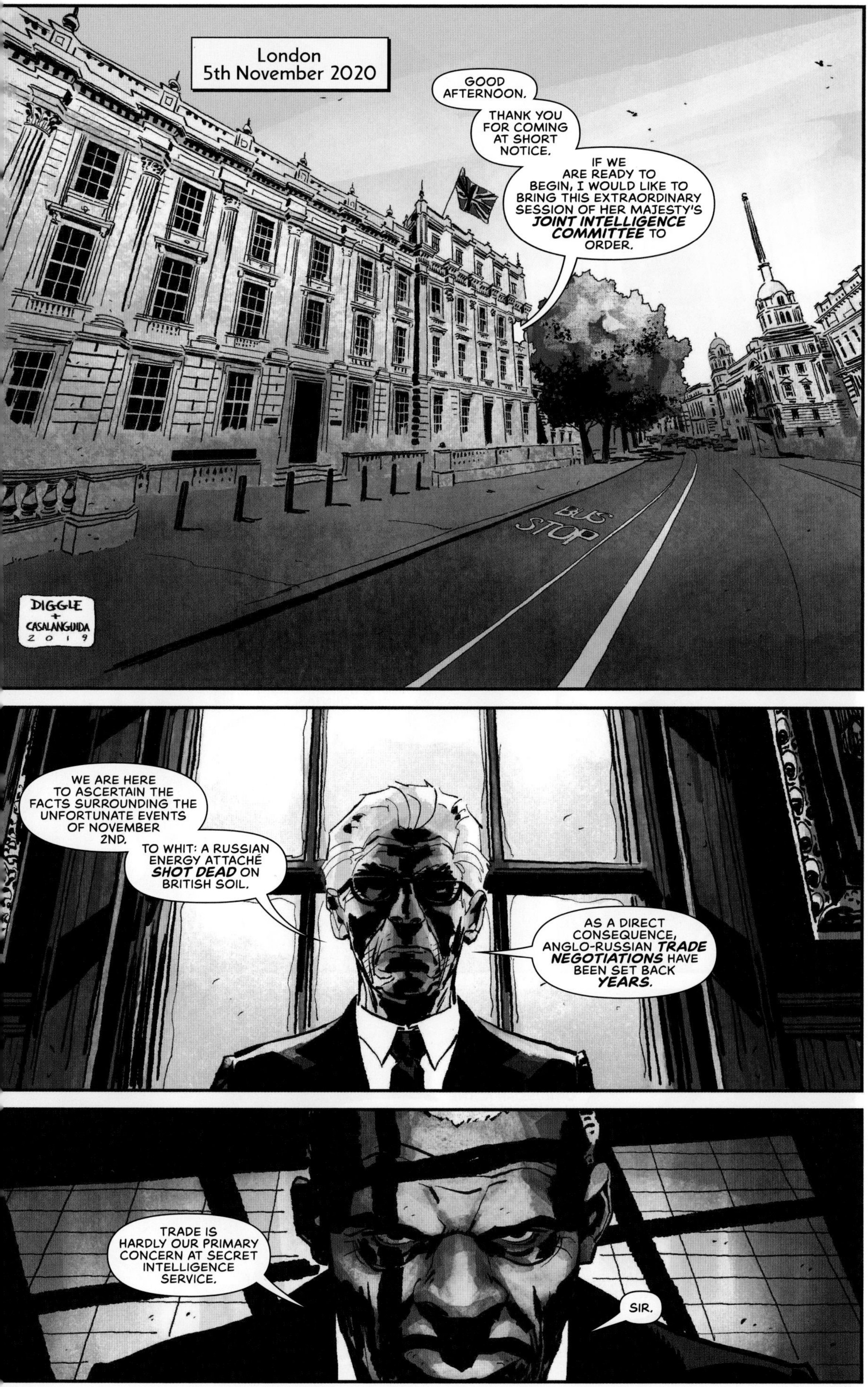
London
5th November 2020
GOOD AFTERNOON.
THANK YOU FOR COMING AT SHORT NOTICE.
IF WE ARE READY TO BEGIN, I WOULD LIKE TO BRING THIS EXTRAORDINARY SESSION OF HER MAJESTY'S ***JOINT INTELLIGENCE COMMITTEE*** TO ORDER.
BUS STOP
DIGGLE + CASALANGUIDA 2019
WE ARE HERE TO ASCERTAIN THE FACTS SURROUNDING THE UNFORTUNATE EVENTS OF NOVEMBER 2ND.
TO WHIT: A RUSSIAN ENERGY ATTACHÉ ***SHOT DEAD*** ON BRITISH SOIL.
AS A DIRECT CONSEQUENCE, ANGLO-RUSSIAN ***TRADE NEGOTIATIONS*** HAVE BEEN SET BACK ***YEARS***.
TRADE IS HARDLY OUR PRIMARY CONCERN AT SECRET INTELLIGENCE SERVICE.
SIR.

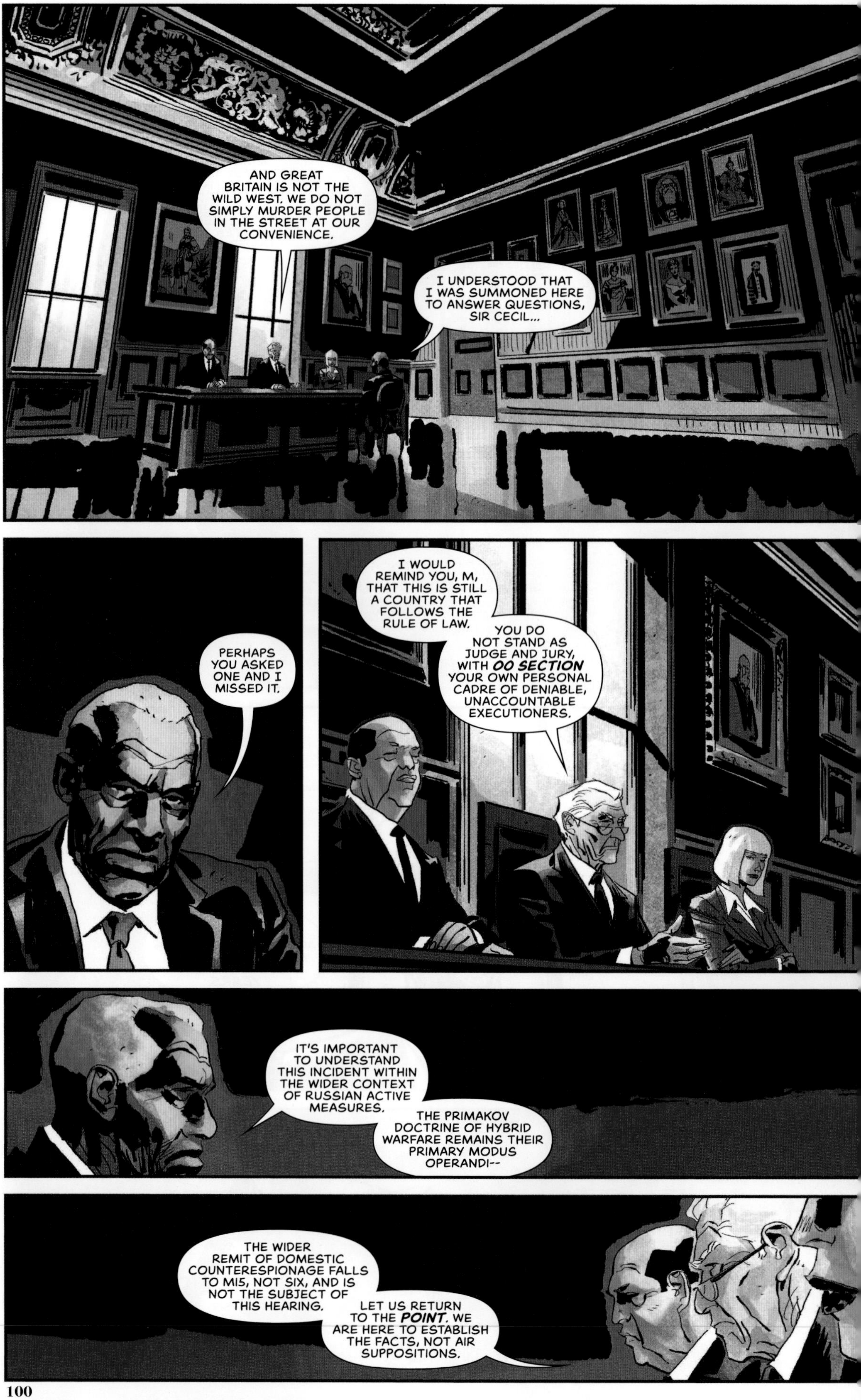
AND GREAT BRITAIN IS NOT THE WILD WEST. WE DO NOT SIMPLY MURDER PEOPLE IN THE STREET AT OUR CONVENIENCE.
I UNDERSTOOD THAT I WAS SUMMONED HERE TO ANSWER QUESTIONS, SIR CECIL...
PERHAPS YOU ASKED ONE AND I MISSED IT.
I WOULD REMIND YOU, M, THAT THIS IS STILL A COUNTRY THAT FOLLOWS THE RULE OF LAW.
YOU DO NOT STAND AS JUDGE AND JURY, WITH *OO SECTION* YOUR OWN PERSONAL CADRE OF DENIABLE, UNACCOUNTABLE EXECUTIONERS.
IT'S IMPORTANT TO UNDERSTAND THIS INCIDENT WITHIN THE WIDER CONTEXT OF RUSSIAN ACTIVE MEASURES.
THE PRIMAKOV DOCTRINE OF HYBRID WARFARE REMAINS THEIR PRIMARY MODUS OPERANDI--
THE WIDER REMIT OF DOMESTIC COUNTERESPIONAGE FALLS TO MI5, NOT SIX, AND IS NOT THE SUBJECT OF THIS HEARING.
LET US RETURN TO THE *POINT*. WE ARE HERE TO ESTABLISH THE FACTS, NOT AIR SUPPOSITIONS.

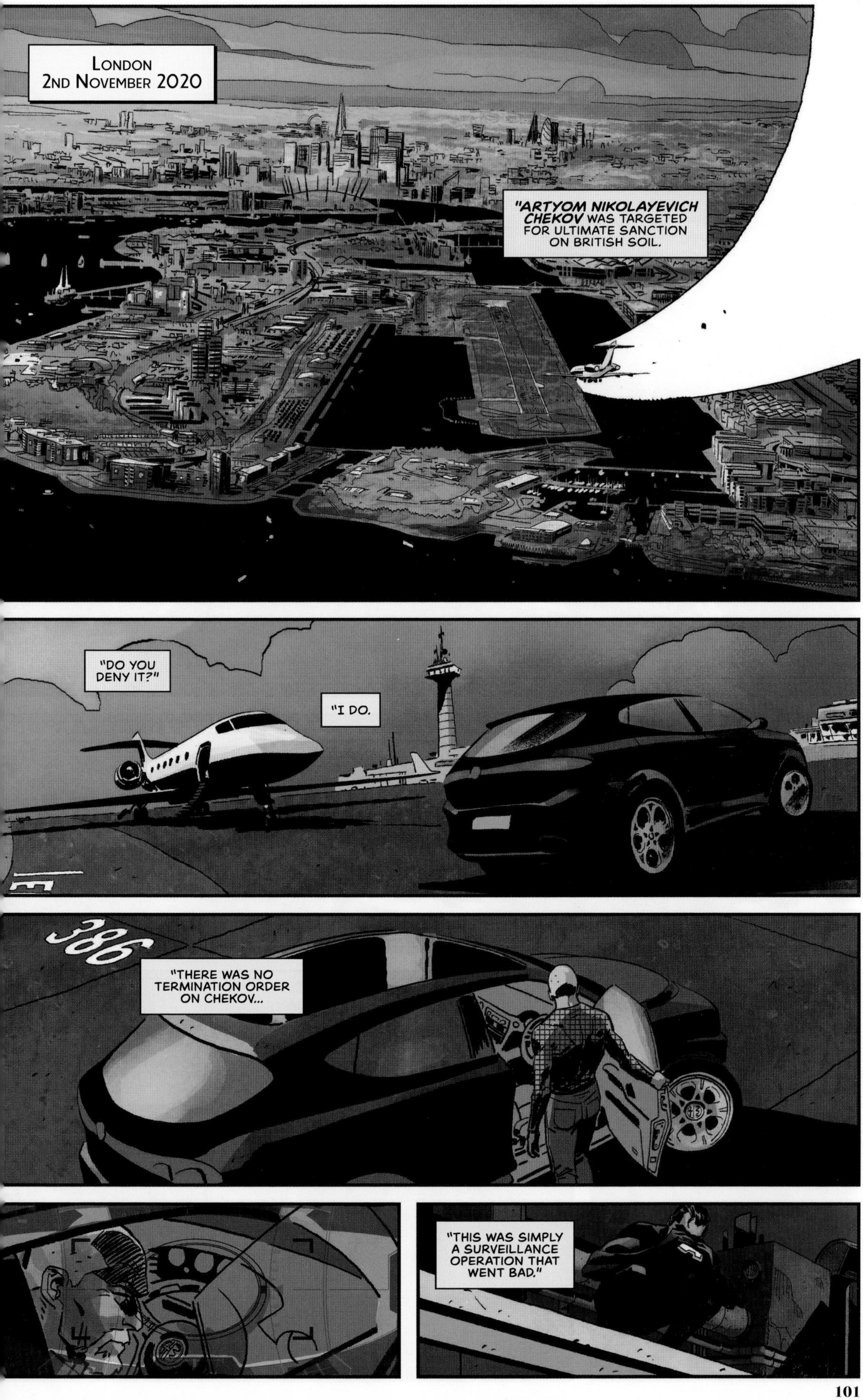
London
2nd November 2020
"ARTYOM NIKOLAYEVICH CHEKOV WAS TARGETED FOR ULTIMATE SANCTION ON BRITISH SOIL.
"DO YOU DENY IT?"
"I DO.
386
"THERE WAS NO TERMINATION ORDER ON CHEKOV...
"THIS WAS SIMPLY A SURVEILLANCE OPERATION THAT WENT BAD."

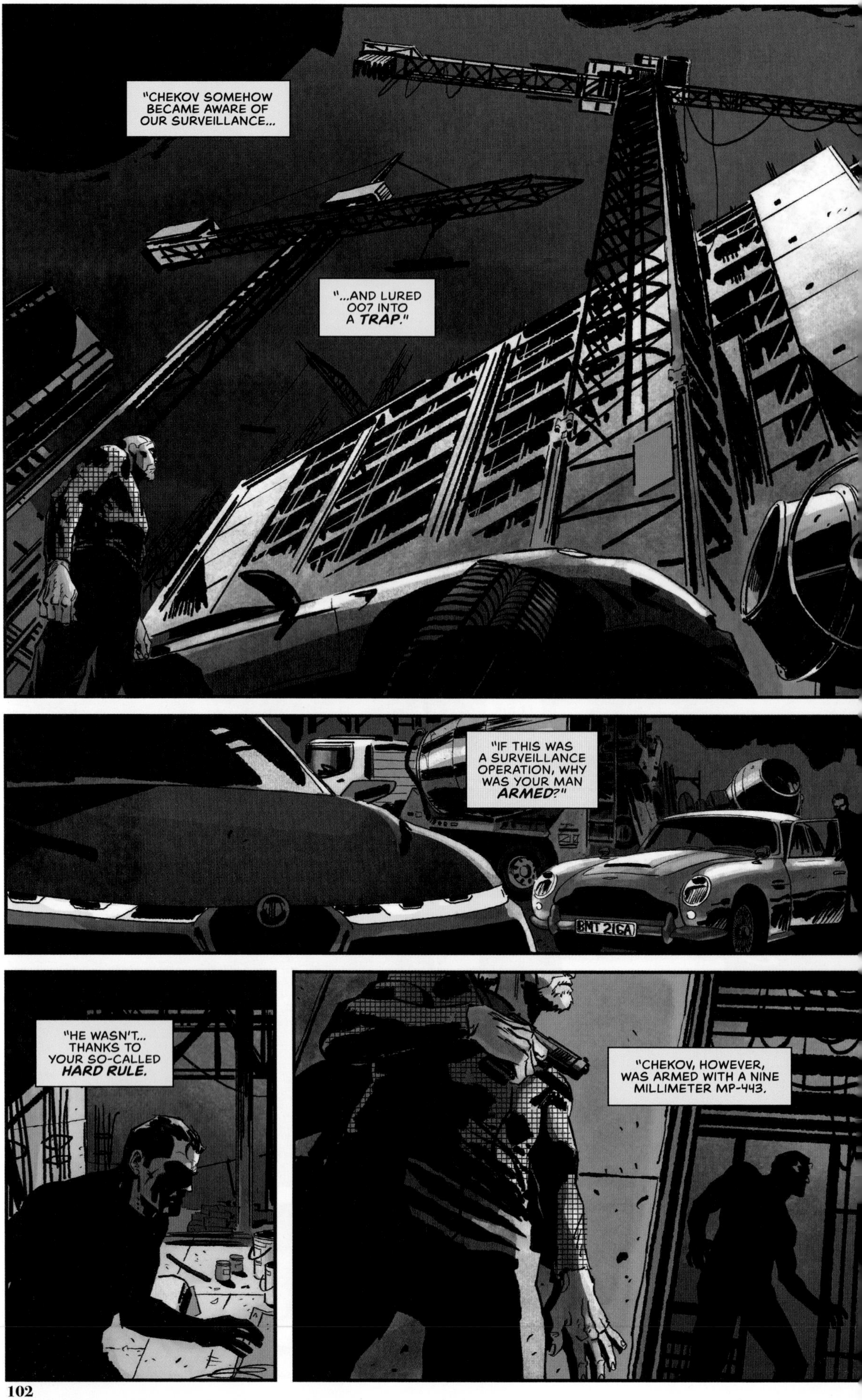
"CHEKOV SOMEHOW BECAME AWARE OF OUR SURVEILLANCE...
"...AND LURED 007 INTO A TRAP."
"IF THIS WAS A SURVEILLANCE OPERATION, WHY WAS YOUR MAN ARMED?"
"HE WASN'T... THANKS TO YOUR SO-CALLED HARD RULE.
"CHEKOV, HOWEVER, WAS ARMED WITH A NINE MILLIMETER MP-443.

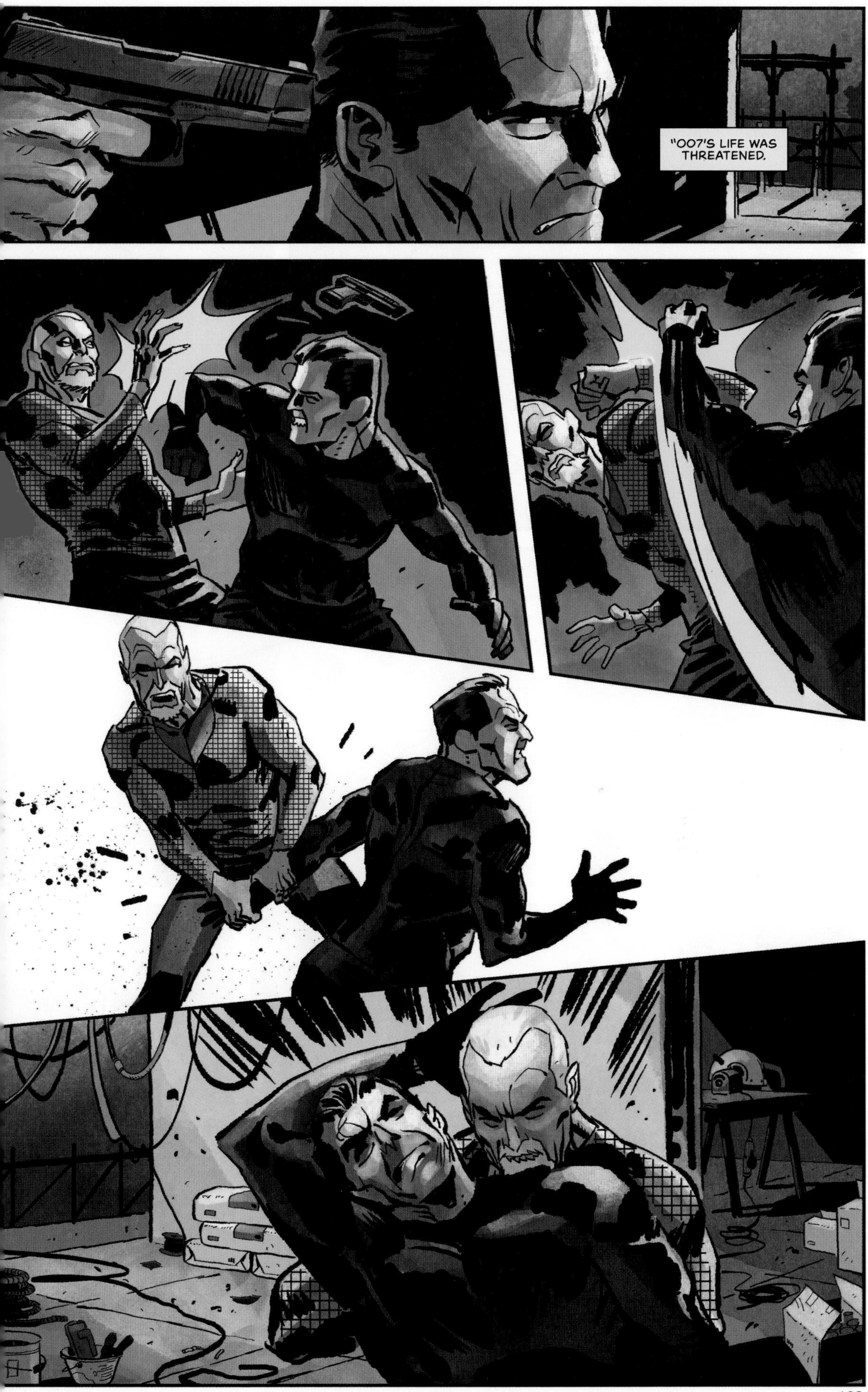
"007'S LIFE WAS THREATENED.

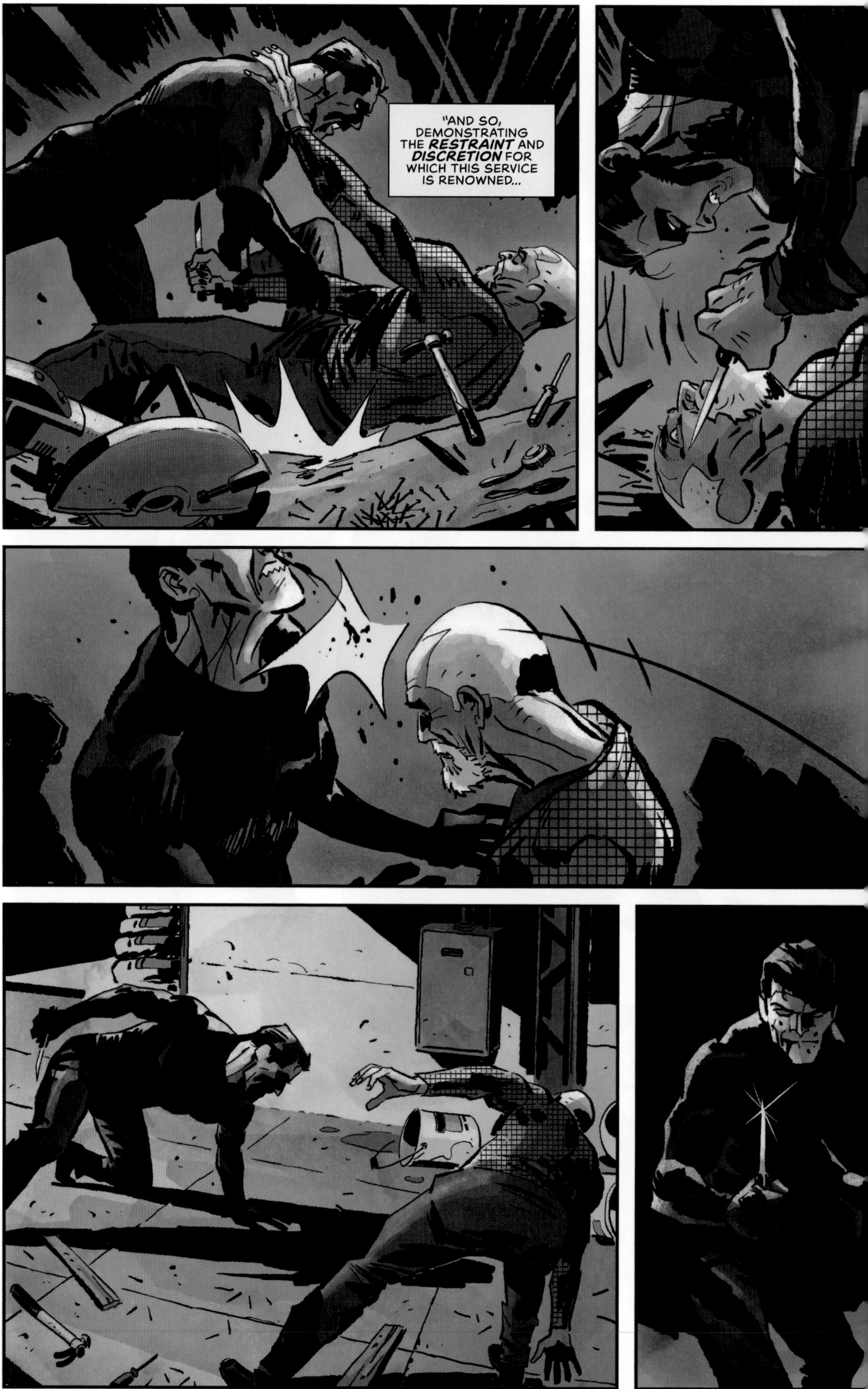
"AND SO, DEMONSTRATING THE RESTRAINT AND DISCRETION FOR WHICH THIS SERVICE IS RENOWNED...

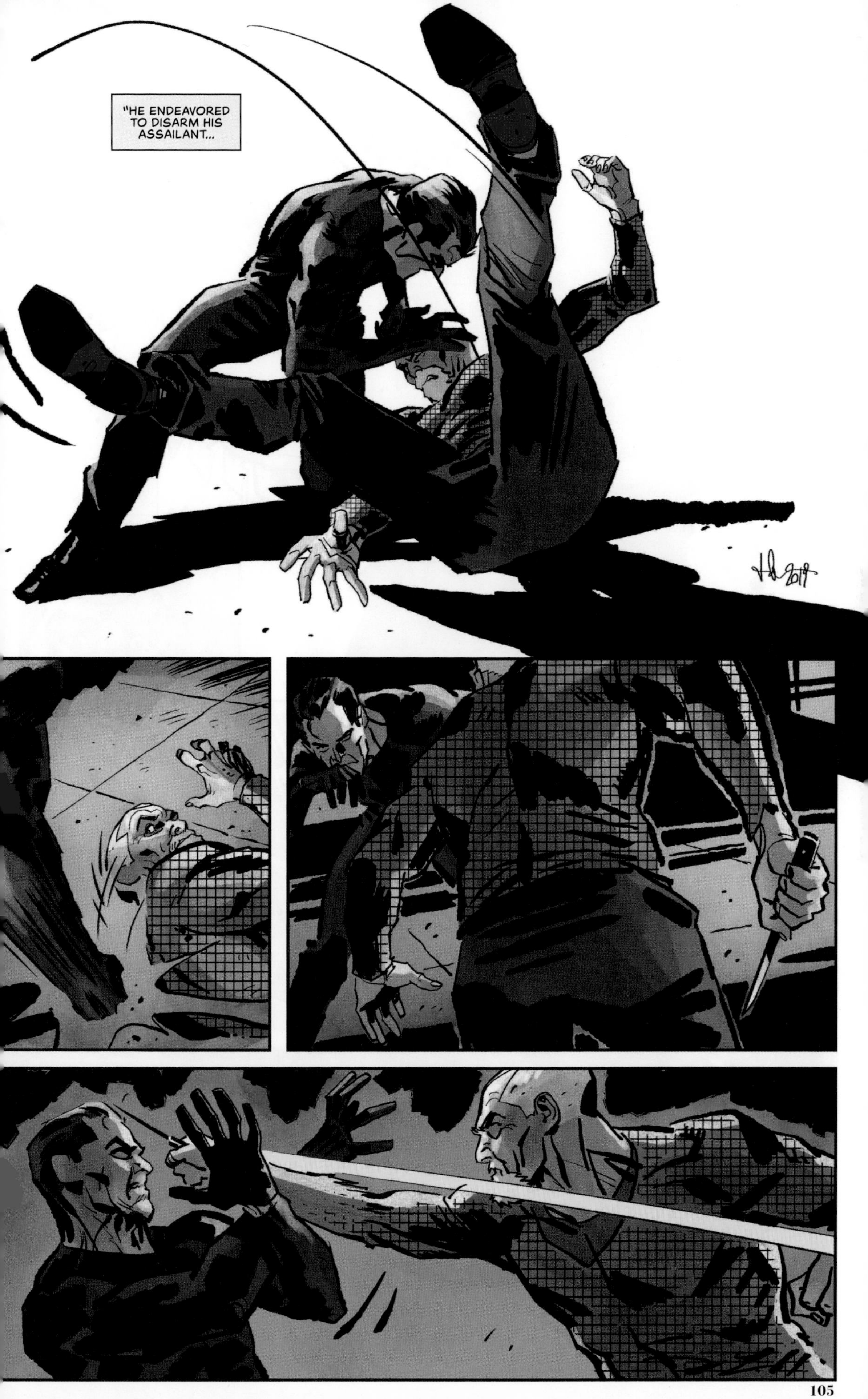
"HE ENDEAVORED TO DISARM HIS ASSAILANT...

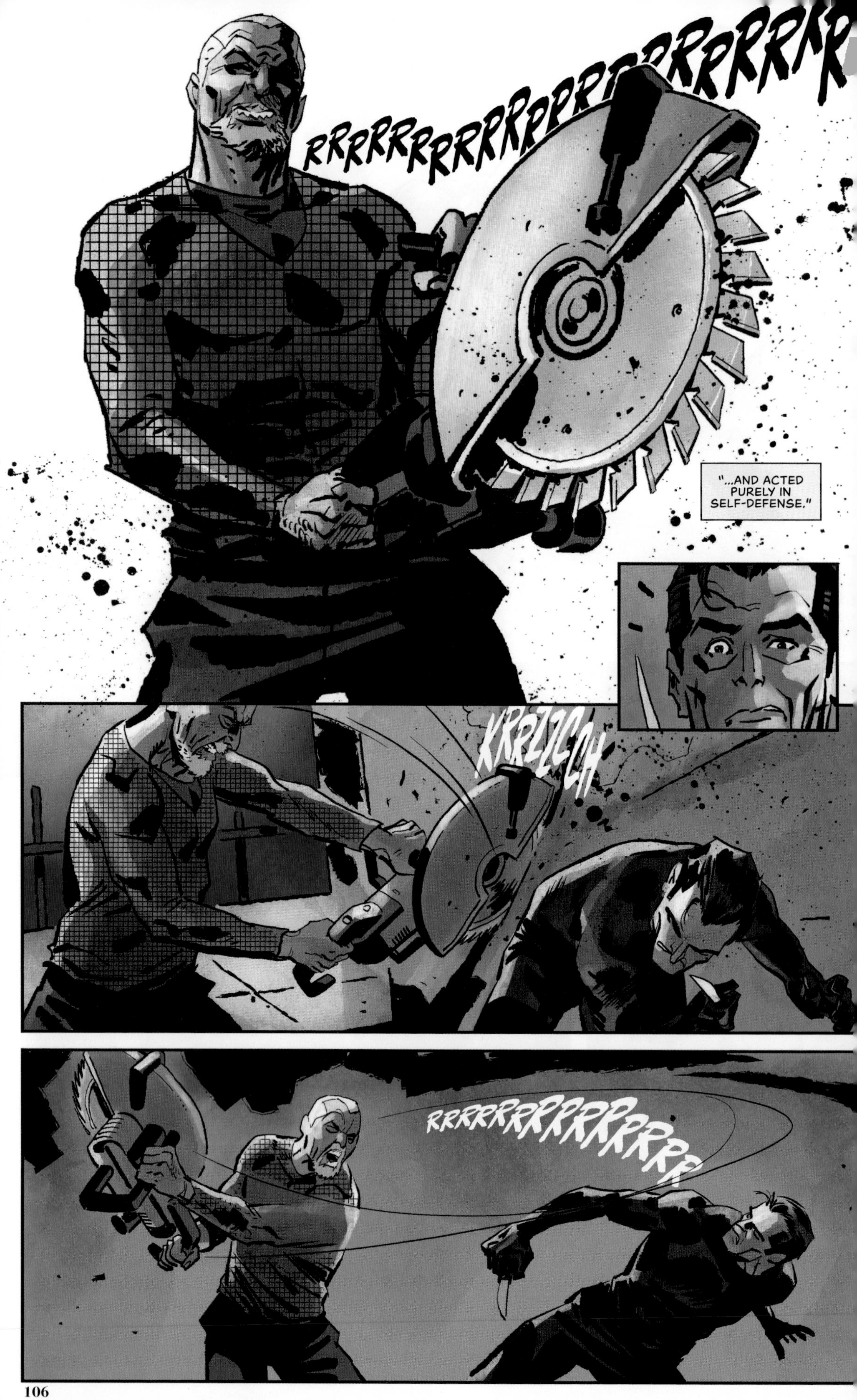
RRRRRRRRRRRRRRRRRRRRRR
"...AND ACTED PURELY IN SELF-DEFENSE."
KRRZZCH
RRRRRRRRRRRRRRR

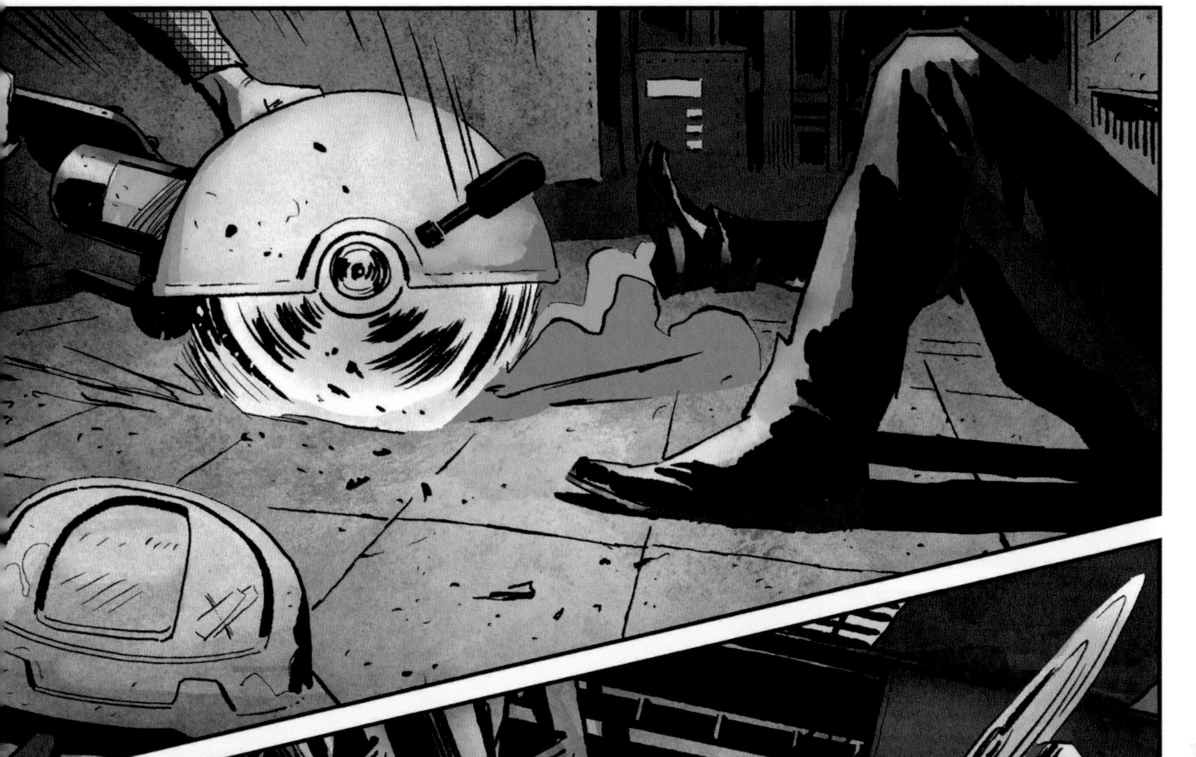

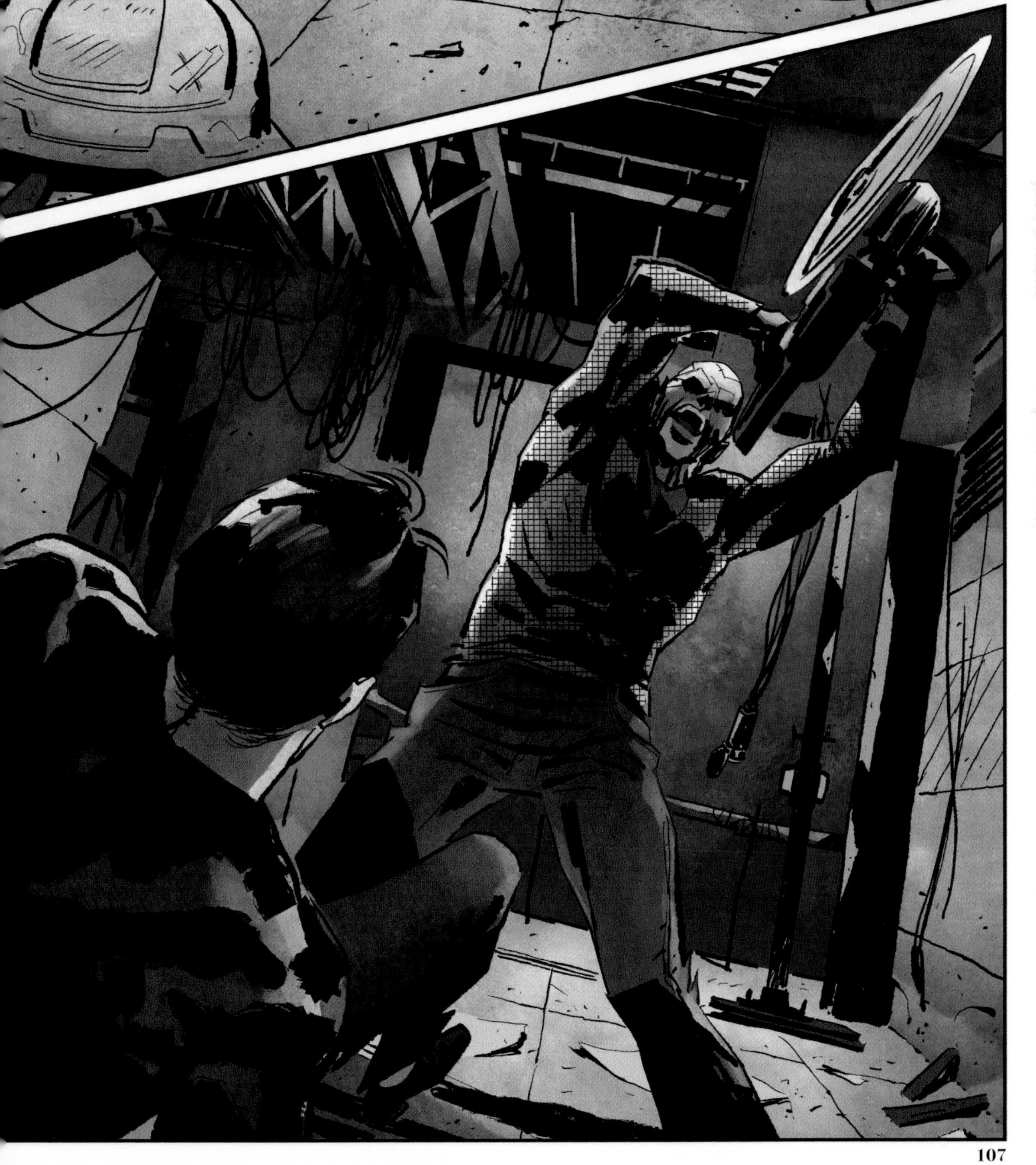

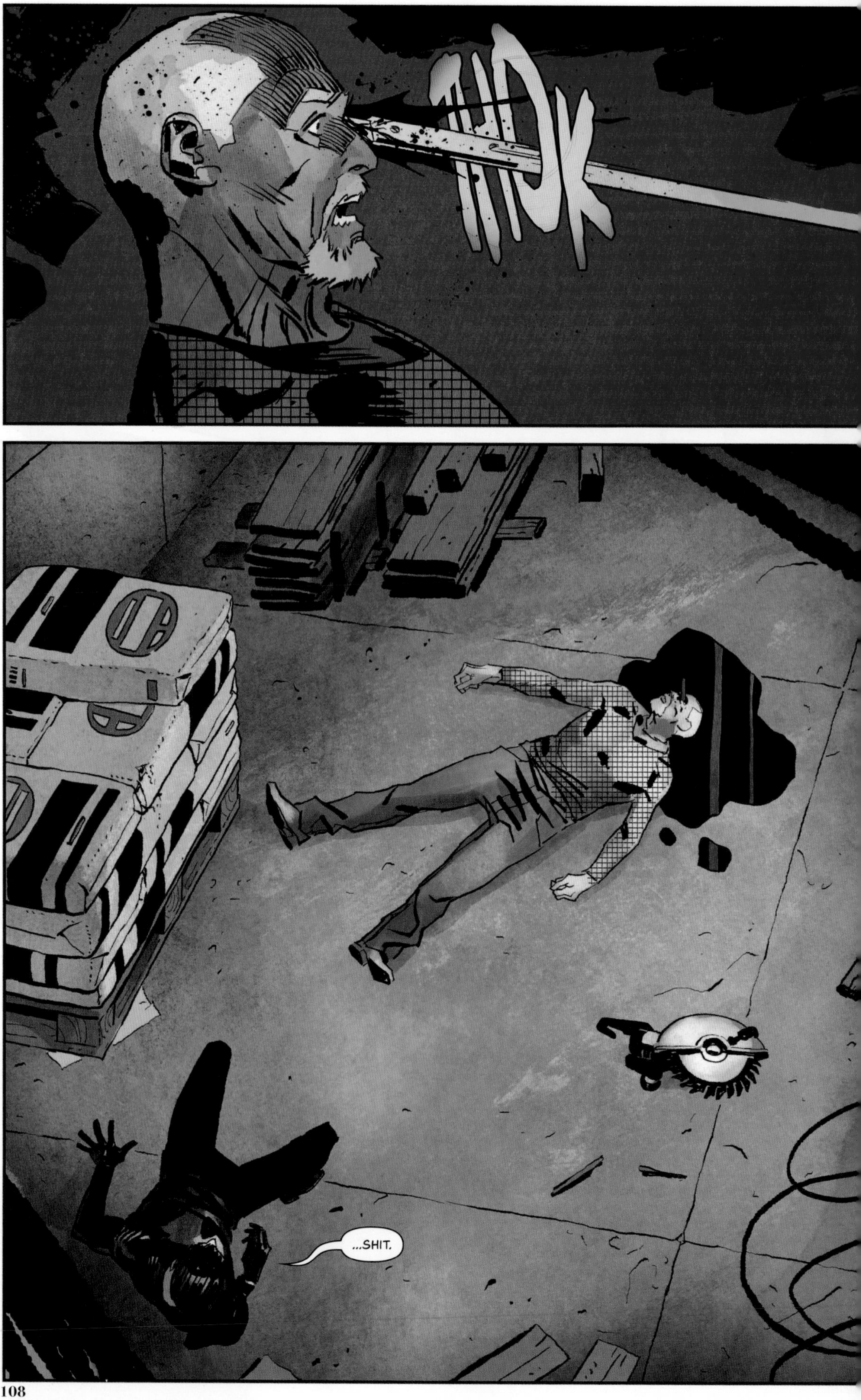
THOK
...SHIT.

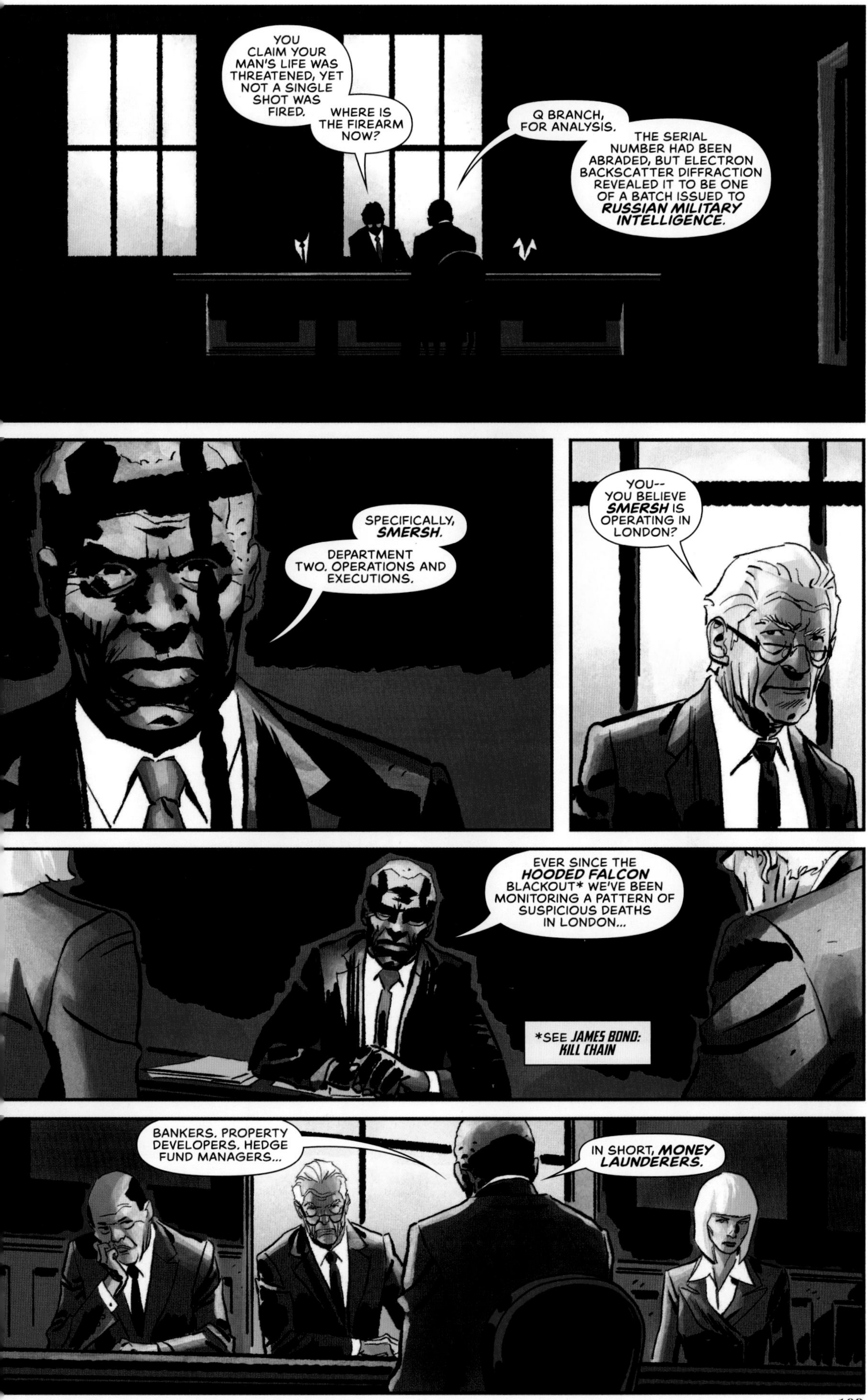
YOU CLAIM YOUR MAN'S LIFE WAS THREATENED, YET NOT A SINGLE SHOT WAS FIRED.
WHERE IS THE FIREARM NOW?
Q BRANCH, FOR ANALYSIS.
THE SERIAL NUMBER HAD BEEN ABRADED, BUT ELECTRON BACKSCATTER DIFFRACTION REVEALED IT TO BE ONE OF A BATCH ISSUED TO ***RUSSIAN MILITARY INTELLIGENCE***.
SPECIFICALLY, ***SMERSH***.
DEPARTMENT TWO. OPERATIONS AND EXECUTIONS.
YOU-- YOU BELIEVE ***SMERSH*** IS OPERATING IN LONDON?
EVER SINCE THE ***HOODED FALCON*** BLACKOUT* WE'VE BEEN MONITORING A PATTERN OF SUSPICIOUS DEATHS IN LONDON...
*SEE ***JAMES BOND: KILL CHAIN***
BANKERS. PROPERTY DEVELOPERS. HEDGE FUND MANAGERS...
IN SHORT, ***MONEY LAUNDERERS***.

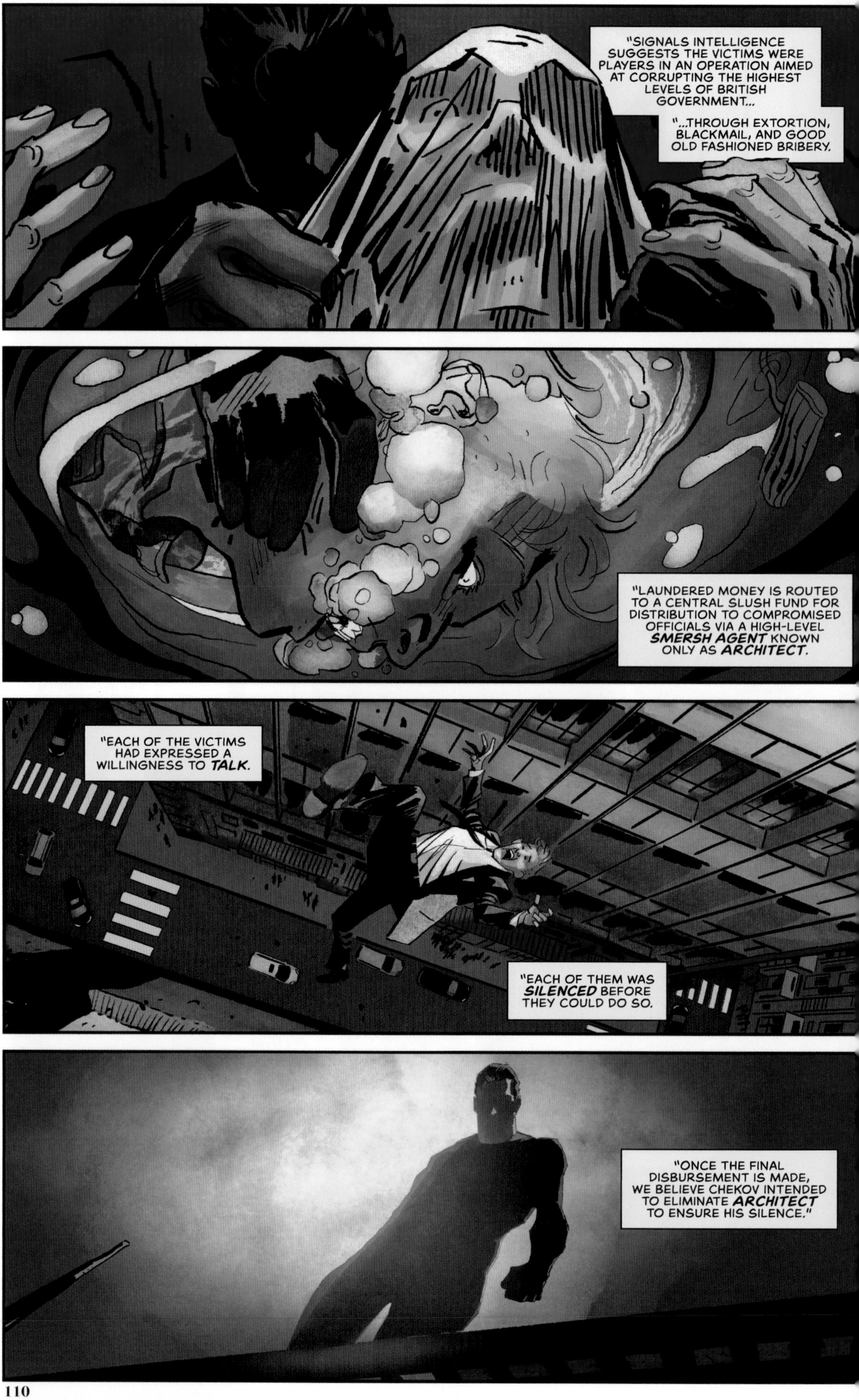
"SIGNALS INTELLIGENCE SUGGESTS THE VICTIMS WERE PLAYERS IN AN OPERATION AIMED AT CORRUPTING THE HIGHEST LEVELS OF BRITISH GOVERNMENT...
"...THROUGH EXTORTION, BLACKMAIL, AND GOOD OLD FASHIONED BRIBERY.
"LAUNDERED MONEY IS ROUTED TO A CENTRAL SLUSH FUND FOR DISTRIBUTION TO COMPROMISED OFFICIALS VIA A HIGH-LEVEL SMERSH AGENT KNOWN ONLY AS ARCHITECT.
"EACH OF THE VICTIMS HAD EXPRESSED A WILLINGNESS TO TALK.
"EACH OF THEM WAS SILENCED BEFORE THEY COULD DO SO.
"ONCE THE FINAL DISBURSEMENT IS MADE, WE BELIEVE CHEKOV INTENDED TO ELIMINATE ARCHITECT TO ENSURE HIS SILENCE."

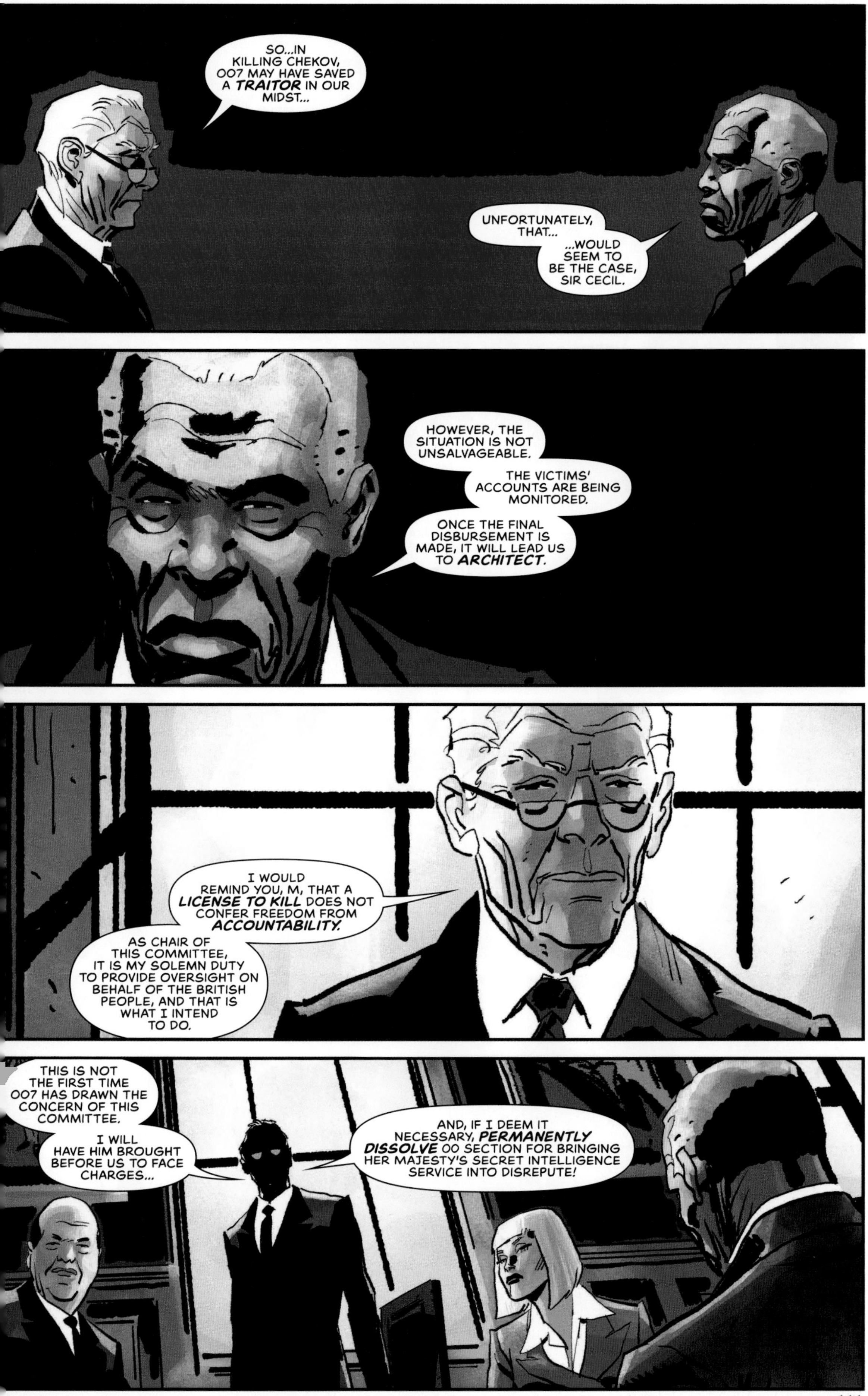
SO...IN KILLING CHEKOV, 007 MAY HAVE SAVED A TRAITOR IN OUR MIDST...
UNFORTUNATELY, THAT...
...WOULD SEEM TO BE THE CASE, SIR CECIL.
HOWEVER, THE SITUATION IS NOT UNSALVAGEABLE.
THE VICTIMS' ACCOUNTS ARE BEING MONITORED.
ONCE THE FINAL DISBURSEMENT IS MADE, IT WILL LEAD US TO ARCHITECT.
I WOULD REMIND YOU, M, THAT A LICENSE TO KILL DOES NOT CONFER FREEDOM FROM ACCOUNTABILITY.
AS CHAIR OF THIS COMMITTEE, IT IS MY SOLEMN DUTY TO PROVIDE OVERSIGHT ON BEHALF OF THE BRITISH PEOPLE, AND THAT IS WHAT I INTEND TO DO.
THIS IS NOT THE FIRST TIME 007 HAS DRAWN THE CONCERN OF THIS COMMITTEE.
I WILL HAVE HIM BROUGHT BEFORE US TO FACE CHARGES...
AND, IF I DEEM IT NECESSARY, PERMANENTLY DISSOLVE 00 SECTION FOR BRINGING HER MAJESTY'S SECRET INTELLIGENCE SERVICE INTO DISREPUTE!

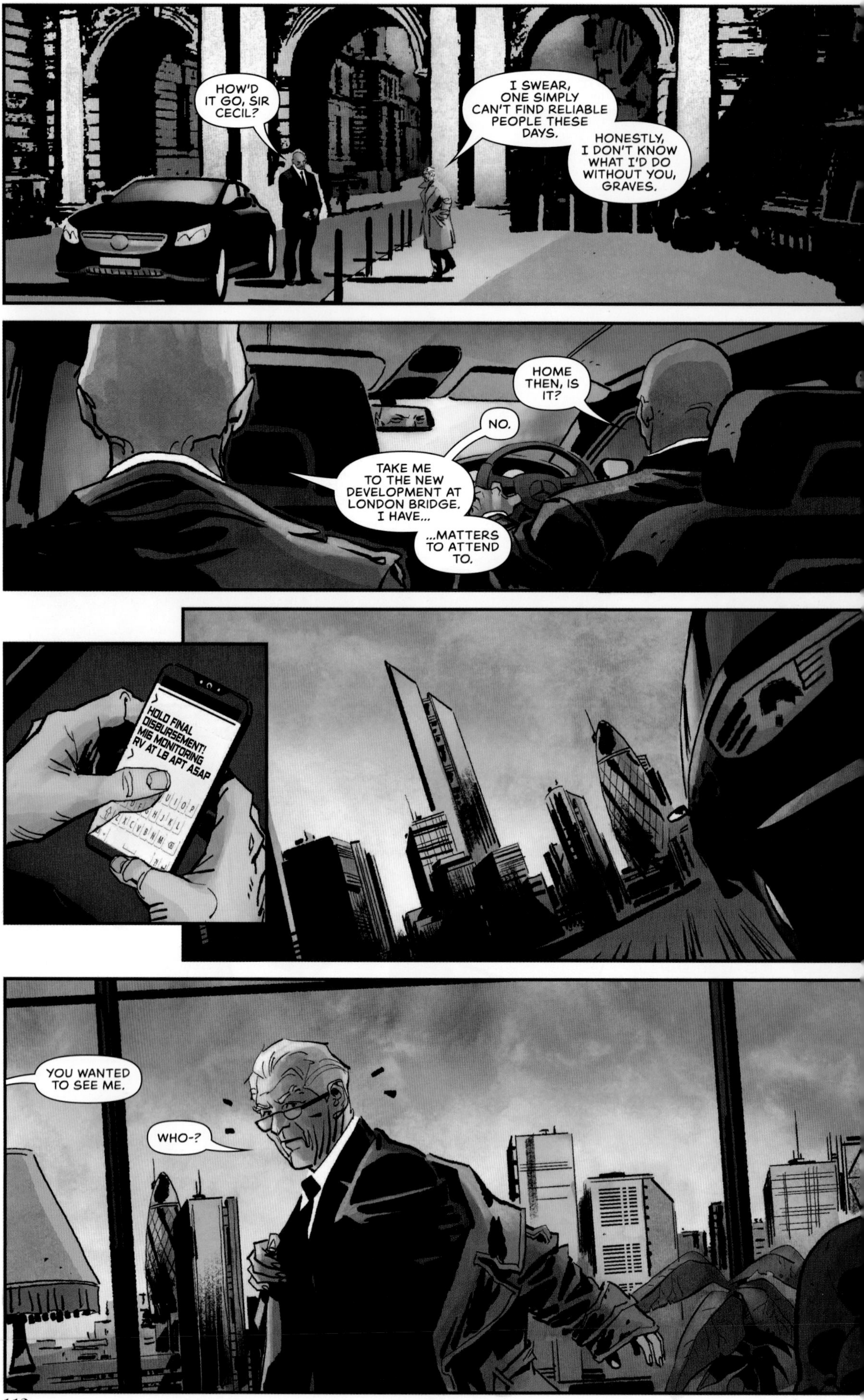
HOW'D IT GO, SIR CECIL?
I SWEAR, ONE SIMPLY CAN'T FIND RELIABLE PEOPLE THESE DAYS.
HONESTLY, I DON'T KNOW WHAT I'D DO WITHOUT YOU, GRAVES.
HOME THEN, IS IT?
NO.
TAKE ME TO THE NEW DEVELOPMENT AT LONDON BRIDGE. I HAVE...
...MATTERS TO ATTEND TO.
HOLD FINAL DISBURSEMENT! MI6 MONITORING RV AT LB APT ASAP
YOU WANTED TO SEE ME.
WHO-?

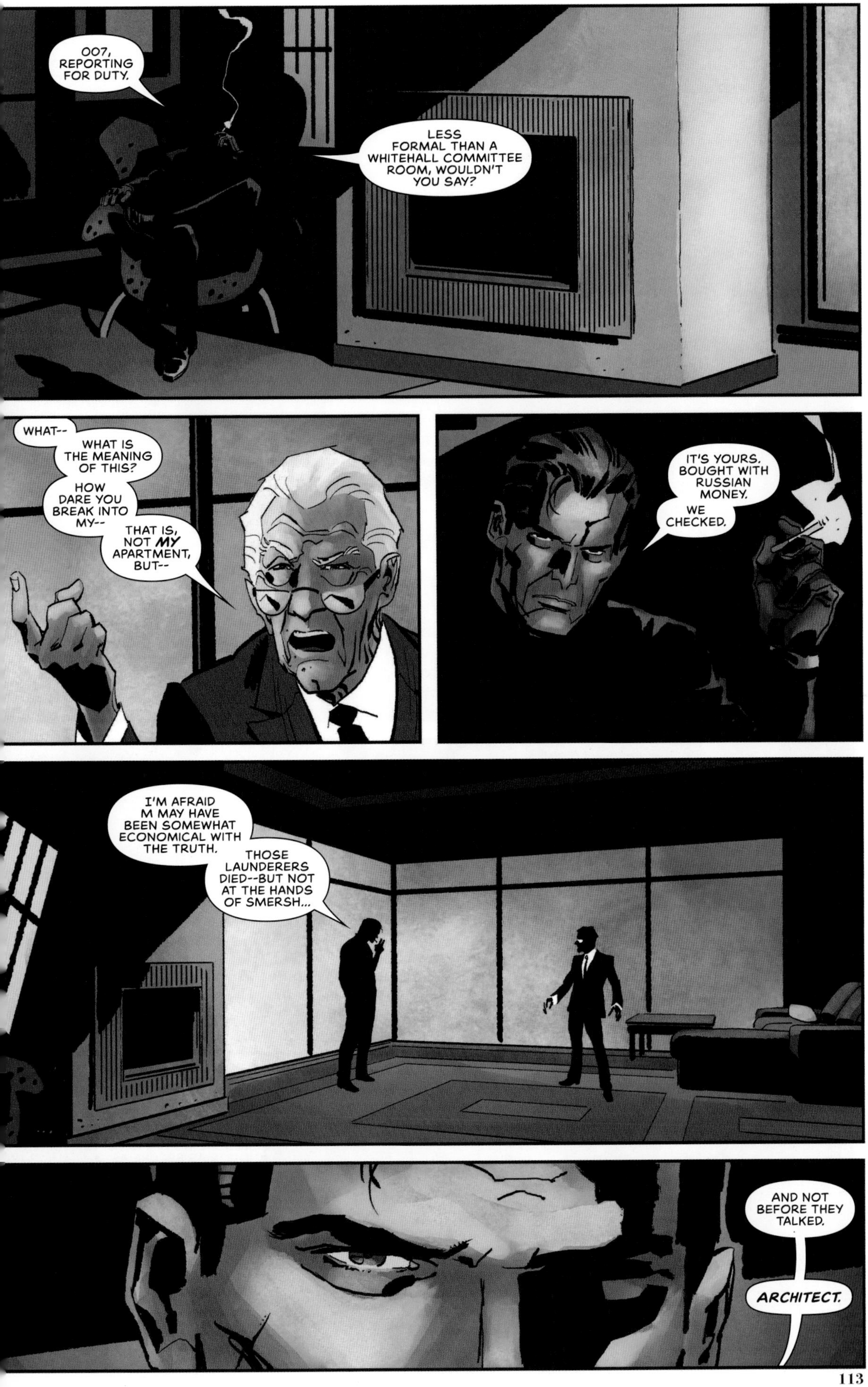
007, REPORTING FOR DUTY.
LESS FORMAL THAN A WHITEHALL COMMITTEE ROOM, WOULDN'T YOU SAY?
WHAT--
WHAT IS THE MEANING OF THIS?
HOW DARE YOU BREAK INTO MY--
THAT IS, NOT *MY* APARTMENT, BUT--
IT'S YOURS. BOUGHT WITH RUSSIAN MONEY.
WE CHECKED.
I'M AFRAID M MAY HAVE BEEN SOMEWHAT ECONOMICAL WITH THE TRUTH.
THOSE LAUNDERERS DIED--BUT NOT AT THE HANDS OF SMERSH...
AND NOT BEFORE THEY TALKED.
ARCHITECT.

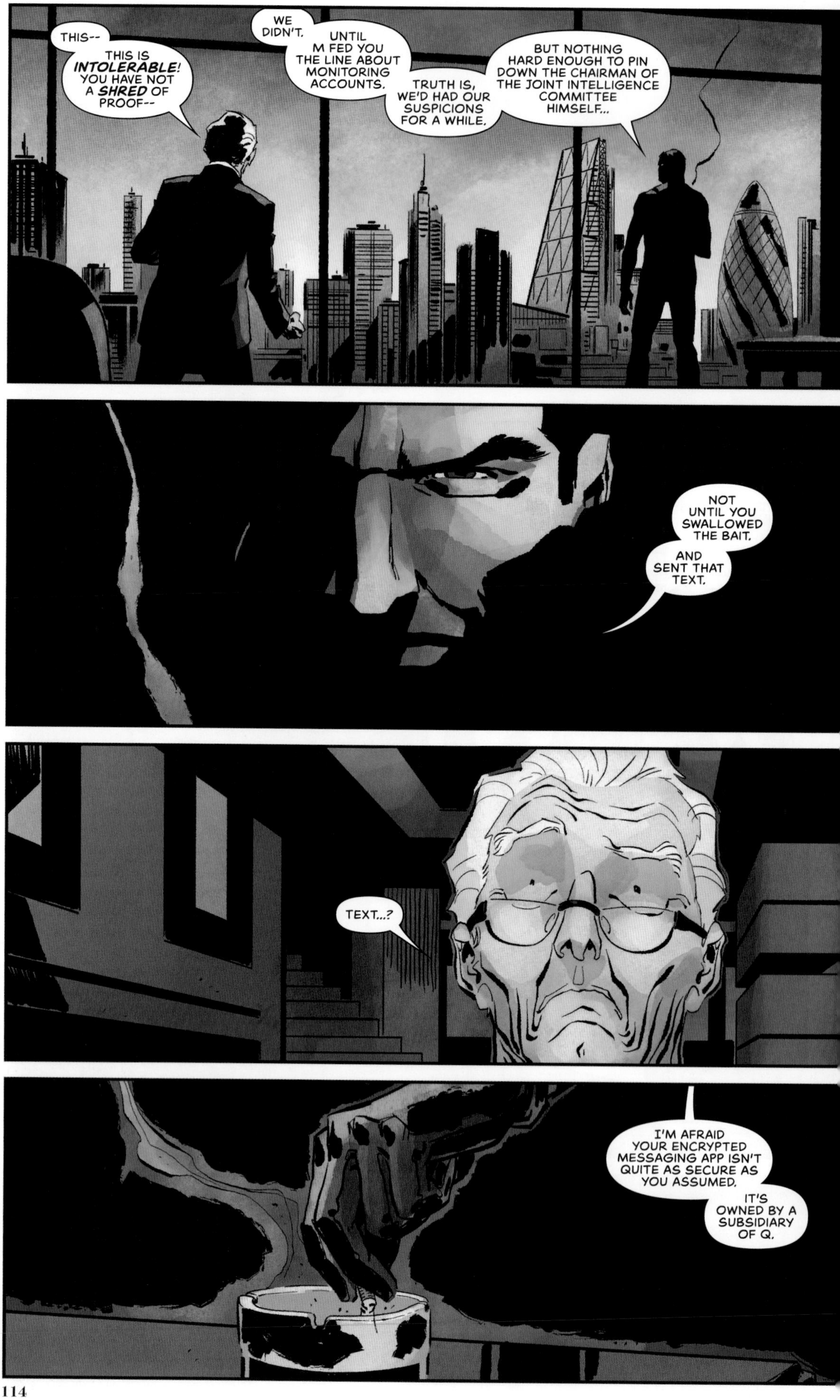
THIS--
THIS IS *INTOLERABLE*! YOU HAVE NOT A *SHRED* OF PROOF--
WE DIDN'T.
UNTIL M FED YOU THE LINE ABOUT MONITORING ACCOUNTS.
TRUTH IS, WE'D HAD OUR SUSPICIONS FOR A WHILE.
BUT NOTHING HARD ENOUGH TO PIN DOWN THE CHAIRMAN OF THE JOINT INTELLIGENCE COMMITTEE HIMSELF...
NOT UNTIL YOU SWALLOWED THE BAIT.
AND SENT THAT TEXT.
TEXT...?
I'M AFRAID YOUR ENCRYPTED MESSAGING APP ISN'T QUITE AS SECURE AS YOU ASSUMED.
IT'S OWNED BY A SUBSIDIARY OF Q.

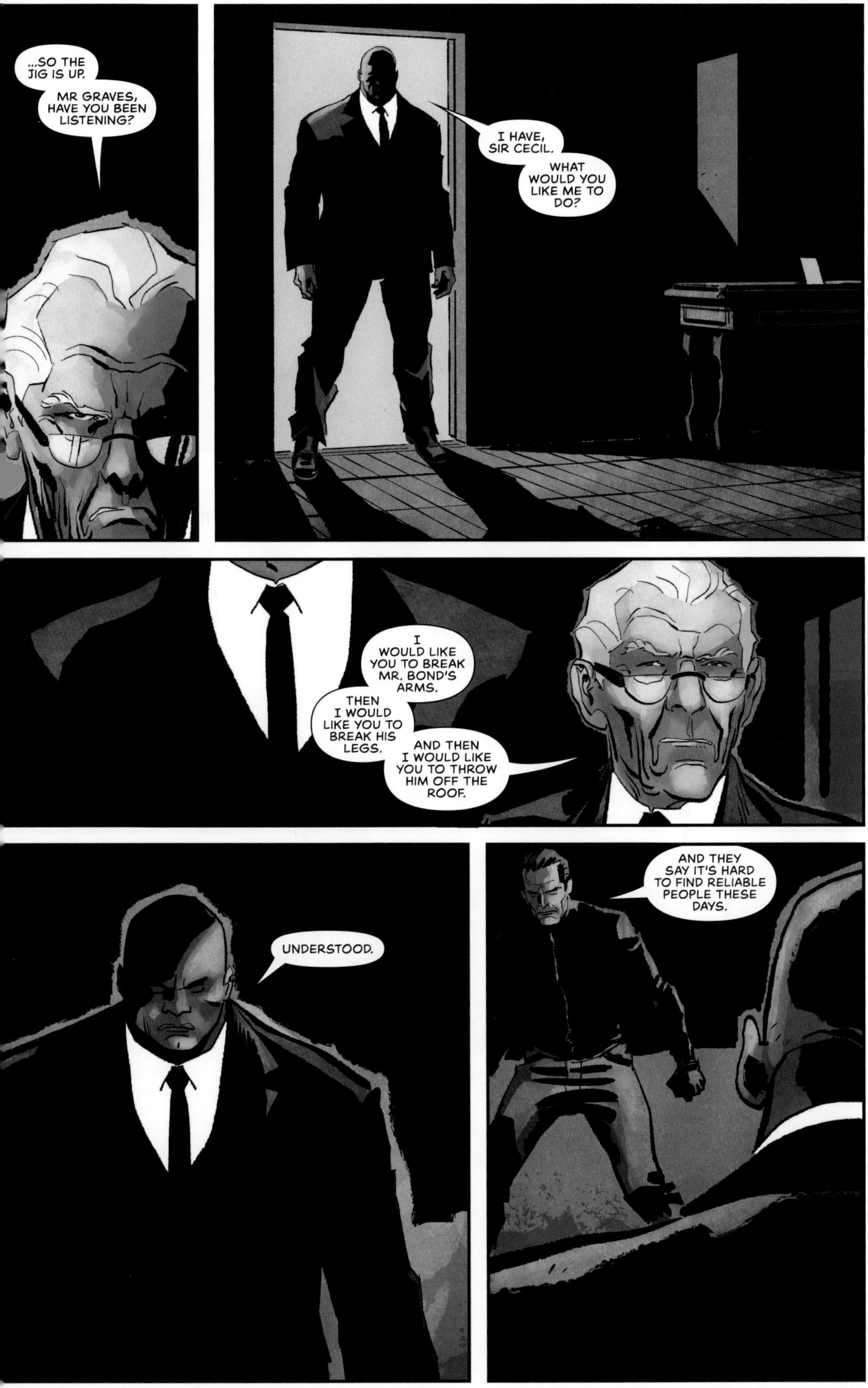
...SO THE JIG IS UP.
MR GRAVES, HAVE YOU BEEN LISTENING?
I HAVE, SIR CECIL.
WHAT WOULD YOU LIKE ME TO DO?
I WOULD LIKE YOU TO BREAK MR. BOND'S ARMS.
THEN I WOULD LIKE YOU TO BREAK HIS LEGS.
AND THEN I WOULD LIKE YOU TO THROW HIM OFF THE ROOF.
UNDERSTOOD.
AND THEY SAY IT'S HARD TO FIND RELIABLE PEOPLE THESE DAYS.

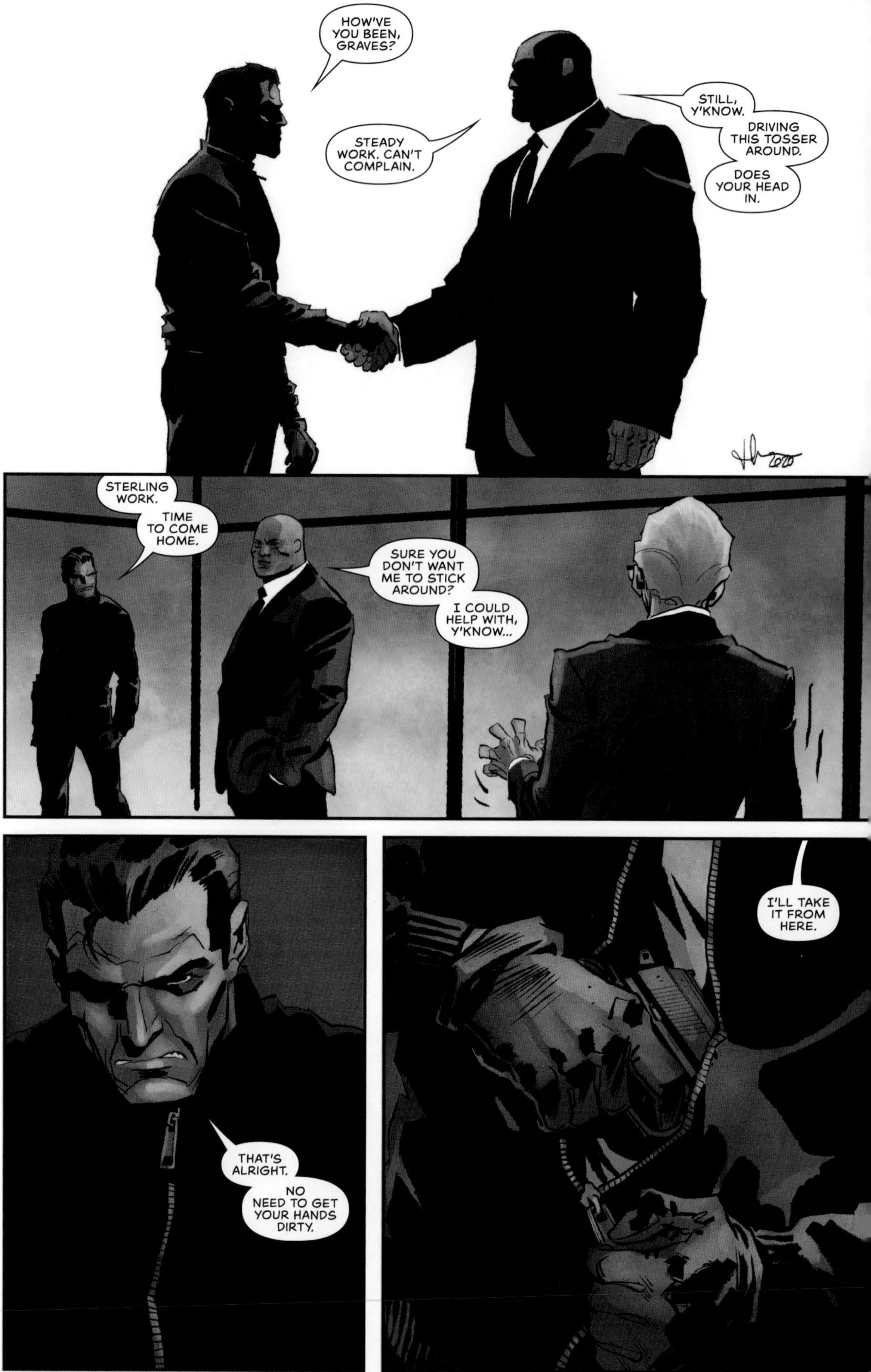
HOW'VE YOU BEEN, GRAVES?
STEADY WORK. CAN'T COMPLAIN.
STILL, Y'KNOW.
DRIVING THIS TOSSER AROUND.
DOES YOUR HEAD IN.
STERLING WORK.
TIME TO COME HOME.
SURE YOU DON'T WANT ME TO STICK AROUND?
I COULD HELP WITH, Y'KNOW...
THAT'S ALRIGHT.
NO NEED TO GET YOUR HANDS DIRTY.
I'LL TAKE IT FROM HERE.

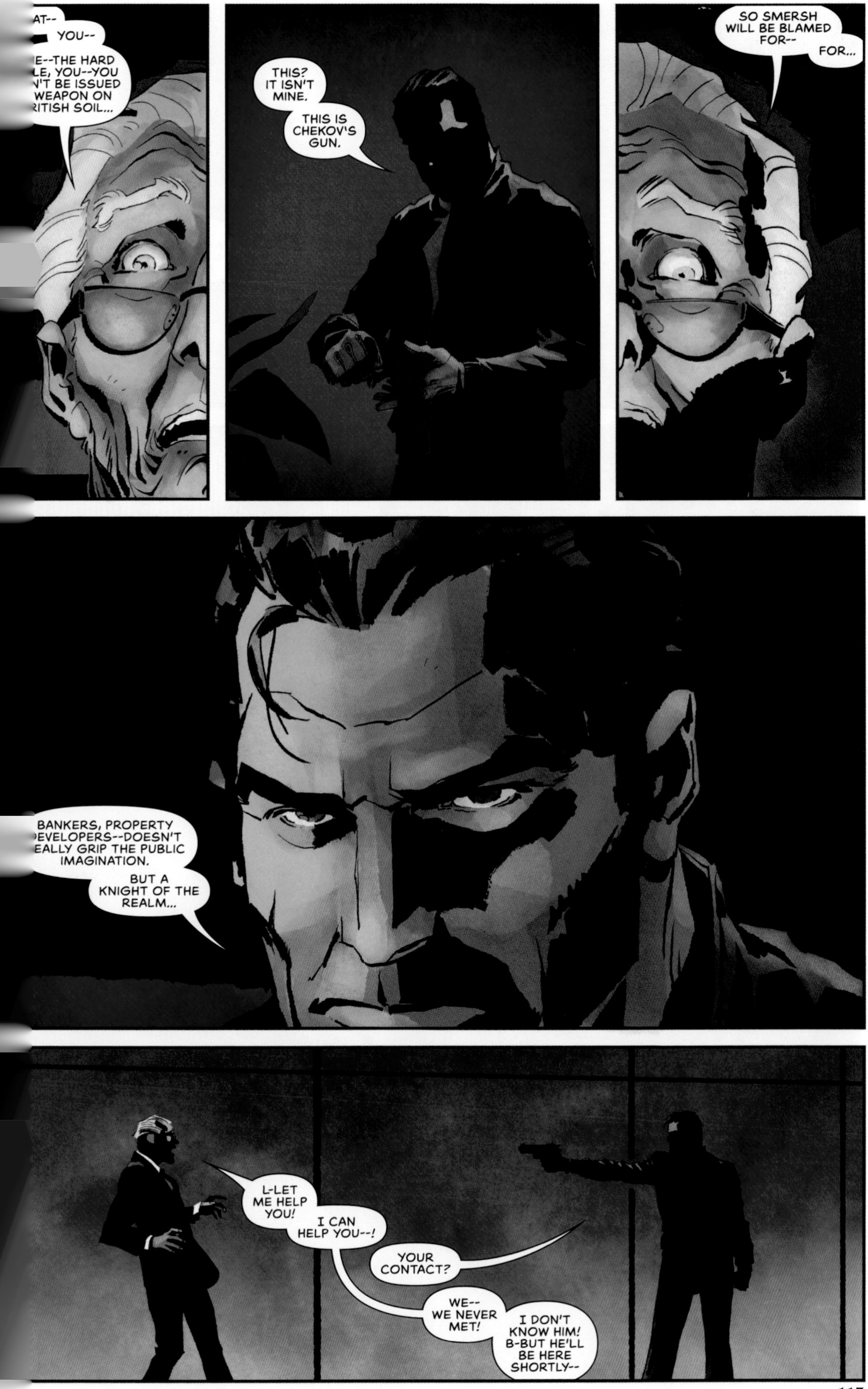
AT--
YOU--
E--THE HARD
LE, YOU--YOU
N'T BE ISSUED
WEAPON ON
RITISH SOIL...
THIS? IT ISN'T MINE.
THIS IS CHEKOV'S GUN.
SO SMERSH WILL BE BLAMED FOR--
FOR...
BANKERS, PROPERTY
EVELOPERS--DOESN'T
EALLY GRIP THE PUBLIC
IMAGINATION.
BUT A KNIGHT OF THE REALM...
L-LET ME HELP YOU!
I CAN HELP YOU--!
YOUR CONTACT?
WE-- WE NEVER MET!
I DON'T KNOW HIM! B-BUT HE'LL BE HERE SHORTLY--

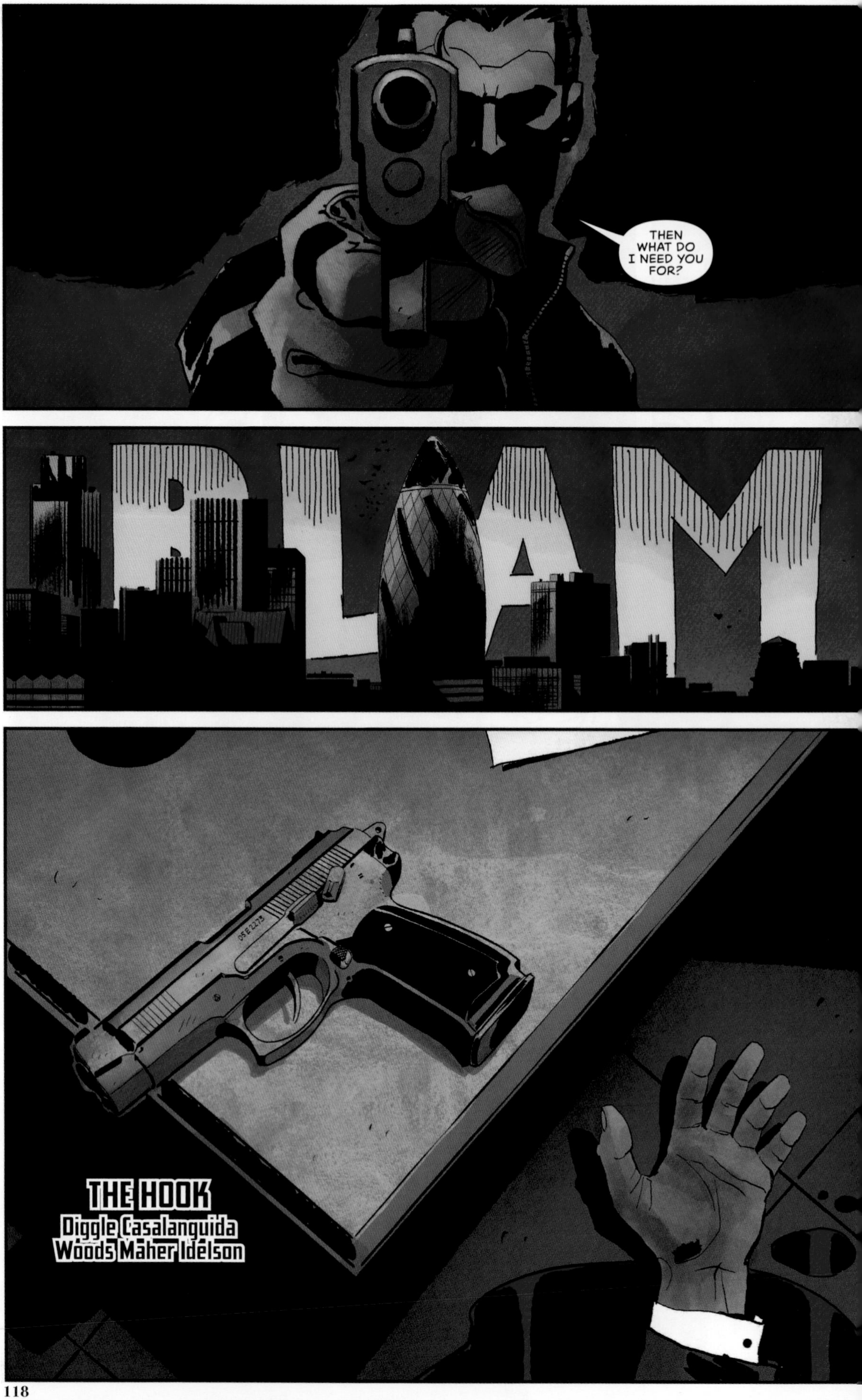
THEN WHAT DO I NEED YOU FOR?
BLAM
THE HOOK
Diggle Casalanguida
Woods Maher Idélson

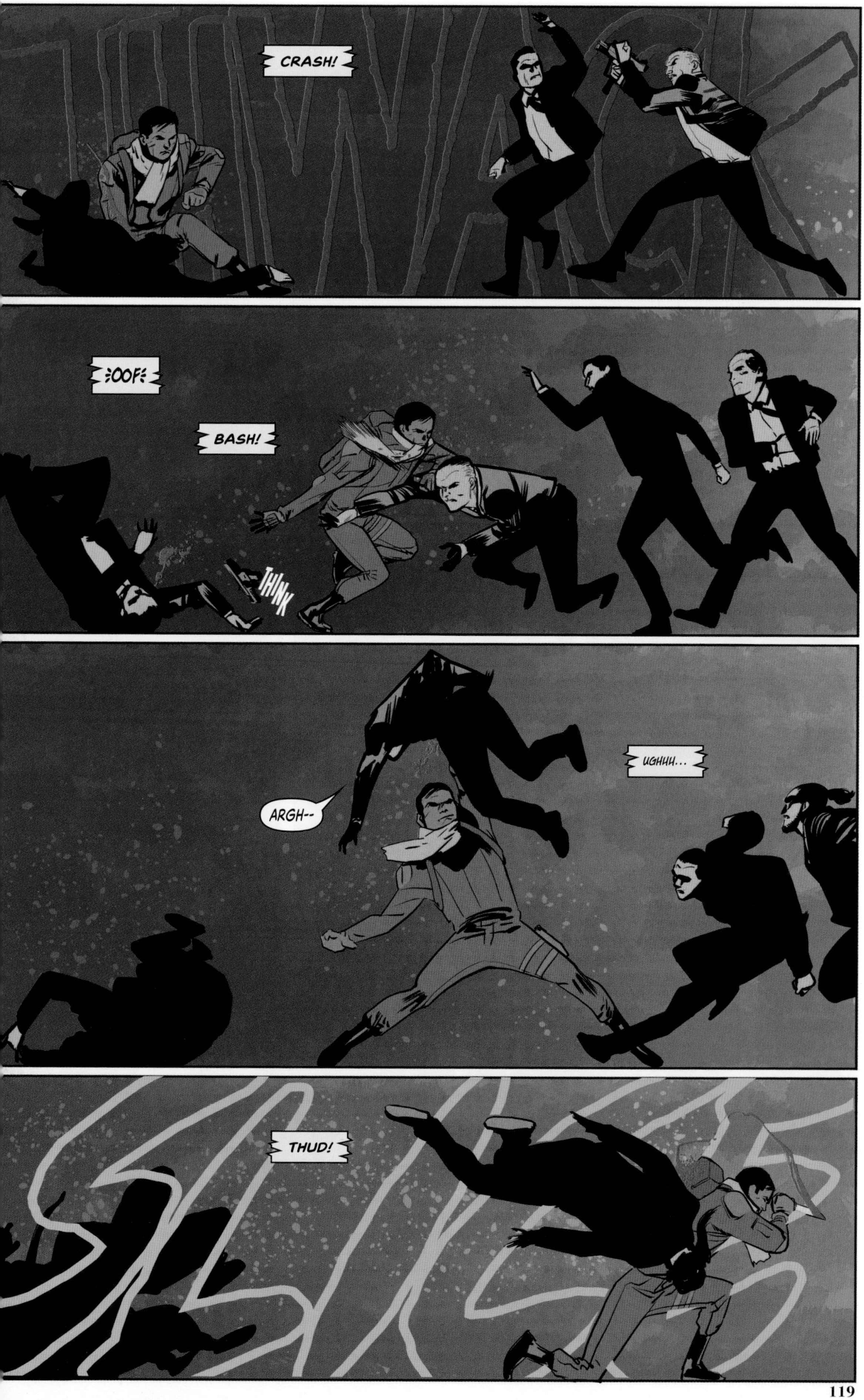
CRASH!
OOF
BASH!
THINK
ARGH--
UGHHH...
THUD!

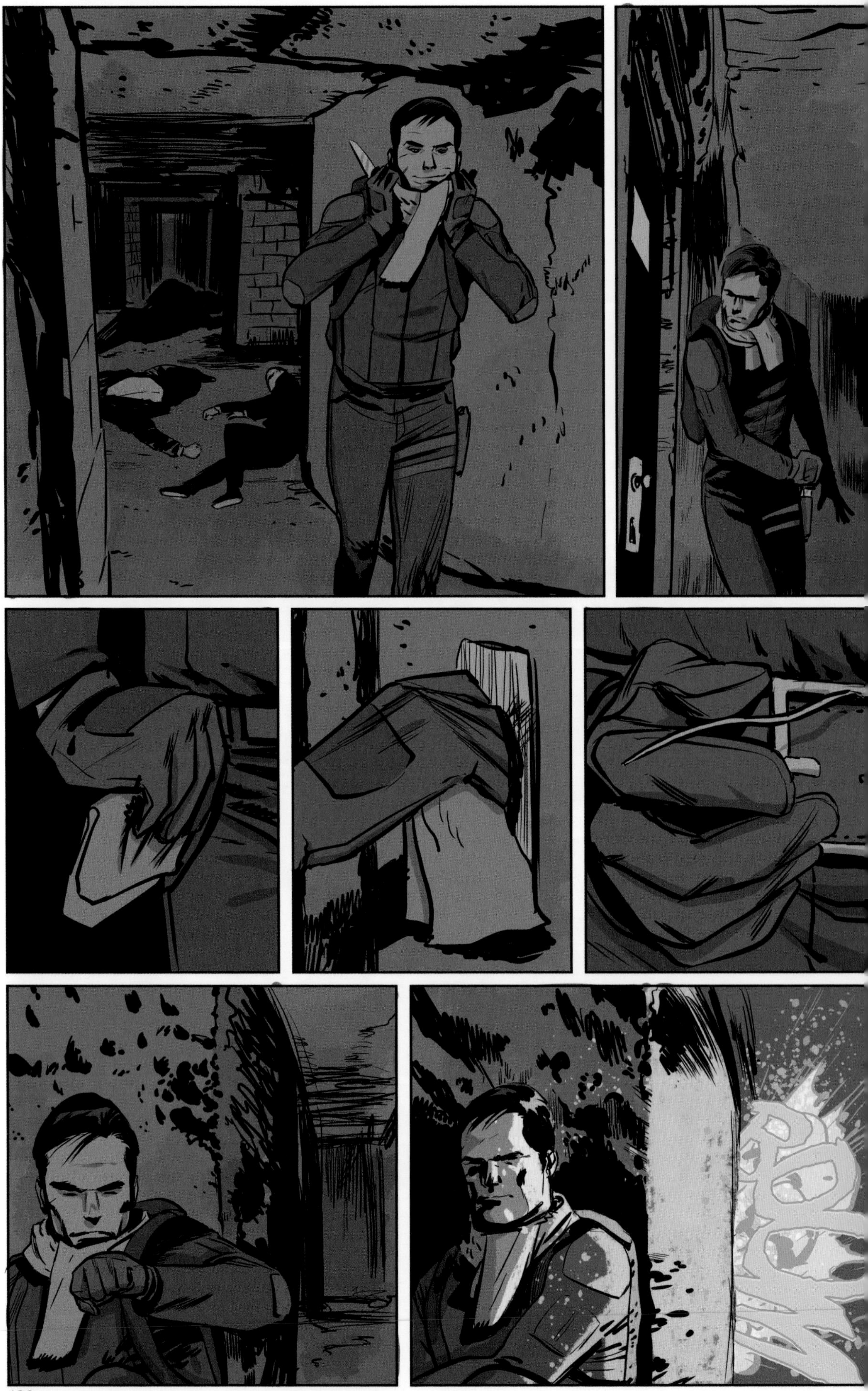

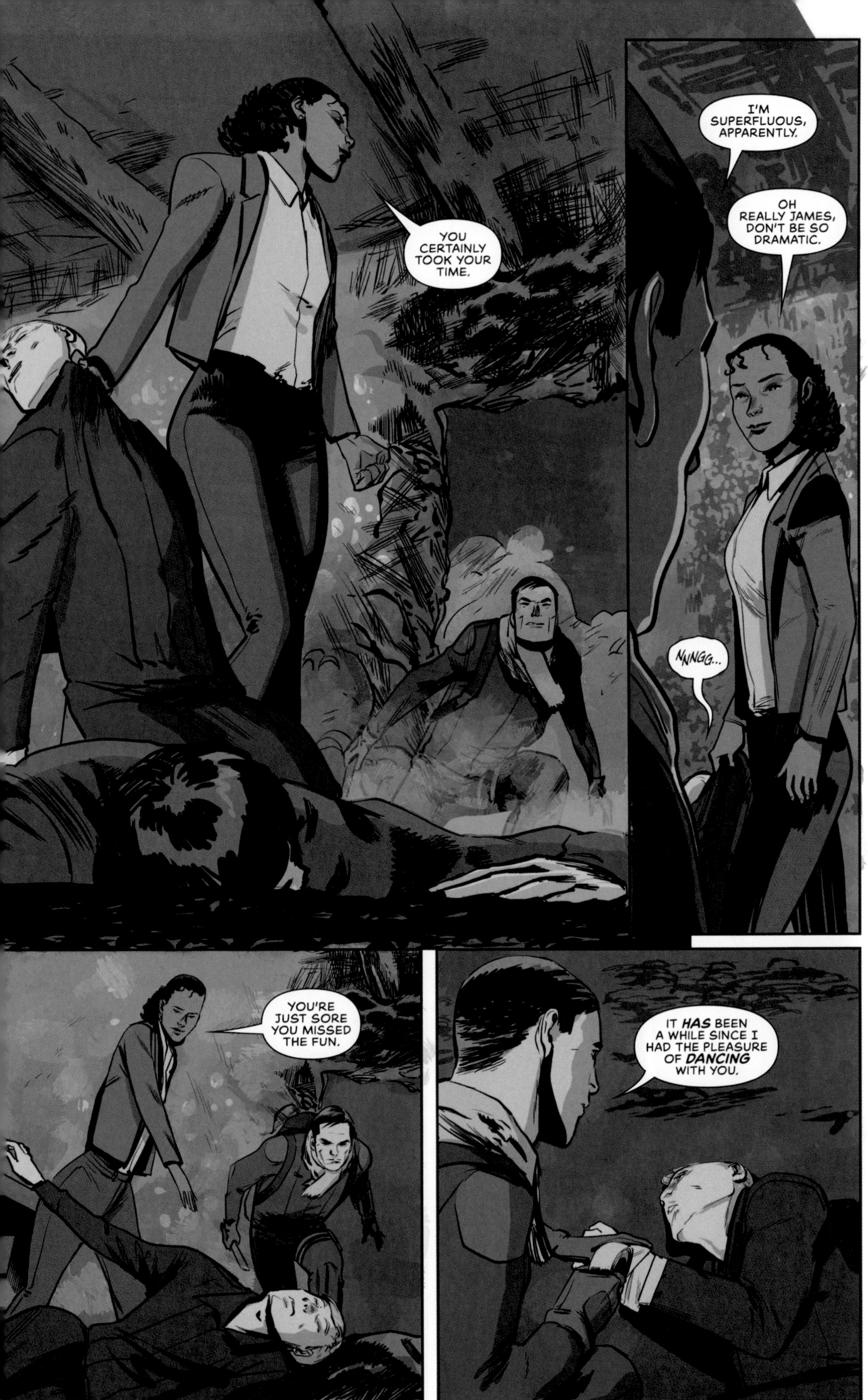
YOU CERTAINLY TOOK YOUR TIME.
I'M SUPERFLUOUS, APPARENTLY.
OH REALLY JAMES, DON'T BE SO DRAMATIC.
NNNGG...
YOU'RE JUST SORE YOU MISSED THE FUN.
IT **HAS** BEEN A WHILE SINCE I HAD THE PLEASURE OF ***DANCING*** WITH YOU.

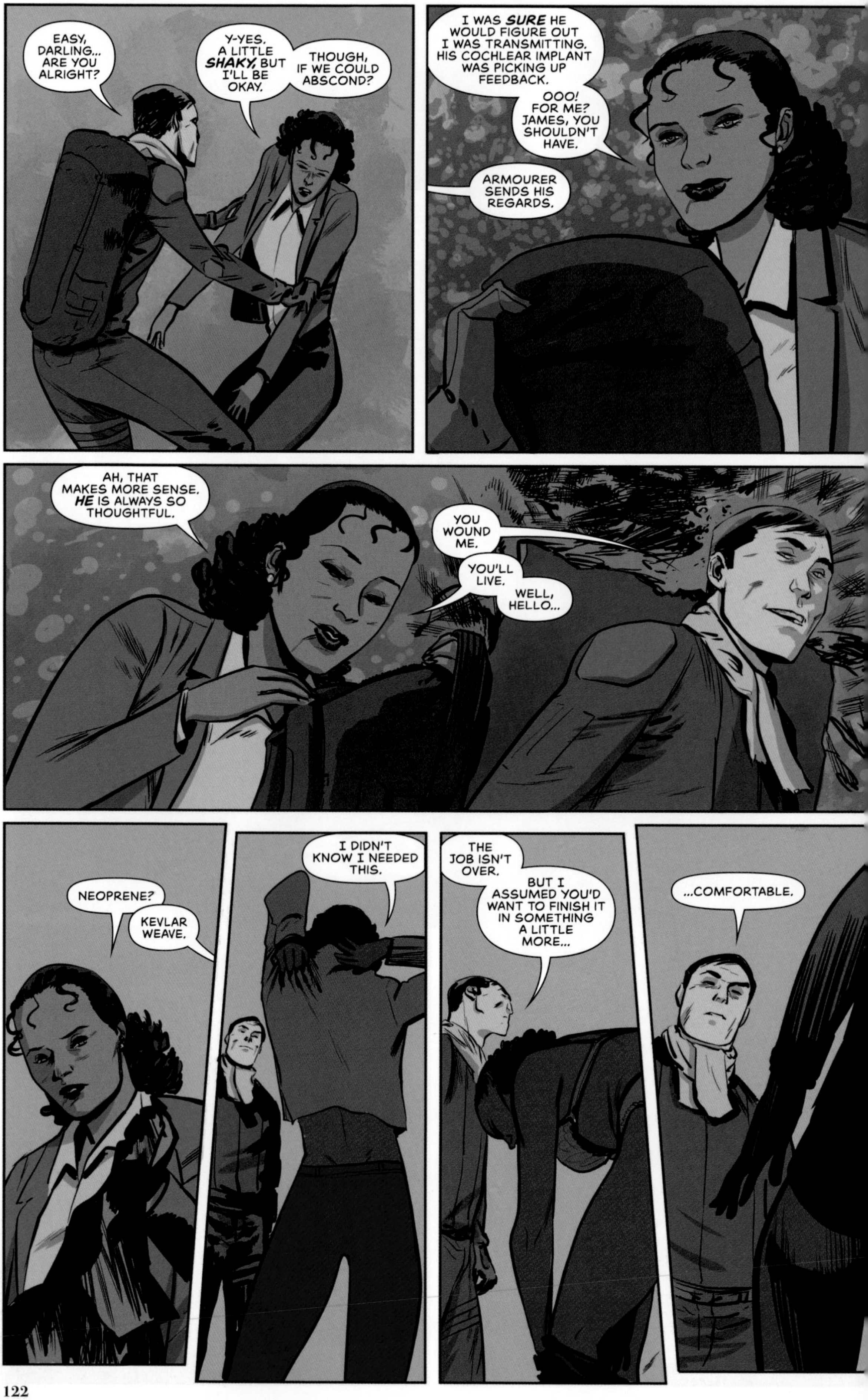
EASY, DARLING... ARE YOU ALRIGHT?
Y-YES. A LITTLE SHAKY, BUT I'LL BE OKAY.
THOUGH, IF WE COULD ABSCOND?
I WAS SURE HE WOULD FIGURE OUT I WAS TRANSMITTING. HIS COCHLEAR IMPLANT WAS PICKING UP FEEDBACK.
OOO! FOR ME? JAMES, YOU SHOULDN'T HAVE.
ARMOURER SENDS HIS REGARDS.
AH, THAT MAKES MORE SENSE. HE IS ALWAYS SO THOUGHTFUL.
YOU WOUND ME.
YOU'LL LIVE.
WELL, HELLO...
NEOPRENE?
KEVLAR WEAVE.
I DIDN'T KNOW I NEEDED THIS.
THE JOB ISN'T OVER.
BUT I ASSUMED YOU'D WANT TO FINISH IT IN SOMETHING A LITTLE MORE...
...COMFORTABLE.

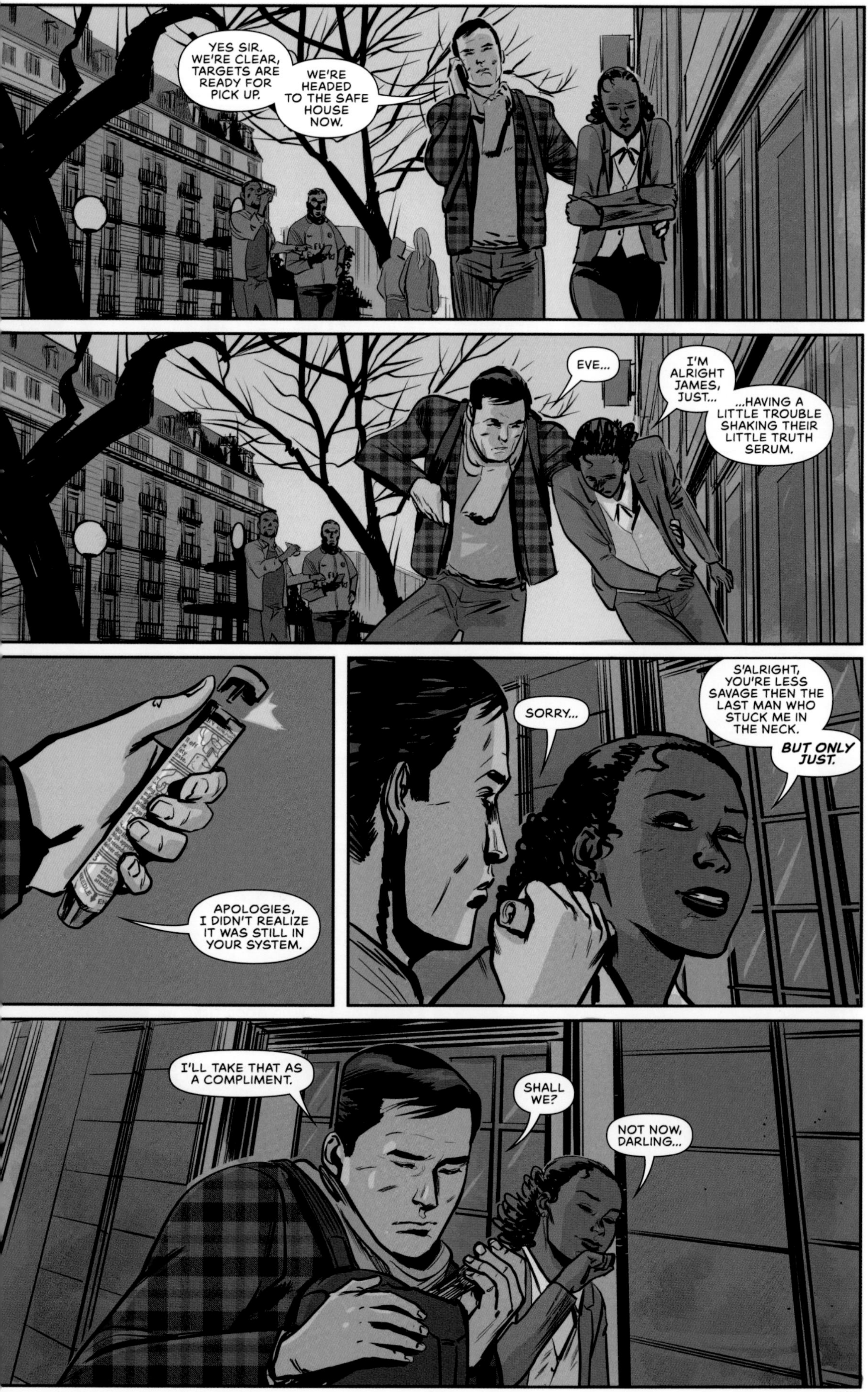
YES SIR. WE'RE CLEAR, TARGETS ARE READY FOR PICK UP.
WE'RE HEADED TO THE SAFE HOUSE NOW.
EVE...
I'M ALRIGHT JAMES, JUST...
...HAVING A LITTLE TROUBLE SHAKING THEIR LITTLE TRUTH SERUM.
APOLOGIES, I DIDN'T REALIZE IT WAS STILL IN YOUR SYSTEM.
SORRY...
S'ALRIGHT, YOU'RE LESS SAVAGE THEN THE LAST MAN WHO STUCK ME IN THE NECK.
BUT ONLY JUST.
I'LL TAKE THAT AS A COMPLIMENT.
SHALL WE?
NOT NOW, DARLING...

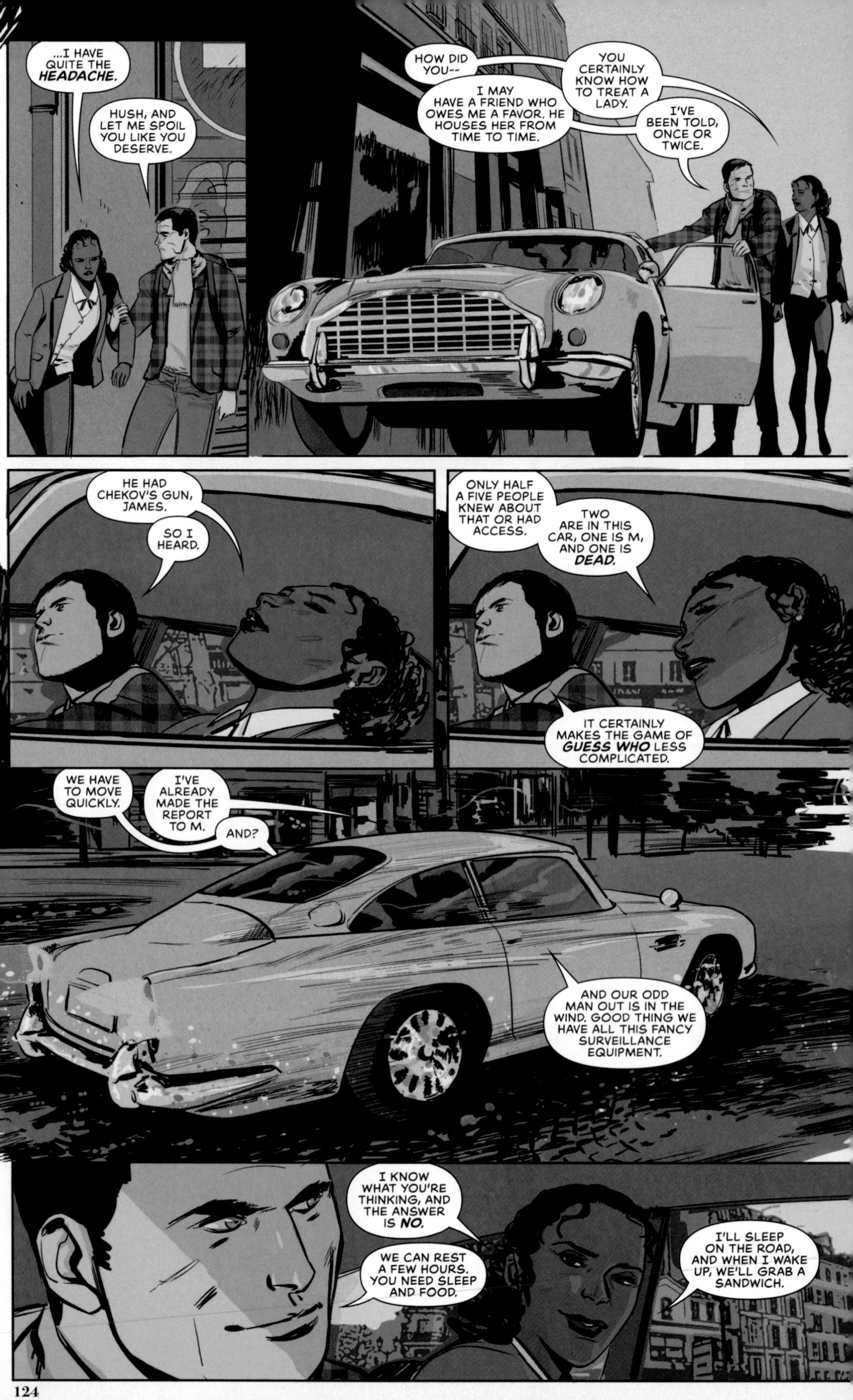
...I HAVE QUITE THE **HEADACHE.**
HUSH, AND LET ME SPOIL YOU LIKE YOU DESERVE.
HOW DID YOU--
I MAY HAVE A FRIEND WHO OWES ME A FAVOR. HE HOUSES HER FROM TIME TO TIME.
YOU CERTAINLY KNOW HOW TO TREAT A LADY.
I'VE BEEN TOLD, ONCE OR TWICE.
HE HAD CHEKOV'S GUN, JAMES.
SO I HEARD.
ONLY HALF A FIVE PEOPLE KNEW ABOUT THAT OR HAD ACCESS.
TWO ARE IN THIS CAR, ONE IS M, AND ONE IS **DEAD.**
IT CERTAINLY MAKES THE GAME OF **GUESS WHO** LESS COMPLICATED.
WE HAVE TO MOVE QUICKLY.
I'VE ALREADY MADE THE REPORT TO M.
AND?
AND OUR ODD MAN OUT IS IN THE WIND. GOOD THING WE HAVE ALL THIS FANCY SURVEILLANCE EQUIPMENT.
I KNOW WHAT YOU'RE THINKING, AND THE ANSWER IS **NO.**
WE CAN REST A FEW HOURS, YOU NEED SLEEP AND FOOD.
I'LL SLEEP ON THE ROAD, AND WHEN I WAKE UP, WE'LL GRAB A SANDWICH.

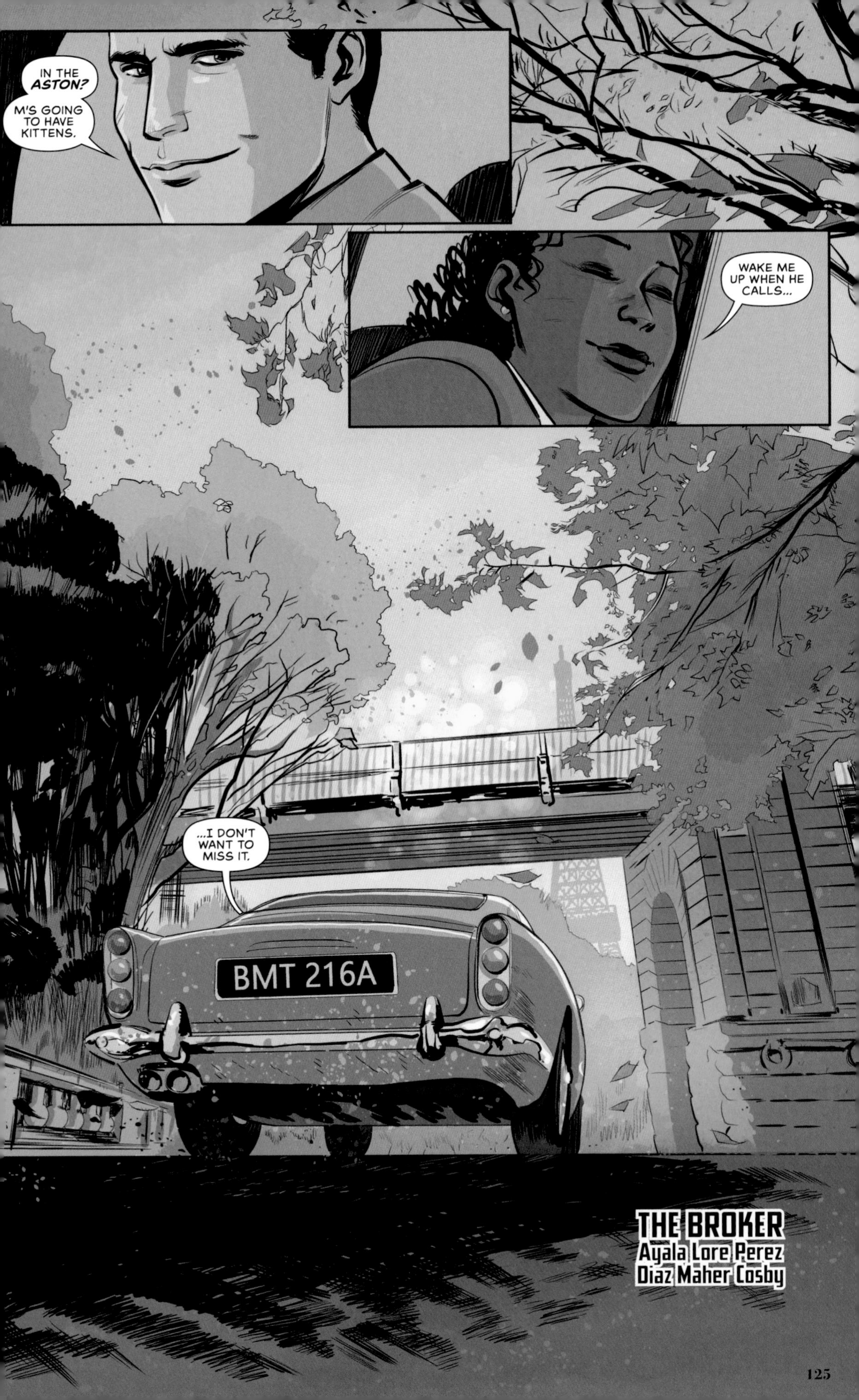
IN THE ASTON? M'S GOING TO HAVE KITTENS.
WAKE ME UP WHEN HE CALLS...
...I DON'T WANT TO MISS IT.
BMT 216A
THE BROKER
Ayala Lore Perez
Diaz Maher Cosby

About the Creators

VITA AYALA is the writer of The Wilds (Black Mask Studios), Xena Warrior Princess and James Bond (Dynamite Entertainment), Livewire (Valiant) and Submerged (Vault).

DANNY LORE is a writer/editor, whose work includes Queen Of Bad Dreams (Vault) and James Bond (Dynamite Entertainment).

JORDI PEREZ is an artist whose work includes Queen Of Bad Dreams (Vault) and Xena Warrior Princess (Dynamite Entertainment).

KIKE J. DIAZ is a colorist, whose work has been seen in Death To The Army Of Darkness!, Red Sonja and James Bond (Dynamite Entertainment).

BENJAMIN PERCY writes Wolverine and X-Force for Marvel. He is known for his work in comics on such series as James Bond, Green Arrow, Nightwing, and Teen Titans. He is also the author of five novels, three story collections, and a book of essays.

KEWBER BAAL is a comic artist based in Brazil. He is best known for do many series for Dynamite Comics, like Jennifer Blood, KISS, Army of Darkness, Jeepers Creepers and James Bond. He loves to draw double spread pages, and chaotic restaurant kitchen fight scenes.

CELESTE WOODS is a Portland-based artist and colorist. She's colored titles such as Charlie's Angels, Red Sonja, and Barbarella. When asked what her favorite color was, she simply said, "All of them. All of them at the same time."

GREG PAK is the writer of World War Hulk and Darth Vader (Marvel), Action Comics and Batman/Superman (DC) and James Bond 007 (Dynamite Entertainment).

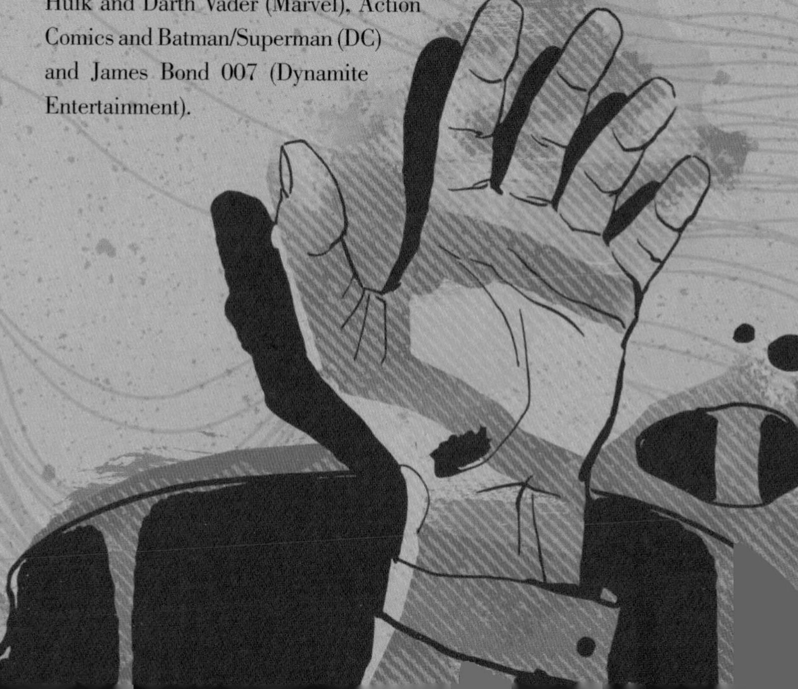

DEAN KOTZ is an artist, whose work includes Butcher Of Paris (Dark Horse), Warlord Of Mars Attacks (Dynamite Entertainment) and Dungeons & Dragons (IDW).

GAIL SIMONE is a fan-favorite writer of comics and animation. She has had well-loved runs on comics titles as diverse as Deadpool (Marvel), Red Sonja (Dynamite), Birds of Prey and Secret Six (DC). Her creator-owned properties Clean Room (Vertigo) and Crosswind (Image) are both being developed for television. She lives in the Oregon boonies with her family and greyhounds.

EOIN MARRON is an Irish comic book artist, best known for his creator-owned crime series Killer Groove (AfterShock Comics) and his work at Dynamite (Centipede, Army of Darkness, James Bond) as well as other publishers including Marvel, BOOM! Studios and IDW.

DEARBHLA KELLY is a colourist, designer and illustrator based in Dublin, Ireland. Her work includes colours on Queen of Bad Dreams (Vault), Red Sonja (Dynamite), Dejah Thoris (Dynamite) and Paradiso (Image), as well as numerous illustrations that you can find on her website. She enjoys reading good stories, watching terrible TV shows and spending too much time with her three cats.

MARK RUSSELL is the writer of Red Sonja and The Lone Ranger for Dynamite Entertainment, The Flintstones and Wonder Twins for DC Comics, and Second Coming for AHOY Comics.

ROBERT CAREY is an artist who has drawn James Bond 007 (Dynamite Entertainment) and Aliens: Resistance (Dark Horse).

ROSHAN KURICHIYANIL is a colorist whose work includes James Bond 007 and The Six Million Dollar Man (Dynamite Entertainment).

ANDY DIGGLE is a writer based in the UK. He is best known for The Losers, which was adapted into the movie starring Jeffrey Dean Morgan, Chris Evans, Zoe Saldana and Idris Elba; and Green Arrow: Year One, which inspired the hit TV show Arrow.

LUCA CASALANGUIDA is a comic artist based in Italy. Loves sea and comics as a child. He drawn for James Bond (Dynamite), Orphans (Bonelli), Rebels (Dark Horse), Adr1ft (Top Cow). He's still drawing for Dylan Dog (Bonelli), Lost Soldiers (Image) and more.

ARIANA MAHER is the letterer for James Bond 007 (2018), as well as the newest James Bond (2019) series. Whenever she manages to save his hide from a scary deadline with her lettering, Dynamite Editor Nate Cosby owes her a beer. Nate owes her 40 beers. That's as many as four tens. And that's terrible.

CHECK OUT THESE GREAT JAMES BOND COLLECTIONS, ALSO FROM DYNAMITE!